RESOURCES FOR EDUCATIONAL EQUITY

A Guide
for Grades
Pre-Kindergarten - 12

Source Books on
Education

Vol. 17

**GARLAND REFERENCE LIBRARY
OF THE SOCIAL SCIENCES (VOL. 444)**

SOURCE BOOKS ON EDUCATION

RESOURCES FOR EDUCATIONAL EQUITY

A Guide
for Grades
Pre-Kindergarten - 12

Merle Froschl
Barbara Sprung

Educational Equity Concepts, Inc.

GARLAND PUBLISHING, INC.
NEW YORK & LONDON 1988

120729

Library of Congress Cataloging-in-Publication Data
Resources for educational equity: a guide for grades
prekindergarten–12 / [edited by] Merle Froschl, Barbara Sprung.
    p. cm. —(Garland reference library of social science ; vol.
444. Source books on education; vol. 17)
    Includes bibliographies and index.
    ISBN 0–8240–0443–4 (alk. paper)
    1. Educational equalization—United States. 2. Education
equalization—United States—Bibliography. 3. Textbook bias—
United States. I. Froschl, Merle. II. Spring, Barbara. III. Series:
Garland reference library of social science ; vol. 444. IV. Series:
Source books on education; vol. 17.
LC213.2.R47   1988
016.37019′0973—dc19   88–16445

                                                                CIP

Design by Renata Gomes

Printed on acid-free, 250-year-life paper
MANUFACTURED IN THE UNITED STATES OF AMERICA

CONTENTS

ACKNOWLEDGMENTS

We would like to acknowledge all the people who helped to make <u>Resources for Educational Equity</u> a reality. First, Marie Ellen Larcada, Editor at Garland Publishing, who approached us with the idea for this book. We acknowledge her vision, her tenacity, and her ability to guide us through to the book's completion.

We also would like to thank Joni K. Miller, Linda Henry, and Joan Spence who, at crucial times in the book's development, provided the necessary typing, word processing, and production skills. Thanks also are extended to Lisset Marin who diligently and competently helped in the preparation of the author index.

We wish to take this opportunity to acknowledge the National Coalition of Sex Equity in Education (NCSEE). This organization of sex equity professionals, many of whom have authored chapters in this guide, has provided leadership in the struggle to equate excellence and equity. The annual NCSEE conference is always a source of professional growth and renewed commitment. We also wish to thank NCSEE members on a personal level for their unfailing support and nurturance of our work.

Finally, we cannot thank enough all the authors of <u>Resources for Educational Equity</u> who worked voluntarily and without financial remuneration to provide the content of this book. They truly are the people who care and strive to provide equality of opportunity for all students.

INTRODUCTION

Merle Froschl and Barbara Sprung

Purpose and Definition

We have assembled Resources for Educational Equity: An Annotated Bibliography and Guide for Grades Pre K-12 as a practical tool for educators. It is the most comprehensive and up-to-date compilation of available resources to help teachers locate the materials they need to create equitable curriculum and classroom environments.

Three basic premises underlie this bibliography and guide. The first is that all forms of bias have a limiting effect on the potential development of students and, therefore, have no place in the educational system. Thus, while its primary focus is girls and women, Resources for Educational Equity is unique in that it takes a comprehensive approach to equity encompassing concerns of sex (it is our belief that educational equity is in the best interest of all students whether female or male), race, and disability.

The second premise is that excellence in education cannot be achieved without the commitment to ensure equity. Too often the recent calls for excellence have ignored issues of equity and have been concerned with excellence only for a few. The third premise grows out of and is related to the second: that the educational system must prepare all its youth to take positions of leadership, thereby enlarging the pool of talent from which this country can draw its strength for the remaining decade of the twentieth century and into the twenty-first.

If written fifteen or even ten years ago, Resources for Educational Equity would have been a very slim volume. During the past ten years there has been an extraordinary growth in the development of classroom resources focusing on educational equity. Except for the "classics," for which there have been no recent substitutes, the overwhelming majority of resources listed in this volume date from 1979 or 1980.

In the early 1970s, activists began to examine and address the bias and stereotyping due to sex, race, and disability that was evidenced in the educational system. During that time, there was documentation of the stereotyping in textbooks and other forms of instructional media, and attention was paid to the absence of women, people of color, and people with disabilities in textbooks and curriculum. Awareness materials were developed pointing to biased attitudes on the part of teachers and administrators, however, equitable instructional resources were still few. While several federal laws and a wide variety of state mandates supported equity in education, it was the Women's Educational Equity Act of 1974 (WEEA) that created the impetus and funds for the development and dissemination of equity materials.[1] The Women's Educational Equity Act also played a key role in defining issues of educational equity to include women and girls of diverse racial and ethnic groups and women and girls with disabilities.

Scope and Format

Given the enormous numbers of materials now available, Resources for Educational Equity is comprehensive yet selective. Materials have been selected first and foremost on their equity content, with quality, timeliness, and relevance also used as important criteria. Its major focus is on instructional materials that can be used directly with students, but it also contains copious references for background readings for educators.

Resources for Educational Equity has been organized topically by subject areas. Each of the eleven chapters has been written by an expert--or pair of experts--in that subject area. Chapters begin with a thoughtful essay followed by annotated, evaluative bibliographic entries. Each chapter reflects the insights and expertise of its author(s).

The book begins, appropriately, with a chapter on Early Childhood Education reflecting another of our beliefs that it is essential to "begin at the beginning" to provide equality of opportunity. This chapter is treated with an interdisciplinary approach that is in keeping with the curriculum of the preschool, Kindergarten, and early elementary grades. Other chapters are organized by grade levels.

There is a chapter on each of the traditional subject areas, e.g. Language Arts and Literature, Mathematics, History, Science, and, as a sign of our technological times, a chapter on Computers as well. Chapters on other educational areas relevant to equity include Sports, Guidance Counseling, and Vocational Education. The inclusion of a chapter on Teenage Childbearing recognizes the importance of including this issue in any contemporary consideration of educational equity. The book ends with a chapter on Libraries and Media Centers that includes references to more general resources and extends educational equity into the larger school environment.

There is a comprehensive approach to every curriculum and subject area, taking into account, whenever possible, issues of sex, race, and disability. Because disability in relationship to educational equity is relatively new, there regrettably are fewer resources listed in this category than there are for sex and race. The one exception is the chapter on Early Childhood Education where resources on disability are plentiful and are incorporated throughout.

Resources on Educational Equity also includes opening essays by Leslie R. Wolfe and Beryle Banfield, leaders in the field of educational equity. Leslie Wolfe, the visionary former Director of the Women's Educational Equity Act Program, eloquently sketches the origins of the Women's Educational Equity Act and the role that the program has played in broadening the definition of educational equity. She also credits WEEA with creating a national network of equity leaders that "ensures that the spirit and purpose of the Women's Educational Equity Act will survive and flourish." Beryle Banfield, a nationally recognized leader in the field of educational equity, addresses the need for a comprehensive approach to equity. Looking at the negative effects of sex, race, and disability bias, she charges educators to become equipped to make the connections between the issues and to understand the "roots of inequity" in order to bring about effective and lasting change.

Chapter Contents

In their chapter on Early Childhood Education, Linda Colón and Ellen Rubin also address the need for a comprehensive equity approach that creates a nonsexist, multicultural, and disability inclusive learning environment from the beginning of the educational experience. They cite

the myriad resources that are available for this effort and
urge early childhood educators to take full advantage of
them.

In the chapter on Computers, Patricia B. Campbell
defines inequities due to gender and socioeconomic status and
notes that these inequities can lead to the transference of
math anxiety to the area of computers. She offers practical
strategies to address the problem including careful review
and purchasing of gender-neutral software, providing positive
role models, making scheduling changes to ensure equality of
access to computers, and requiring all students to use
computers rather than leaving it to a self-selection process.

Melissa Keyes's and Pamela J. Wilson's approach to
Guidance Counseling is not a response to "kids in trouble."
Rather it is a well thought-out plan for each student that
begins with an emphasis on development and promotes "unbiased
instruction and the deliberate support of opportunity
regardless of sex, race, or disability." The authors also
charge the schools with the task of encouraging students to
try nontraditional career options, and they say that guidance
counseling must include instruction in decision-making,
problem-solving, communication skills, and interpersonal
relationships.

"Women's history was one of the first disciplines to
arise out of the contemporary feminist movement," states
Frances Arick Kolb at the beginning of the History chapter.
She then goes on to trace the development of the field from
the late 1960s, beginning with "contribution history," which
included the contributions made by women through the ages;
moving on through "social history," which investigated
ordinary women's lives and defined the autonomous "culture of
women," and finally, the current phase, which is
"transforming historical thought." The chapter also
discusses the origins of Women's History Week, its growth
into Women's History Month, and the important resources
provided by the National Women's History Project.

Frances Arick Kolb also brings a historian's perspective
to the chapter on Language Arts and Literature. She begins
by giving a chronological overview from the late 1960s
through the 1980s of feminist discoveries about the gross
underrepresentation of women and people of color in virtually
all forms of literature, starting with picture books and
progressing through basal readers, textbooks, novels, and
classics. She cites as well the sex-role stereotyping and

racial bias that was common in the few female and black characters that did appear. As in the History chapter, Frances Kolb traces the positive changes that feminist scholarship has wrought on the field of literature. She acknowledges the positive changes made by educational publishers as a result of consultations with feminists. She also documents how scholars have moved from criticism of stereotyping and underrepresentation to profoundly broadening the definition of literature through the introduction of nontraditional sources such as oral interviews, diaries, and autobiographies of ordinary women.

In the chapter on Mathematics, Joy Wallace compares the different and unequal treatment of girls in mathematics classes and relates the importance of a good education in mathematics to the job market. She cites factors such as the lack of teacher preparation at the early levels of education, lack of expectations on the part of parents and teachers regarding the mathematics performance of girls and children of color, low self-esteem, biased guidance and counseling, and the competitive and "right answer" approach that prevails at the secondary level as contributing to the problem. Joy Wallace also offers many positive strategies for change including cooperative learning techniques, provision of positive role models, making math relevant to the real world, using manipulatives and hands-on teaching approaches, involving parents in math activities, and addressing math anxiety.

In the chapter on Science, Marylin Hulme and Walter Smith give an overview of the data that document the low participation of women and people of color in the sciences, particularly the physical sciences, mathematics, and engineering. They trace this lack of participation back to the high school level when students do not take the courses that prepare them for higher level college courses. The authors identify four major areas of concern: 1) liking science, 2) lack of problem-solving and visual-spatial skills, 3) perceiving science as a male domain, and 4) seeing the utility of science.

The chapter on Sports by Linda Villarosa documents the enormous gains in women's sports brought about by Title IX. She also speaks of the fervent efforts on the part of women athletes who benefited from Title IX to have the Grove City decision, which severely limited the effectiveness of the Act, rescinded. Happily, these efforts paid off through the Civil Rights Restoration Act of 1988. Linda Villarosa suggests four strategies for an equity approach to physical education: 1) recognize and address sex-role stereotyping as it arises, 2) emphasize cooperative games and health activities, 3) advocate for female coaches, and 4) create specific sports opportunities for girls.

Teenage Childbearing by Michele Cahill underscores the importance of school continuation and achievement in pregnancy prevention and in ameliorating the negative effects of teenage parenting. She sees the school as the place to instill motivation and a sense of options other than motherhood, as well as providing a strong grounding in basic skills. She states unequivocally that "if educational equity is the goal, it is essential that a school make a commitment to assisting young mothers to graduate."

Barbara Bitters, in the chapter on Vocational education, offers a definition of vocational sex equity as one that provides "an environment in which individuals can consider options and make choices based on their abilities and talents, not on the basis of gender expectations." She provides data on sexual harassment, salary differentials between males and females, and on the particular problems faced by women of color, women with disabilities, and female heads of households in the workforce. And she traces these problems to biased attitudes and practices in the field of vocational education. Barbara Bitters closes the chapter with many practical strategies that sex equity activists can employ at the local and state levels.

The final chapter of this guide is Libraries and Media Centers, a compilation of equity resources by Marylin Hulme. She sees librarians as being in a key position to effect system-wide change within a school by building an equitable collection of materials that is open and representative. Strategies for accomplishing this task include bringing a focus on equity to reviewing the collection, developing collection strategies, and examining selection policies.

Conclusion

For readers who wish to examine the theoretical background of educational equity and to learn more about educational strategies, two recent publications are recommended: <u>Handbook for Achieving Sex Equity through Education</u>, edited by Susan S. Klein and <u>Sex Equity in Education: Readings and Strategies</u> by Anne O'Brien Carelli.

The Handbook, focusing on how sex equity can be achieved in and through education, is a compendium of articles, research, and bibliographical references by nationally known leaders in the field of sex equity. It addresses issues of sex-role development and psychology, research, administration, specific populations, curriculum content areas, and general educational practices. Sex Equity in Education is a textbook that discusses the problems and provides solutions to encourage educators to eliminate sex-role stereotyping. Topics covered include early childhood and sex-role socialization, educators' response to contemporary families, teaching practices, administration, equity in math, science, and technology, and bias in textbooks. These two books provide the perfect companion pieces to the practical curriculum approach taken by Resources For Educational Equity.

It is our sincere hope and intent that Resources for Educational Equity be used as widely as possible to help educate all students from preschool through twelfth grade free of the limits imposed by the use of biased and stereotyped materials. By providing equality of opportunity we will ensure that our children and our youth, our most important assets for the future, develop to their fullest potential.

Notes

1. Federal education laws that promote equity include Title VI of the Civil Rights Act of 1964 (nondiscrimination on the basis of race, color, or national origin), Title IX of the Education Amendments of 1972 (nondiscrimination on the basis of sex), Section 504 of the Rehabilitation Act of 1973 (nondiscrimination on the basis of disability), and Public Law 94-142--The Education of All Handicapped Children Act of 1975. To provide incentives for state and local compliance with Title IX, Congress also passed program statutes and appropriated funds primarily through the Women's Educational Equity Act of 1974, Title IV of the 1964 Civil Rights Act, and the Vocational Education Amendments of 1976.

2. Susan S. Klein, ed., Handbook for Achieving Sex Equity through Education (Baltimore: Johns Hopkins University Press, 1985); Anne O'Brien Carelli, ed., Sex Equity in Education: Readings and Strategies (Springfield, IL: Charles Thomas Publishers, 1988).

THE WOMEN'S EDUCATIONAL EQUITY ACT: IMPETUS AND INSPIRATION

Leslie R. Wolfe

Once upon a time, in 1971, when the extent of sexism in education and employment was only dimly understood (and only by those called feminists), a young woman working for a Congressional education subcommittee asked for a promotion. Arlene Horowitz still remembers what her boss told her: "He said that I couldn't have a promotion, even though he knew I deserved it, because -- as he put it -- 'I just can't see women in positions of responsibility.'"[1]

Arlene Horowitz, hurt and angry, decided to do something about the sex-role stereotyping that so clearly restricted her opportunities and those of other women. She talked to Bernice Sandler, the founding director of the Project on the Status and Education of Women of the Association of American Colleges, and other feminists working for equity for women in higher education. And together, they developed an audacious plan. They would draft a piece of legislation that would make educational equity for women more than a dream. Together, they wrote what later became the Women's Educational Equity Act (WEEA) of 1974; to this day, Arlene Horowitz says that this was "the single most important thing I have ever done in my life, or will ever do."[2]

This volume, <u>Resources for Educational Equity</u>, is evidence that Arlene Horowitz's assessment was correct, for the book owes much to the Women's Educational Equity Act. And so, I am especially grateful that the editors believed it was important for the readers of this book to understand WEEA's crucial role in the development and dissemination of many of the equity materials described in these chapters.

Before WEEA, it was virtually impossible to find any educational materials, whether for teacher training, curriculum reform, or any other purpose, that did not perpetuate sex and race stereotypes. In addition, existing materials either totally excluded people with disabilities or portrayed them in negative and discriminatory ways. Thanks to WEEA, that is no longer the case. Indeed, many of the this book's authors have been WEEA grantees; and many of the materials they discuss were developed with WEEA funds.

Of equal significance, I believe, is the role that WEEA has played in defining issues of educational equity to include women and girls of diverse racial and ethnic groups and women and girls with disabilities. While this will be the focus of my comments, first the history of WEEA must be told.

History of WEEA

The original WEEA, drafted by feminists with a vision of equal educational opportunity, was introduced into the House of Representatives by a feminist Member of Congress from Hawaii, Patsy Mink, who used every legislative strategy her extensive experience had taught her to ensure passage of the bill. She introduced the bill first in 1972 and reintroduced it in 1973, holding brief hearings at that time. Then, while Congresswoman Mink was endeavoring to incorporate her bill into the omnibus Elementary and Secondary Education Act (ESEA) in 1974, a feminist on Senator Walter Mondale's staff, Ellen Hoffman, joined in and ensured that WEEA also would appear in the Senate version of ESEA. And on August 21, 1974, the Women's Educational Equity Act became law.

The explicit purpose of the new law was to provide educational equity for women in the United States. To achieve this goal, WEEA authorized the Office of Education (now the Department of Education) to create a program to award grants and contracts for the development of new curriculum and training models that would attack sex bias in education at every level, from preschool through adult education.

WEEA's first grants were awarded in 1976 and, by 1979, many important landmark projects had been supported. Highly regarded materials on Title IX were developed and presented in workshops for state and community educational personnel. These materials, developed by Shirley McCune and her staff at the Resource Center on Sex Equity, remain among the best training materials for Title IX implementation. In addition, because so many local, grassroots women's organizations had no experience in writing proposals and felt, therefore, that they could not compete for grants, the WEEA Program (at the insistence of the National Advisory Council on Women's Educational Programs) funded proposal writing workshops around the country.

WEEA grants supported staff development projects at all

levels, career development programs for rural high school students, academic and social skills programs for women in the penal system, and projects that gave students active roles in implementing Title IX. WEEA also funded several women's studies projects, including efforts to infuse the new scholarship on women into the liberal arts curriculum, to develop textbooks on women in American and world history, and to produce new curriculum materials for preschool and elementary school classrooms. In addition, WEEA projects addressed math anxiety and avoidance among female students and teachers and developed strategies for moving women into educational administration.

By 1978, when WEEA was scheduled to be reauthorized, both the strengths and weaknesses of its implementation had become clear. Many feminists (myself included) were concerned that the Office of Education's failure to set priorities for the WEEA Program had resulted in the relative exclusion of important considerations: less traditional, more feminist projects; various population groups (primarily women of color); certain levels of education (junior high school); particular types of grantees (grass-roots feminist and community-based nonprofit organizations); and projects designed to make long-term institutional change. Because it was clear that Congress would never appropriate funds for WEEA in the billions necessary to infuse equity into every school district and college, we believed it was essential that WEEA's limited resources be focused on certain areas of greatest need.

Because of continued advocacy for WEEA by feminist organizations, especially the National Coalition for Women and Girls in Education, the law was reauthorized in 1978 with substantial improvements. We called it the "new" WEEA when it became law on November 1, 1978, and it required the Department to establish priorities for funding under the Act, in response to these concerns.[4]

New Priorities

When I became Director of the WEEA Program in August of 1979, funding priorities for the "new" WEEA were developed in response to hundreds of suggestions from public comments, from the Coalition, from the Advisory Council, and from other concerned advocates for educational equity. The staff shared a vision of WEEA as a feminist program -- a program that would express our government's commitment to the ideals of

equality and justice by transforming the educational
experiences of girls and women.

We envisioned the "new" WEEA as a program that would
focus important resources on addressing the self-defined
educational needs of women of color, a program that would
jointly attack sexism and racism as the two-headed monster of
discrimination and oppression. We envisioned a program that
would fund important activities designed to eliminate the
institutional structures and patriarchal assumptions that
maintained inequity. We envisioned a program that would take
the lead in addressing double discrimination and stereotyping
on the basis of both sex and disability and that would end
the invisibility of women with disabilities in our curriculum
and consciousness. We envisioned a program that would lead
the way in showing parents, teachers, and policymakers why
equity is essential to educational quality and how it can be
implemented in every part of the country, at every level of
education, and in every aspect of the educational system.

The priorities established in 1980, which remain WEEA's
priorities despite the upheavals of the Reagan years, reflect
this vision. They include an emphasis on projects that will
assist schools to comply with both the "letter" and the
"spirit" of Title IX -- to make long lasting change in their
own administration and pedagogy. They focus on the most
recalcitrant "persistent barriers" to educational equity --
those bastions of sex and race bias that seem impossible to
change but must be addressed.

The priorities attempt institutional change in the
administration of our schools, rather than simply attempting
to improve women's credentials so that they can continue
applying for top level jobs. WEEA established a priority
that would support projects that influence educational
leaders and policymakers for equity. Thus, we expressed our
belief in the importance of educating the hiring officials
rather than pouring money into programs to provide more
administrative training for women, many of whom already were
over-qualified for administrative jobs but simply were not
hired!

And the priorities clearly state the WEEA Program's
policy that its most important work would be to focus
national attention on the severe and destructive impact of
combined sex, race, and disability bias, stereotyping, and
discrimination. And so we established two crucial funding
priorities; one focusing on racism and sexism and the other

on disability discrimination and sexism.[6]

WEEA Projects

Invaluable materials and programs have been developed by WEEA grantees during the past five years. WEEA projects have addressed critical Title IX compliance issues -- physical education and sports, in-classroom sex segregation, health services for women on campus, for instance. They also have addressed compliance-related issues (the "spirit" of the law) -- curriculum reform, teacher and parent training, and development of community support networks for equity. WEEA projects are as diverse as possible; they have developed new curricula for high school social studies and arts classes focused on the cultural experiences of Chicana women in the United States, training and awareness seminars for Chinese American women, research seminars for black women policymakers and researchers, and teacher training programs to reshape negative teacher expectations for students of color, to name only a few. Leadership and skills development projects have produced models and materials to improve the status of transitional black women in the Southeast, of rural Chicana farmworkers, of Indian women living on the reservation, and black women in an urban university.

As the first funder of projects addressing the educational needs of women and girls with disabilities, WEEA has been invaluable. Curriculum materials include new approaches to training disabled teenage girls and young women with disabilities in their civil rights and educational and career opportunities. Career education materials for K-3 also have been developed, as have outstanding new preschool and elementary curriculum resources showing children and adults with disabilities interacting with their nondisabled peers.

This essay would fill the entire book if I were to list all of the important materials developed in whole or in part with WEEA funds as well as those inspired by WEEA's priorities and by the continuing leadership of present and former WEEA grantees. For it is this powerful national network of advocates for equity that makes all of the difference and ensures that the spirit and purpose of the Women's Educational Equity Act will survive and flourish.

The Future of WEEA

Indeed, WEEA was reauthorized by Congress again -- despite strongly expressed Reagan Administration and New Right hostility. The "newest" WEEA, which became law in October of 1984, has been strengthened and improved with a new purpose -- "to provide educational equity for women and girls who suffer multiple discrimination, bias or stereotyping based on sex and on race, ethnic origin, disability or age." Thus, our most recent victory has been to ensure that the funding priority created in 1980 now is mandated by law.

A final word, from feminist Lucy Stone in 1855, captures our purpose and persistence: "In education, in marriage, in everything, disappointment is the lot of woman. It shall be the business of my life to deepen this disappointment in every woman's heart until she bows down to it no longer." The movement for educational equity already has defined the "disappointment." This volume offers us the resources for ending it and ensuring that our educational system prepares the coming generations for life in an egalitarian world where all are judged, not by race or sex or disability, but as Martin Luther King dreamed, only by the "content of their character."

Notes

1. Conversation with Arlene Horowitz, December, 1985.

2. Ibid.

3. For a more detailed discussion of the passage and implementation of the Women's Educational Equity Act, from 1974 through 1980, see Mary Ann Millsap and Leslie R. Wolfe, "A Feminist Perspective in Law and Practice: The Women's Educational Equity Act," in Marguerite Ross Barnett and Charles C. Harrington, Readings on Equal Education, Volume 8, Race, Sex, and National Origin: Public Attitudes of Desegregation, New York: AMS Press, Inc., 1985.

4. Another important provision of the reauthorized Women's Educational Equity Act was the addition of a new purpose for the program, to provide specific grants to local educational agencies and other institutions and organizations to assist them in implementing Title IX at the local level.   These local implementation grants, however, could only be awarded

if Congress appropriated more than $15 million for the WEEA Program. Since that has never happened, the local assistance grants have never been awarded (although the late Patricia Roberts Harris requested $20 million for 1981 when she was Secretary of HEW, that request was withdrawn by the new Reagan Administration in January of 1981).

5. For additional information about the recent history of the WEEA Program, see A Clash of Ideologies: The Reagan Administration Versus The Women's Educational Equity Act (published by PEER and available for $2 per copy from PEER, 1413 K Street, N.W., 9th floor, Washington, DC 20005) and Judith Paterson, "Equity in Exile: The Reagan War on Equality," Ms. Magazine, November 1984, pages 18-20.

6. In 1986 and 1987, the Reagan Administration chose to fund a few grants in the priority for Title IX compliance and to reserve the bulk of WEEA's grants for projects in a more general "other" category, thus essentially eliminating, for the remainder of the Reagan Administration, the focused funding that had been WEEA's hallmark since 1980.

7. For a complete description of the reauthorized WEEA, see PEER Policy Paper #3, The New Women's Educational Equity Act: Still Alive and Making a Difference, Spring 1985 (published by PEER and available for $1 per copy).

SEX, RACE, AND DISABILITY:

TRIPLE THREAT TO EDUCATIONAL EQUITY FOR GIRLS AND WOMEN

Beryle Banfield

Educational equity for women cannot be adequately addressed without taking into account the factors of race and disability as well as that of sex. There are women who experience institutional discrimination purely on the basis of sex. There are women who suffer institutional discrimination because of sex and race. Still others encounter institutional barriers based on sex and disability. Finally, there are those who are triply jeopardized because of sex, race, and disability.

All of these women feel the impact of institutionalized discrimination as it is reflected in the denial of full and equal opportunity for education and training. To treat the issue of educational equity for women as purely one of sex equity is not to recognize that even if all institutional barriers based on sex were to be removed, women of color would still be victimized by institutional discrimination based on race.[1] It is also to ignore the fact that women and girls with disabilities are underserved by the educational system and do not receive the type of training or education that would enable them to reach their full potential and become economically self-sufficient.[2] It becomes important, therefore, to understand the connections between discrimination based on sex, race, and disability and to focus on all three issues as they relate to educational inequities.

It is also essential to examine the reasons these inequities developed, how they were perpetuated and maintained, and the impact of unequal educational opportunities on the lives of all girls and women. Finally, we need to become aware of the implications for the development of effective programs designed to achieve educational equity.

Roots of Inequity

Educational inequities based on sex, race, and disability are deeply rooted in national tradition and practices. These practices are a direct outgrowth of the attitudes and values that informed the development of United States society. The white males who determined the shape that the society was to take came to these shores with very well defined attitudes. Their attitude toward sex roles was effectively demonstrated by the fact that the signing of the Mayflower compact was limited to the males on board. Attitudes toward race and sex were demonstrated by the refusal to respect the right of Native American women to participate in treaty negotiations, as previously had been their custom. This attitude was further underscored by the legislation conceived and enacted that transformed African American women into chattels that produced more chattels for the profit of the slavemaster. Of course, since women with disabilities also were excluded from American history, one can only infer that they, too, were treated as nonpersons.

Institutionalization of Inequity

Discrimination based on sex and race became institutionalized as the law, business, religion, and government combined to enforce societal inequities through a series of rules and restrictions that effectively limited women's access to educational and employment opportunities. For the slave woman this meant the imposition of a life of long, hard, unpaid labor. For her, education was rigidly proscribed, and those brave black women who taught slave girls and women to read did so on pain of death. For the white woman, the laws and statutes meant consignment to those jobs designated as women's work and only as much education as was deemed necessary to fulfill those roles.

The societal attitudes that unquestioningly accepted inequities based on sex, race, and disability as natural and desirable social arrangements were fueled by social and occupational stereotypes developed to justify such discriminatory treatment. These stereotypes acquired validity as they were sanctioned and spread through textbooks and tradebooks, literature, the movies, and more recently, the electronic media. These negative images thus became part of the national consciousness determining the ways in which the people affected by these stereotypes were perceived and treated.

Acceptance of negative social and occupational stereotypes has been translated into educational practices and programs that have served to perpetuate educational inequities. These have ranged from teacher education courses based on social and educational philosophies derived from theories of sex and race inferiority to the use of educational materials that foster social and occupational stereotypes of sex, race, and disability. Acceptance of these stereotypes also has led to inappropriate career counseling practices particularly in the case of girls and women of color and girls and women with disabilities.

Impact of Inequity

The devastating effects of institutional barriers supported by social stereotyping were highlighted in a recent report on women's work issued by the National Academy of Science. The report acknowledged the large gains in female employment in the 1970s and the increase in the number of females in traditionally male occupations. Affirmative action programs were credited for these positive results. The report, however, emphasized that women are still largely limited to sex-segregated occupations such as secretaries, registered nurses, and bookkeepers and specifically cites discrimination and institutional barriers in their education, training, and employment as the cause. Social stereotyping was cited as a major factor that will continue to limit women's progress.[4]

Recent statistics provide ample proof of the extent to which institutional discrimination based on sex, race, and disability limit the earning power of women. In 1985, the mean annual income for full-time workers was as follows: for every $1.00 earned by white males, white females earn $.61.2, black women earned $.54.8 and Hispanic women earned $.51.7.[5] White female workers with disabilities earn less than one-third the salary of their male counterparts and black female workers with disabilities earn less than that.[6]

Research has shown that negative stereotypic perceptions tend to be internalized by those victimized by these negative presentations.[7] The logical result is a poor self-concept and acceptance of the limited occupational roles to which they have been consigned. Given this circumstance, the phenomenon of math avoidance by female students socialized to accept mathematics as a male subject should come as no surprise, nor should the failure of female students of color to choose mathematics as an elective in high school.

Implications for Educational Practices and Programs

There are definite implications that there is a need for educational and instructional practices designed to reduce the deleterious effects of negative social and occupational stereotyping based on sex, race, and disability.

It is clearly indicated that the attack on negative social and occupational stereotypes should begin on day one of a child's school experience. It has been established that by the time a child enters school, his or her perceptions of the societal roles assigned to individuals on the basis of sex and race already have begun to develop.[8] Because of the failure of the media to present persons with disabilities in positive and productive roles, a child most likely already has received negative messages concerning the way in which society regards people with disabilities.

This suggests that corrective and preventive strategies need to be employed in the early childhood years. Corrective strategies help to counteract those negative perceptions that might already have begun to develop. Preventive strategies forestall the hardening of negative perceptions and the acceptance of additional negative stereotypes. This means establishing a classroom environment that sends messages different from those perpetuated by the media and society at large. Teacher behavior, use of language, and choice of instructional materials should be guided by the need to reduce the effect of societal and occupational stereotypes based on sex, race, and disability.

On a simple level, children in the early grades can be taught to analyze their picture books, nursery rhymes, and readers for the kinds of messages they send in terms of sex, race, and disability. From the middle grades upward, students can analyze advertisements in magazines and on television, and be guided to explore the historic and economic reasons for the development of negative stereotypes. High school students should be able to make predictions concerning the economic future of white women, women of color, and women with disabilities. Activities for both female and male students should involve awareness, consideration of solutions, and development of strategies to reduce the limiting effect of social and occupational stereotyping. In addition, students need to be provided with the type of counseling that enables them to make course choices that prepare them for increased career options and to succeed in those subjects.

Negative stereotypes based on sex, race, and disability support institutional discrimination against girls and women and lead to inequitable educational practices, which ultimately result in economic disadvantages for women. This is the cycle we must break, and the resources in this volume provide a way for educators to reach that goal.

Notes

1. See Council on Interracial Books for Children, Facts Sheets on Institutional Racism and Understanding Institutional Racism (1841 Broadway, New York, NY 10023).

2. See the Council of Chief State School Officers Resource Center on Sex Equity, Concerns, Issue IX, June 1983, special issue on "Sex Equitable Education for Disabled Students"; and Interracial Books for Children, Bulletin, vol. 8, nos. 6 and 7, 1977, special issue on "Handicapism."

3. Discussed in John Terrell and Donna Terrell, Indian Women of the Western Morning (New York: Dial Press, 1974) and Shirley Hill Witt, Tuscaroras (New York: Crowell, 1972).

4. Barbara F. Reskin and Heidi I. Hartmann, eds., Women's Work, Men's Work: Segregation on the Job (Washington, DC: National Academy Press, 1986).

5. National Commission on Working Women, Pay Equity – A Fact Sheet (Washington, DC, 1985).

6. Bureau of the Census data from March 1982, cited in Concerns, Issue IX, June 1983.

7. See Candace Garrett Schau, "Educational Equity and Sex Role Development" and Selma Greenberg, "Educational Equity in Early Education Environments" in Handbook for Achieving Sex Equity Through Education, ed by Susan S. Klein (Baltimore and London: The Johns Hopkins University Press, 1985).

8. See Interracial Books for Children Bulletin issue on "Children, Race and Racism: How Race Awareness Develops," vol. 11, nos. 3 and 4, 1980.

Resources for
Educational Equity

EARLY CHILDHOOD EDUCATION

Linda Colón and Ellen Rubin

Learning Begins at Home

Beginning at birth a child is actively learning from clues in her/his environment. Family members become the child's first educators, and children rapidly form a view of "the way things are supposed to be," based on their early family experiences. These experiences become guidelines by which other experiences are interpreted and evaluated. As children mature, these early beliefs become reinforced or are replaced by other beliefs that "work better" for making sense of the world.

Of course, the preceding scenario is a simplified view of the complex social, emotional, and intellectual development that takes place during a child's first few years of life. The important point, however, is that by the time they enter a child care or preschool setting, children already have a baseline of experiences that influence their perception of the world.

The Equity Role of Early Childhood Educators

As the recent findings of the High Scope Perry Preschool Project document, early childhood education can have a positive, long-term impact, helping children to achieve more in school and in their adult lives.[1] At the same time, early childhood education can limit children's potential by perpetuating sex-differentiated attitudes and behaviors, by reinforcing racially or ethnically biased attitudes, or by perpetuating negative attitudes about people with disabilities.

Addressing the "Isms"

For the most part, preschoolers come into the classroom with a fairly well-developed concept of gender-based social roles and racial differences that have been learned through family and community experiences, television, books, games, toys, and friends.[2] They learn negative stereotypes about being a person of color (racism) and about being a female (sexism) in this society.

In terms of disability, many children have had no experience with a person who is disabled (unless the child or a significant other in her/his life is disabled). This lack of direct experience, combined with negative media images and societal messages about people with disabilities, lead to the development of biased attitudes (handicapism). While efforts have been made to address issues of sex and race bias at the early childhood level, less has been done to counteract disability bias.

Negative messages are destructive to <u>all children</u>--to children of color, to white children, to girls, to boys, to children with disabilities, to children who are poor, and to those who are rich. Thus, it becomes critical that educators address these issues in age-appropriate ways, by creating learning environments that are "inclusive." An inclusive environment is one that is nonsexist, multicultural, and includes images and actual role models of people with disabilities. Such an environment expands young children's perceptions of the world and helps them extend their own experiences to include a wide range of people different from themselves.

Eliminating Language Bias

Choice of language is reflective of personal and societal attitudes and prejudices. Attitudes can be transmitted in a number of ways: how and when one says something; through the choice of words, gestures, facial expressions, body language; or by what one chooses or does not choose to say. Language, for example, plays a large role in perpetuating bias. Words and expressions of speech can instantly convey individual or societal prejudices towards specific groups. The damaging effects of sexist language, such as use of the generic "he" or referring to women of any age as "girl," have become familiar and are avoided by most educators. Similarly, racist stereotypes, such as referring to a black man of any age as "boy" or to a black woman as "the girl," have been virtually eliminated from popular speech patterns. It is widely understood that such terms convey second class status and dependency and hinder the development of a positive self image.

Drawing a parallel from sexist and racist language, "handicapist language" has a similar negative effect on self-image, but this is not yet well recognized by educators or the general public. The word "invalid" means "not valid" and the word "crippled," which comes from the word "creep," are only two examples of the negative images conveyed through language that educators must begin to examine and eliminate. Also, the word handicapped is believed to be derived from a begging term, "cap-in-hand," an image that arouses pity rather than respect.

In addition to developing attitudes and beliefs that are conveyed through language, young children typically mimic their teachers' speech patterns, right down to using exact expressions and intonations. Therefore, bias-free language becomes one of the most basic and essential equity tools of the early childhood classroom.

The Benefits of Equity in Early Childhood

The benefits of creating an early childhood learning environment that is nonsexist, multicultural, and includes images and actual role models of adults and children with disabilities are long-term, freeing children to develop their full potential and a positive sense of self-esteem. Providing equity at the preschool level:

o helps children understand, respect, and appreciate differences

o acquaints children with the reality of the world around them

o extends children's range of experience

o enhances children's self-image and self-esteem

o allows children to develop to their fullest potential

Plentiful Resources

Given the appropriate resources, early childhood educators can create an equitable classroom environment for all children, regardless of sex, race, or disability. It is fortunate that picture books, posters, toys, games, and teacher resources that promote equity are plentiful at this level.

While resources are necessary to create a physical environment in the classroom that dispels stereotypic views, it is equally important to provide opportunities for concrete equity experiences such as worksite and community trips, to arrange to have positive role models visit classrooms, and to encourage children and teachers to share personal experiences.

The following list of resources has been selected to help create a learning environment that is nonsexist, multicultural, and includes images of adults and children with disabilities. While some of the resources do not meet all these criteria simultaneously, they are included because they focus on at least one of the three equity areas and have additional qualities that make them worth noting.

The bibliography is divided into three sections: <u>Picture Books</u>, <u>Classroom Materials</u>, and <u>Teacher Resources</u>, which includes training and curriculum guides, organizations, articles, and publishers/distributors of bias-free materials.

Notes

1. John R. Berrueta-Clement, Lawrence J. Schweinhart, W. Steven Barnett, Ann S. Epstein, and David P. Weikart, <u>Changed Lives</u> (Ypsilanti, MI: High Scope Press, 1984).

2. James Olden, et al., "Racial Awareness in Kindergarten Children: A Decade of Progress?" <u>Integrateducation</u>, Spring, 1981, pp. 98-100. As reported in "Perspectives," an essay written by Beryle Banfield and Robert B. Moore, which appeared in <u>Resources for Early Childhood</u> (New York: Garland, 1983).

BIBLIOGRAPHY

Picture Books

Adoff, Arnold, illustrated by Emily McCully. <u>Black Is Brown Is Tan</u>. New York: Harper and Row, 1973.
   A story poem about a multiracial family delighting in each other and in the good things of the earth. The joy they feel extends to everyone who reads the book.

Baker, Pamela, illustrated by Patricia Bellan Gillen. <u>My First Book of Sign</u>. Washington, DC: Kendall Green Publications, imprint of Gallaudet Press, 1986 (second printing, 1987).
   Children of many races and cultures sign 150 words in clear, colorful pictures. Words are arranged in easy to find alphabetical order. For added clarity, a description of each sign is included in the index. A must for anyone interested in learning the manual alphabet (finger spelling) or basic words in sign language.

Bang, Molly, illustrated by author. <u>Ten, Nine, Eight</u>. New York: Greenwillow Books, 1983.
   A unique, gentle bedtime story and number book that provides a reassuring countdown to the land of dreams.

Baylor, Byrd, illustrated by Peter Parnall. <u>I'm in Charge of Celebrations</u>. New York: Charles Scribner's Sons, 1986.
   Captures some of the special experiences of the southwest desert country. The brightly-colored desert scenes enhance the story's beauty.

Brenner, Barbara, photographs by George Ancona. <u>Bodies</u>. New York: E. P. Dutton, 1973.
   Presents a good way to begin thinking about bodies and how they work. The black-and-white photographs are multiracial and nonsexist.

Cairo, Shelley, Jasmine Cairo, and Tara Cairo, photographs by Irene McNeil. <u>Our Brother Has Down's Syndrome</u>. Toronto,

Canada: Annick Ltd., 1985.

Clear photographs of a toddler who has Down's Syndrome show him in a variety of situations with his family, teacher, and classmates. Unfortunately, the text is not as appealing as the photos. Although it provides information about this type of disability and some insight into life with a family that has a small child with Down's Syndrome, there is no real story line. However, it is included despite its shortcomings since age-appropriate books on this topic are so rare.

Caines, Jeannette, illustrated by Pat Cummins. <u>Just Us Women</u>. New York: Harper and Row Publishers, 1982.

Lively illustrations and simple text combine to create just the right mood for a very special trip—easy, carefree, and warm. One drawback is that they refer to having taken a long time as "we had a lot of girl talk to do".

Children's Television Workshop. <u>Sesame Street Sign Language Fun</u>. New York: Random House/Children's Television Workshop, 1980.

As the Muppets act out simple sentences, Linda Bove, a member of the National Theatre of the Deaf, illustrates the signs. Most illustrations are nonsexist, but some words are not, e.g., "policeman" (which can be changed to read "police officer"). Also available from: The National Association for the Deaf (bookstore), 814 Thayer Ave., Silver Springs, MD 20910.

Clifton, Lucille, illustrated by Thomas DiGrazia. <u>My Friend Jacob</u>. New York: E. P. Dutton, 1980.

This is the story of eight-year-old Sam and his seventeen-year-old friend, Jacob, who is mentally retarded. It focuses on the friendship, the activities the boys share, and the things they do for each other. The soft black-and-white sketches are multiracial.

Crews, Donald, illustrated by author. <u>Bicycle Race</u>. New York: Greenwillow Books, 1985.

Bright colors and numbered helmets help the reader to follow the race and learn about counting at the same time. The multiracial drawings show both women and men participating, and a woman is shown repairing her own bike.

Clifton, Lucille, illustrated by Ann Grifalconi. <u>Everett Anderson's Goodbye</u>. New York: Holt, Rinehart, and Winston, 1983.

A young boy tries to come to grips with his father's death. The story captures the true and painful feelings of loss, from denial and anger to depression and, finally, acceptance.

Father Gander, (alias Dr. Douglas Larch). <u>Father Gander Nursery Rhymes: The Equal Rhymes Amendment.</u> Santa Barbara, CA: Advocacy Press, 1985.

In this volume, Father Gander "amends" traditional nursery rhymes so that they offer more equitable world views. This book is important because our most popular rhymes reveal a male dominated, able-bodied, monocultural fairyland filled with sexism, anger, violence, environmental, and nutritional ignorance.

Flournoy, Valerie, illustrated by Jerry Pinkney. <u>The Patchwork Quilt</u>. New York: E.P. Dutton/Dial Books for Young Readers, 1985.

Tanya's grandmother works daily to make a quilt of memories using scraps from family members' clothing. When Grandmother becomes ill, Tanya and her mother finish the quilt together. A beautifully illustrated story of sharing, trust, and family life.

Goldsmid, Paula, illustrated by Janice Schopler. <u>Did You Ever</u>. Chapel Hill, NC: Lollipop Power, Inc., 1971.

A book that invites children to think of all the different things they may want to do. Possibilities range from kissing a kangaroo to washing a whale. Boys and girls are shown participating equally.

Greenfield, Eloise, illustrated by George Ford. <u>Darlene</u>. New York: Methuen, 1980.

Darlene, a young girl who uses a wheelchair, is feeling homesick while spending a morning with her uncle and cousin. Darlene resists her cousin's attempts to play with her, but finally becomes absorbed in games and in her uncle's guitar playing. In typical child-fashion, when Darlene's mother returns, Darlene doesn't want to go home. <u>Darlene</u> is outstanding because the child's disability is secondary to the plot; it shows a positive view of a black family; and has

a male caregiver as a main character. Unfortunately, Darlene
is out of print, but can be found in libraries.

Hines, Anna Grossnickle, illustrated by author. Daddy Makes
the Best Spaghetti. New York: Carion Books/Ticknor and
Fields, A Houghton Mifflin Co., 1986.
  A sparkling picture book that depicts parents sharing
everyday routines that are transformed into joyful games.

Hazen, Nancy, illustrated by author. Grown-Ups Cry Too/Los
Adultos Tambien Lloran. Chapel Hill, NC: Lollipop Power,
1973.
  Depicts a wide range of emotions: sadness, anger,
fatigue, fear, and happiness as expressed in Stanley Kramer's
family. Stanley explains the reasons for a baby's crying;
relates experiences that have made him cry; and tells about
many different situations in which his mother and/or father
and grandmother cried, too. This nonsexist, multiracial book
is not inclusive of people with disabilities, but it is a
good story to stimulate discussions about emotions.

Head, Barry, and Jim Seguin, designed by Frank Dastolfo and
photographed by Walter Seng. Who Am I? Northbrook, IL:
Hubbard, 1975.
  A girl who is hearing-impaired is shown playing, loving
her family, and learning. The title words, "Who Am I?" are
the only words in the book, and they appear periodically
throughout the text. The full-color photo illustrations are
nonsexist, multiracial, and inclusive. The book is part of a
set of books, audio cassettes, videotapes, and films
entitled, "I Am, I Can, I Will," set of materials created by
Mr. Rogers, but is available separately. (Also see Nadas,
Betsy P., Danny's Song.)

Henriod, Lorraine, illustrated by Christa Chevalier.
Grandma's Wheelchair. Chicago: Albert Whitman and Co.,
1982.
  About the warm relationship between grandma and her
four-year-old grandson, Thomas. Grandma uses a wheelchair,
and Thomas spends a lot of time riding in her lap while they
do things together. Grandma is depicted as a capable, active
homemaker. Information about wheelchair use is an integral
part of the story.

Homan, Dianne, illustrated by Mary Heine. <u>In Christina's Toolbox</u>. Chapel Hill, NC: Lollipop Power, Inc., 1981.
     Christina loves building and fixing things. The books shows all the things Christina can make and fix, and how proud she is of what she can do. It also introduces children to different tools and their uses.

Isadora, Rachel, illustrated by author. <u>Max</u>. New York: Macmillan Publishing Co., 1976.
     Young ball players and ballet dancers will share Max's delight when he discovers that dance class is a great way to warm up for a home run.

Jonas, Ann, illustrated by author. <u>The Quilt</u>. New York: Greenwillow Books, 1985.
     A young girl gets a patchwork quilt made by her mother and father from baby clothes and other favorite material. She falls asleep reminiscing about the patches, which come to life in her dreams.

_____. <u>The Trek</u>. New York: Greenwillow Books, 1985.
     A child, on her way to school, sees a large variety of animals hidden in everything she and her friend pass. If you use your imagination you, too, will see more each time you make this trip.

_____. <u>When You Were a Baby</u>. New York: Greenwillow Books, 1982.
     About all those things that babies can't do. It is a wonderful affirmation of what a toddler CAN do. It is a must for any small child who has an infant sibling.

Kaufman, Curt and Gita, photographs by Curt Kaufman. <u>Rajesh</u>. New York: Antheneum, 1985.
     This story depicts Rajesh, who was born missing both legs and one hand, in his first year of school. In his mainstreamed classroom, everyone learns about being different. This is one of the few children's books about a person with a disability that is written in the first person. The photographs reflect the multicultural nature of this classroom.

Lasker, Joe, illustrated by author. <u>He's My Brother</u>.
Chicago: Albert Whitman and Co., 1974.
   The story of Jamie, who is developmentally disabled, as
told by his brother. Balances the things Jamie can do well
with the things he does more slowly. It deals with the
frustration, hurt, and anger that Jamie experiences, as well
as the joys he feels. Softly colored and black-and-white
illustrations set a contemporary but gentle tone for this
realistic, nonsexist, and multiracial book.

Leaf, Munro, illustrated by Robert Lawson. <u>The Story of
Ferdinand</u>. New York: Penguin, 1977.
   A classic story (originally from 1936) about a
nonstereotyped bull. He is gentle, quiet, peace-loving, and
fond of flowers. He does not like to fight, charge, or roar,
but he is still a great bull. It subtly criticizes
prescribed roles. Also available in Spanish text and in
braille.

Lewin, Hugh, illustrated by Lisa Kopper. <u>Jafta's Father</u>.
Minneapolis: Carolrhoda Books, Inc., 1983.
   Jafta's lives with his mother in South Africa. His
father works in the city and only returns in the Spring. The
story centers around this special time of the year when Jafta
sees his father and they share many special moments. Text
includes words that may be new, but there is a glossary.

_____. <u>Jafta's Mother</u>. Minneapolis: Carolrhoda Books, Inc.,
1983.
   A child lovingly describes his mother. Jafta's
description awakens one's own fond memories.

Litchfield, Ada B., illustrated by Eleanor Mill. <u>A Button in
Her Ear</u>. Chicago: Albert Whitman and Co., 1976.
   Angela is a spunky girl of about eight who is hearing-
impaired. She is shown playing baseball and with her
friends, both boys and girls. Angela describes how she
misinterprets what she hears and how difficult it is for her
to hear what her friends and her teacher are saying. When
her parents take her to the doctor, he refers them to a
hearing specialist who is a black woman. The softly colored
and black-and-white illustrations are multiracial.

_____. A Cane in Her Hand. Chicago: Albert Whitman and Co., 1977.

Valerie, who is visually impaired, describes how she learns to use the long cane so she won't bump into things any more. Depicts Valerie at her visit to the eye doctor; in school, where her teacher is helpful and supportive; and with her friends both male and female.

_____, illustrated by Sonia Lasker. Captain Hook, That's Me. New York: Walker Publishing Co., 1982.

When Judy's family moves to a new town, Judy is concerned about how her new classmates will react to the prosthetic hook, which replaces her hand. This book is a must if there is a child in the school who uses a hook. Judy and her friend, Harry, call each other names which you may want to paraphrase or leave out altogether. While it is true that children often call each other names, it should not be encouraged.

_____, illustrated by Gail Owens. Making Room for Uncle Joe. Chicago: Albert Whitman and Co., 1984.

Uncle Joe, comes to live with Amy, Danny, Beth and their parents. At first, it is hard to have Uncle Joe move in. The children, especially Beth, don't know how to relate to him. Uncle Joe has Down's Syndrome and has lived for a long time in an institution. It takes time for Uncle Joe to get used to his new home and family; and it takes his family time to get used to him. They do, and when a place in a group home becomes available, the family decides together that Uncle Joe should stay where he belongs—with his family.

Mack, Bruce, illustrated by Marian Buchanan. Jesse's Dream Skirt. Chapel Hill, NC: Lollipop Power, Inc. 1979.

Jesse is proud of the skirt he and his mother made—just like the one in his dream. When he wears his skirt to day-care some of the children make fun of him while others support him. His teacher, who is a man, is very sensitive and supportive and helps the other children discuss their feelings.

Marron, C. A., illustrated by Chaya Burstein. No Trouble for Grandpa. Milwaukee: Raintree Publishers, 1983.

David and baby sister Amy are going to stay with their grandpa. David, who uses a wheelchair, is not happy about sharing this visit to grandpa's with Amy. The story shows a positive model of an older male caregiver as Grandpa demonstrates his ability to nurture both David and Amy. David's mobility impairment is not discussed in the text, but is evident in the pictures.

Maury, Inez, illustrated by Lady McCrady; translated into Spanish by Norah E. Alemany. My Mother the Mail Carrier/Mi Mama la Cartera. Westbury, NY: The Feminist Press, 1976.
    A story with many timely themes. Lupita is the daughter of a single mother who works as a mail carrier. She is proud of her mother's career and has career aspirations of her own. Each page has both English and Spanish text.

Mitchel, Joyce S., illustrated by True Kelley. My Mommy Makes Money. Boston: Little, Brown and Co., 1984.
    Mommies can do all kinds of jobs and this book describes on-the-job details. The lively and cheerful illustrations and humor add fun to this picture book depicting mommies who are car salespersons, ministers, and surgeons, among others.

Nadas, Betsy P., designed by Frank Dastolfo and William Panos. Danny's Song. Northbrook, IL: Hubbard, 1975.
    Danny, a boy who uses crutches, is shown interacting with his sister and brother. The story stresses the many things he does well and deals with his frustrations caused by having to do some things more slowly. This book is part of a set of books, audio cassettes, videotapes, and films entitled, "I Am, I Can, I Will" by Mr. Rogers, but is available separately. (See also Head, Barry, Who Am I?)

Newth, Philip. Roly Goes Exploring. New York: Philomel Books, 1981.
    A simple story with cut-out "shapes" to feel as well as to see. The text of this unique book is in both braille and in print to be enjoyed by sighted and blind children. Since Roly is a circle that is referred to as "he," to make the story nonsexist, you can alternate using "she" or "he."

Omerod, Jan. 101 Things To Do With a Baby. New York: Lothrop, Lee & Shepard Books, 1984.
    A lovely book for growing families to share. Shows mother, dad, and sister taking care of a very active baby.

Poix, Carol de, illustrated by Stephanie Sove Ney, translated by Martha P. Cotera. <u>Jo, Flo and Yolanda</u>. Chapel Hill, NC: Lollipop Power, 1973.

This delightful nonsexist story about triplets talks about the ways the girls are the same as well as the many ways they are different. Depicts a Hispanic family living in a multiracial neighborhood.

Rosenberg, Maxine B., photographs by George Ancona. <u>My Friend Leslie</u>. New York: Lothrop, Lee & Shepard, 1983.

Karen tells us about her friend Leslie, a classmate who has multiple disabilities. The story describes a typical day in school, including all the activities that Leslie, Karen, and other children do. Leslie is shown working independently as well as accepting assistance from her peers. Accommodations are made to enable Leslie to participate fully. A realistic portrayal of a successful mainstreaming effort.

Sargent, Susan, and Donna Aaron Wirt, illustrated by Allan Eitzen. <u>My Favorite Place</u>. Nashville: Abingdon Press, 1983.

This story is full of the multisensory experiences of a child's trip to the ocean. It is not until the end that the reader finds out that the girl, who is shown actively swimming and playing in the waves, is blind. Helps young children understand the use of the senses other than vision -- hearing, touch, smell, and taste.

Severance, Jane, illustrated Jan Jones. <u>Lots of Mommies</u>. Chapel Hill, NC: Lollipop Power, Inc., 1983.

A story of a nontraditional family. Emily has three mommies who care for her. Emily's classmates are surprised and enlightened when they get to see these three mommies in action.

Scott, Ann Herbert, illustrated by Glo Coalson. <u>On Mother's Lap</u>. New York: McGraw-Hill, 1972.

An Eskimo boy happily discovers there is room on his mother's lap for both him and the new baby.

Simon, Norma, illustrated by Joe Lasker. <u>All Kinds of Families</u>. Chicago: Albert Whitman and Co., 1976.

All kinds of families doing all kinds of things are

depicted in soft, warm-color drawings. Included in family scenes are a boy who uses a wheelchair and an older person with a cane. Scenes of a funeral, a wedding, and a visit to a parent in jail are interspersed with picnic scenes, holiday scenes, and other traditional family activities. Nonsexist and multiracial.

Surowiecki, Sandra Lucas, illustrated by Patricia Riley Lenthal. Joshua's Day. Chapel Hill, NC: Lollipop Power, 1972.
    Joshua lives in a one-parent home. His mother, who is a photographer, drops him off at a day care center where he interacts with many friends.

Waber, Bernard, illustrated by author. Ira Sleeps Over. Boston, MA: Houghton Mifflin, 1972.
    Rather than risk ridicule, a little boy hesitates to bring his teddy bear on an overnight visit to a friend. When he discovers his friend has a teddy bear, too, Ira runs home to get his.

Wandro, Mark and Joani Blank, illustrated by Irene Trivas. My Daddy Is a Nurse. New York: Harper and Row, 1981.
    In this book, children will meet ten daddies at work. The simple but informative text and lively illustrations help children to understand that daddies come in all shapes and sizes and can be caring and gentle in their work, as well as with their families.

Whitehouse, Jeanne Peterson, illustrated by Debora Ray. I Have a Sister, My Sister Is Deaf. New York: Harper & Row, 1977 paperback edition, 1984.
    Two sisters, one of whom is deaf, are shown doing many things together. Talks about what it is like to have a sister who is deaf and provides information about how she communicates with her family and friends. There is a good balance between what the child who is deaf can and can't do.

Williams, Vera B., illustrated by author. The Great Watermelon Birthday. New York: Greenwillow Books, 1980.
    A watermelon give-away results in a community birthday party for one hundred children, relatives, friends, and pets. The whimsical drawings highlight the unusual celebration.

_____. <u>Cherries and Cherry Pits</u>. New York: Greenwillow Books, 1986.
   Bidemmi's drawings and storytelling brings diverse people together as they enjoy sharing cherries. The text is written and illustrated through a child's perspective.

Zaslavsky, Claudia, illustrated by Jerry Pinkney. <u>Count on Your Fingers African Style</u>. New York: Thomas Y. Crowell, 1980.
   The traditional finger-counting methods of several different African peoples are illustrated. Shows how people who use different languages can find a common language through hand signs.

Zolotow, Charlotte, illustrated by William Pene Du Bois. <u>William's Doll</u>. New York: Harper and Row, 1972.
   Now a classic, this well-written book is about a boy who wants a doll to nurture, and about the negative reactions of his family and friends to his request. Williams's grandmother buys him a doll and gives a moving account of the importance of the development of gentle and nurturing qualities in prospective fathers.

Classroom Materials

<u>All About Me and Let's Be Friends: Book and Record Sets</u>. Gryphon House, Inc., 3706 Otis St., P.O. Box 275, Mt. Rainier, MD 20712.
   Picture books and accompanying cassettes (or 45 rpm records) consist of an original "Miss Jackie" song (sheet music on back page). The black-and-white photographs by David Giveans are nonsexist, multiracial, and inclusive of children with disabilities.

<u>Feeling Free Posters</u>. Human Policy Press, P.O. Box 127, Syracuse, NY 13210.
   A set of three color posters includes: "If You Thought the Wheel Was a Good Idea, You'll Love the Ramp!" featuring different views of ramps, with children using a variety of wheeled vehicles (including a wheelchair); "We All Fit In," depicting children with disabilities interacting; and "Any Questions?" showing a boy using Canadian crutches. Also available is "Hi, Friend," a Dick Bruna poster illustrating one child pushing another in a wheelchair.

Free to Be...You and Me. A project of the Ms. Foundation, Inc. New York: McGraw-Hill Book Company, 1974.
A collection of delightful nonsexist stories and songs that expands children's view of themselves and of their future. Dispels myths and challenges stereotypes. Also available as a record.

Inclusive Play People. Educational Equity Concepts, Inc., 114 E. 32nd St., Suite 306, New York, NY 10016.
Six charming and sturdy wooden figures provide a unique variety of work and family roles for use in block building and dramatic play. Approximately 6" high and made of 3/4" poplar, the figures are nonsexist, multiracial/ethnic, and include both disabled and nondisabled people of various ages. A unique, hands-on materials for early childhood classrooms.

Mainstreaming for Equity Kits and Posters. Educational Equity Concepts, Inc., 114 East 32nd St., Suite 306, New York, NY 10016.
The Kits contain books, posters, hands-on materials, and ideas for activities that present a unique approach to the language arts and social studies curriculum grades K-2 and 3-6. The 17" by 22" posters are available separately. The multicultural posters, which are grouped around themes of Families, School, and Communcation, depict disabled and nondisabled children and adults interacting in a variety of situations.

New Friends. The Chapel Hill Training Outreach Project, Lincoln Center, Merritt Hill Rd., Chapel Hill, NC 27514.
This program includes a do-it-yourself pattern for making a child-size rag doll that can be adapted to depict several different disabilities. Also available are a New Friends Trainer's Notebook and New Friends Mainstreaming Activities to Help Young Children Understand and Accept Individual Differences.

Our Helpers. Media Materials, Inc., 2936 Remington Ave., Baltimore, MD 21211-1891.
Originally created by the Non-Sexist Child Development Project, these twelve multiracial stand-up figures feature females and males in counterpart jobs. Includes postal workers, doctors, nurses, police officers, construction workers, office workers. Sturdy cardboard, 10" high.

Play Scenes Lotto. Media Materials, Inc., 2916 Remington Ave., Baltimore, MD 21211-1891.

Originally created by the Non-Sexist Child Development Project, these multicultural color photographs depict children in a wide variety of play activities unhampered by sex-role stereotypes. Four lotto boards and 24 matching cards promote visual discrimination, perceptual skills, and language-expressive activities.

Teacher Resources

Baker, Gwendolyn Calvert. **Planning and Organizing for Multicultural Instruction.** Reading, MA: Addison-Wesley, 1983.

Presents a rationale for and conceptual approach to multicultural education. Also included are a step-by-step method for developing a multicultural curriculum and a variety of teaching strategies and techniques that cover all content areas.

Bracken, Jeanne, and Sharon Wigutoff. **Books for Today's Children: An Annotated Bibliography of Nonstereotyped Picture Books.** Old Westbury, NY: The Feminist Press 1979.

A review of 143 recommended nonsexist picture books for children. Selections focus on books that portray girls and women in self-actualizing situations, boys and men expressing their emotions, and situations that address life experiences previously ignored in literature for young children.

Bulletin. Council on Interracial Books for Children, Inc., 1841 Broadway, New York, NY 10023.

Several issues of this newsletter provide excellent resources for creating an equitable early childhood environment. Volume 8, Numbers 6 and 7, 1977 is a special issue on disability bias and how it is reinforced in children's books and other media. Volume 14, Numbers 7 and 8, 1983, a special double issue on early childhood education, includes an article that contains suggestions for creating an inclusive early childhood classroom. Volume 11, Numbers 3 and 4, 1980 is devoted to "Children, Race and Racism: How Race Awareness Develops."

Claudia's Caravan. P.O. Box 1582, Alameda, CA 94501.

An organization that specializes in multicultural and

multilingual materials including books, records, and games.
Write for a catalog.

Equal Play. Women's Action Alliance, Inc., 370 Lexington
Ave., New York, NY 10017.
     Many issues of this newsletter focus on early childhood
education and nonsexist materials and resources; several are
devoted to a discussion of mainstreaming and an inclusive
early childhood classroom environment.

Dillard, John M., Lloyd R. Kinnison, and Barbara Peel.
"Multicultural Approaches to Mainstreaming: A Challenge to
Counselors, Teachers, Psychologists, and Administrators."
Peabody Journal of Education, Volume 57, No. 4, July 1980,
pp. 276-290.
     One of the few articles that brings together two
important issues--multicultural education and mainstreaming.
The authors state the need to consider the personal and
cultural experiences of all students. They also point out
the importance of using differences as a positive force in
the development of a society that professes respect for the
intrinsic worth of every individual.

Edwards, Carolyn P., with Patricia G. Ramsey. Promoting
Social Development in Young Children. New York: Teacher's
College Press 1986.
     Based on a Piagetian understanding of how children
construct knowledge of themselves and their world, the
authors examine the social, moral, and cognitive growth of
children ages two to six. Includes ideas for creating
thinking games with young children as well as sections on sex
roles and cultural diversity.

Froschl, Merle, Linda Colon, Ellen Rubin, and Barbara Sprung.
Including All of Us: An Early Childhood Curriculum About
Disability. New York: Educational Equity Concepts, 1984.
     Discusses why and how learning about disability benefits
all children's cognitive, social, and emotional growth.
Activities are grouped into three curriculum areas:
Same/Different, incorporating hearing impairment; Body Parts,
incorporating visual impairment; and Transportation,
incorporating mobility impairment. (Also distributed by
Gryphon House, 3706 Otis St., P.O. Box 275, Mt. Rainier, MD
20712.)

Froschl, Merle and Barbara Sprung, eds. <u>Beginning Equal: A</u>
<u>Manual About Nonsexist Childrearing for Infants and Toddlers</u>.
New York: Women's Action Alliance, 1983.

A series of workshop materials for caregivers and/or
parents that explore gender issues as they relate to very
young children.

Greenberg, Selma. <u>Right From the Start: A Guide to Nonsexist</u>
<u>Childrearing</u>. Boston, MA: Houghton Mifflin, 1978.

Nonsexist childrearing affects every aspect of family
life. Discipline, sibling rivalry, the terrible twos and the
tendency of boys to be "bad" and girls to be too "good," are
only some of the issues covered in this humorous but
comprehensive look at nonsexist parenting.

Gryphon House, Inc., Early Childhood Books, 3706 Otis St.,
P.O. Box 275, Mt. Rainier, MD 20712.

Gryphon House is committed to supplying educators with
books that are nonsexist, multiracial, and, more recently,
inclusive of people with disabilities. They have a
comprehensive collection of quality books for children and
teachers.

Jenkins, Jeanne Kohl, and Pam McDonald. <u>Growing Up Equal</u>.
Englewood Cliffs, NJ: Prentice-Hall, Inc., 1979.

A resource and activity book for parents and educators
that provides suggestions to help children develop in a
nonsexist environment and encourages all children to explore
their abilities and interests.

Kamien, Janet, illustrated by Signe Hanson. <u>What If You</u>
<u>Couldn't...?</u> New York: Charles Scribner's Sons, 1979.

This informative and simply-written book provides basic
information about what it is like to be disabled. The
drawings show a variety of active children and adults with
disabilities.

Kendall, Frances E. <u>Diversity in the Classroom: A</u>
<u>Multicultural Approach to Education of Young Children</u>. New
York: Teachers College Press, 1983.

Provides the reader with a variety of ways to achieve
education that is multicultural. Combines theoretical
background with a wealth of practical suggestions. Includes

an annotated bibliography of multicultural children's books, a checklist to help teachers determine which aspects of their curriculum need more emphasis on cultural diversity, and sources for multicultural materials and curriculum.

Klein, Susan S. Handbook for Achieving Sex Equity Through Education. Baltimore & London: Johns Hopkins University Press, 1985.
    The authors view education as the primary vehicle for equalizing opportunities and potential success of individuals who come from lower status groups in our society. The volume covers curriculum areas, research, and administration and teacher training issues. The chapters on "Educational Equity and Sex-Role Development" by Candace Garrett Schau and on "Educational Equity in Early Childhood Environments" by Selma Greenberg are of special importance to early childhood education.

Lollipop Power, Inc., P.O. Box 1171, Chapel Hill, NC 27514.
    A feminist collective that writes, illustrates, and publishes books to counteract sex stereotyping and role models presented by society to young children. A list of currently available books, as well as an information sheet for writers and illustrators interested in submitting material to the collection, can be obtained by sending a stamped, self-addressed envelope to the above address.

Nuegebauer, Bonnie, Ed. Alike and Different: Exploring Our Humanity with Young Children. Redmond, WA: Exchange Press, Inc., 1987.
    A book for teachers of young children that addresses issues of race, gender and disability with an emphasis on appreciating diversity. A positive approach to help educators increase their own awareness and address diversity in the classroom. Includes a good bibliography of resources.

Ohio State University, College of Education. "Sex Equity in Education." Theory Into Practice. Volume 25, Number 4, Autumn 1986.
    Addresses questions about the most effective ways of achieving sex equity in education. Some of the topics covered include: sex equity in parenting and parent education, in bilingual education, in computer learning, and in the education of girls and women with disabilities.

Ramsey Patricia G. Teaching and Learning in a Diverse World. New York: Teacher's College Press 1987.

Includes sections on child development theory and research and gives examples of how teachers might apply this information in their classrooms. Provides general goals and a model for incorporating a multicultural perspective into all phases and areas of teaching. Questions are included that will enable teachers to reflect on their own experiences, the special social contexts of their teaching and their current practices. An excellent tool for preservice and inservice teachers as well as administrators.

Rubin, Ellen and Emily S. Watson. "Disability Bias in Children's Literature," The Lion and the Unicorn: Literature of American Minorities, Volume 11, No. 1, April 1987. Baltimore: Johns Hopkins University Press.

Discusses the negative effects of disability bias in books for children from early childhood through elementary school and up. New books and classics are included, and positive and negative examples are compared. While the focus is on disability, sex and race bias also are taken into account.

Saracho, Olivia N. and Bernard Spodek, eds. Understanding the Multicultural Experience in Early Childhood Education. Washington, DC: National Association for the Education of Young Children, 1983.

Examines how early childhood programs can celebrate the unique contributions of each cultural group while fostering children's competence and flexibility. Also reviews classroom practices and materials.

Scheffler, Hannah H. Resources for Early Childhood: An Annotated Bibliography and Guide for Educators, Librarians, Health Professionals, and Parents. New York: Garland Publishing, Inc., 1983.

This comprehensive reference guide includes annotated bibliographies and essays written by early childhood leaders on the following topics: Pregnancy, Child Development, the Family, Parenting, Health, Nutrition, Children's Play, Child Care, Schooling, Multicultural Education, Special Needs, Nonsexist Education, Film and Television. The book is national in scope and includes listings of community and educational services throughout the country.

Sprung, Barbara. Non-Sexist Education for Young Children: A
Practical Guide. New York: Citation Press, 1975.
    This first curriculum for nonsexist early childhood
education contains practical, how-to approaches and ideas,
including a "Checklist for a Non-Sexist Classroom." The book
is full of anecdotes from teachers, children, and parents.
Available from: Educational Equity Concepts, Inc., 114 E.
32nd St., Suite 306, New York, NY 10016.

Sprung, Barbara, Merle Froschl, and Patricia B. Campbell.
What Will Happen If...Young Children and the Scientific
Method. New York: Educational Equity Concepts, Inc., 1985.
    This early childhood curriculum guide fosters visual-
spatial, problem-solving, and creative-thinking skills and
provides strategies to ensure that all children, particularly
girls, children of color, and children who are poor, develop
these essential skills from beginning in preschool. Takes
familiar components of the early childhood classroom, such as
blocks, sand, and water, and expands them to explore math and
science concepts in age-appropriate ways. (Also available
from Gryphon House, Inc., 3706 Otis St., P.O. Box 275, Mt.
Rainier, MD 20712).

TABS: Organization for Equal Education of the Sexes, Inc.,
438 Fourth St., Brooklyn, NY 11215.
    This organization offers a number of posters that can be
used in the early childhood classroom. Of particular
interest is the one of Linda Bove, a member of the National
Theatre of the Deaf and a regular cast member of Sesame
Street, that shows her signing "I love you."

Williams, Leslie R. and Yvonne De Gaetano. ALERTA: A
Multicultural, Bilingual Approach to Teaching Young Children.
Institute for Urban and Minority Education, Teachers College,
Columbia University. Menlo Park, CA: Addison-Wesley
Publishing Co., 1985.
    A comprehensive multicultural, bilingual program that
includes curricular activities, parent involvement, and staff
development. The curriculum stems from a child-centered
philosophy that draws on the cultures of the children's
families and community. Included in the guide are
instructions for creating teacher-made learning materials
that reflect the surrounding community of the school and
celebrate the cultural heritage of the children.

COMPUTERS

Patricia B. Campbell

Computers in the Classroom

Microcomputers have taken education by storm. In two years, the numbers of computers in use in the schools quadrupled from about 250,000 to more than one million. During 1985, approximately fifteen million students and 500,000 teachers used computers in school-based instructional programs.[1] Students are learning to program with BASIC, LOGO, and PASCAL; they are learning word processing as a writing tool; they are using spread sheets to learn math problem-solving; and they are using a wide variety of computer-assisted instruction of programs to learn everything from ABC's to physics.

Computers have been found to be highly effective aids to learning. Studies of computer-assisted instruction (CAI) have concluded that "there appears to be rather strong evidence for the effectiveness of CAI over traditional instruction where effectiveness is measured by standardized achievement tests." Computer-assisted instruction has been found to increase the speed of learning as well. In addition, there is some evidence that learning to program can have positive effects on thinking skills.[2]

Lack of Equity

With the introduction of microcomputers in education in the early 1980s, concern arose that "the computer revolution is upon us, but some of us are being left out." The "some of us being left out" have been found to be overwhelmingly female, poor, and/or nonwhite. Statistics showing the 3:1 to 8:1 ratio of males to females in computer camps and after-school programs; the greater number of computers in the schools and homes of wealthier school districts; the greater number of boys in voluntary computer classes; and the lack of software for non-English speaking students underscore the problem. Research also has revealed that when computer use is extremely limited, as it is in lower-income areas schools, sex differences are even greater.[3]

An awareness of inequities in computer use based on sex and socioeconomic status came soon after use of microcomputers in education began. In a variety of journals and popular periodicals, articles appeared concluding that, if nothing were done, computer inequities would lead to girls becoming "computer anxious" in much the same way so many of them had become "math anxious."

Computers as a Male Domain

Several different reasons were put forth to explain girls' lower computer use. The first was that computers were seen as number-crunching monsters that historically were tamed by mathematical or engineering geniuses. Teachers and administrators generally thought that computers were designed to do math. Since math teachers were those most apt to have computer experience and since even the name "computer" came out of mathematics, most early microcomputer use in education was in mathematics. Since math was seen as a "male domain," so were computers.[4]

Computers were seen as being primarily for boys and men. Newspaper, magazine, and TV ads in the early 1980s showed boys not girls. Movies featuring computers and computer whizzes, from War Games to The Last Starfighter, all featured boys. Girls were, at best, hangers on. One computer manufacturer even announced publicly that its marketing strategy was designed to attract boys and their fathers. The message came through to parents as well as children. Parents were more apt to buy computers for their sons and were more apt to enroll their sons in private computer camps and after-school computer programs.[5] The message came through in school as well, where groups of boys would physically remove girls from the computers or otherwise intimidate them. And there have been reports of school principals who limited computer use to boys because "they will be the engineers."[6]

In addition, most computer software tends to focus on stereotypically masculine areas and reward structures. Games such as Big Math Attack, Demolition Division, and Math Invaders emphasize war and violence. So-called "school" software programs developed by the well-known Weekly Reader were advertised under the headline "Wreck 'Em, Ram 'Em, Rescue 'Em." Other games such as Math Baseball, offered rewards for correct answers that are traditionally of more interest to boys than to girls. In short, software "developed by boys, about boys, for boys" does not encourage girls' computer use.

Strategies for Change

As awareness grew about the reason for inequitable computer use, strategies for change emerged. First, individual teachers made informal efforts to increase girls' computer use. These efforts, instituted with no additional funding or training, had a positive impact on girls' enrollment. Strategies focused on providing positive female role models, requiring both girls and boys to take introductory computer courses, and scheduling free computer time rather than leaving it to free choice.

While individual efforts could be effective, they also were hit and miss. Many teachers were not aware there was a problem, and others didn't know what to do about it. In the early 1980s, the Women's Educational Equity Act Program and a few other federal programs and private foundations began to fund projects to increase computer equity for girls and women and for students of color of both sexes. Several different types of projects were funded. One type of project developed and tested effective strategies to increase girls' computer usage, including published books or kits, inservice training, and dissemination efforts. Programs such as the Lawrence Hall of Science's EQUALS in Computer Technology program and the Project on Equal Education Rights' National Center for Computer Equity follow this model.[7]

A second type of project, based on research conducted to determine students' interests, produced software designed to appeal to girls as well as boys. For example, the Bank Street College of Education chose whales as the topic of its Voyage of the Mimi video/computer materials only after that finding whales are one of the few science topics[8] in which girls and boys of all races are equally interested.

A third type of project focused on providing services directly to students. Playing to Win, for example, addressed the lack of computer access experienced by poor people by setting up a computer center in the East Harlem section of New York City that is available to community residents for a very low cost. The center offers computer literacy courses for parents and children, training programs, and computer terminals for individual use.[9]

Progress Toward Equity

Efforts toward increasing computer equity have met with some success. Some computer software evaluation guidelines, such as those used by the Educational Products Information Exchange and the Boston Computer Society, incorporate equity concerns. Also, a wider variety of educational software is being developed, and computer use in nonmath areas such as writing and language arts is increasing. Indeed, <u>Classroom Computer Learning</u>'s 1986 software competition was co-chaired by a member of the EQUALS project, ensuring that equity was a criterion.

As computer use in education and issues of computer equity come of age, new concerns have surfaced. The major issue is whether there should be a separate area of "computer equity" for girls. In a 1985 article, Brady and Slesnick question whether developing separate software for girls is the right approach.[10] The "separate software" approach assumes that there are things girls like and things boys like and that there is little commonality between the two. Opponents to this approach claim that it both refutes the research and threatens to perpetuate stereotypes of girls' and boys' interests. The alternative, software that is "gender neutral," designed to interest both girls and boys in nonstereotyped ways, is offered as a better way to stop inequity while also having a greater chance of being used in the average classroom.

This issue also relates to programs. The question becomes whether it is better to have separate programs and classes for girls or to define good computer use as equitable computer use and design programs that involve all students. As might be expected in such a new area, no resolution has yet been made of these issues. The resources listed in the bibliography come from both perspectives.

The following bibliography has been divided into five areas. The first area, <u>Computer Equity Programs</u>, includes programs throughout the United States that emphasize computer equity. While some of the programs are national in scope, such as the National Center for Computer Equity, others such as Equity and Technology, focus on one state or region. Each of the programs has materials available at low or no cost.

The second area, Teacher Resources, focuses on books, kits, and reports generated to increase educator awareness of the issues behind computer equity and inequity and to provide possible solutions to various problems. Some of the resources, such as The Neuter Computer: Computers for Girls and Boys and IDEAS for Equitable Computer Learning, have been extensively tested; however, it must be remembered that this field is so young that it has not yet been possible to test for long-term impact of strategies and proposed solutions.

The third area, Periodicals, contains two types of listings: Special Issues on Computer Equity and Educational Computing Periodicals: Computer Equity Articles.

The fourth area, Computer Packages and Programs, includes the software packages designed specifically to interest girls. These are supplemented by a sample of exemplary software that, while not designed specifically for girls, encompasses characteristics such as high student interest, nonviolence, high student control, and chance for success that cause it to be of interest to a wide variety of students.

Since the major responsibility for software selection must ride with the teacher, the fifth area, Guidelines for Evaluating Software, provides a list of evaluation guidelines and some specific guidelines that emphasize equity.

Notes

1. Center for Social Organizations of Schools, Instructional Uses of School Computers: Reports from the 1985 National Survey, Issue 1 (June 1986).

2. Dean Jamison, Patrick Suppes, and Stuart S. Wells, "Effectiveness of Alternative Instructional Media: A Survey," Review of Educational Research, vol. 44, no. 1 (1973), pp. 1-66. John Lipkin, Equity and Microcomputer Use in Education (Washington, DC: National Institute of Education, 1983). Richard Mayer, Jennifer Dyck, and William Vilberg, "Learning to Program and Learning to Think: What's the Connection?" Communications of the ACM, vol. 29, no. 7 (July 1986), pp. 605-610.

3. Patricia B. Campbell, "The Computer Revolution: Guess Who's Left Out?" Interracial Books for Children Bulletin, vol. 15, no. 3 (1984), pp. 3-6.

4. Patricia B. Campbell, "Hidden Equity: Incorporating Equity in Existing Computer Based Programs," paper presented to the annual meeting of the American Educational Research Association (Chicago: April 1985).

5. Irene Miura and Robert Hess, "Sex Differences in Computer Access, Interest and Usage," paper presented to the American Psychological Association (Anaheim, CA: 1983).

6. Jo S. Sanders and Antonia Stone, <u>The Neuter Computer: Computers for Girls and Boys</u> (New York: Neal Schuman, 1986).

7. For information about EQUALS, contact Nancy Kreinberg, Director, Lawrence Hall of Science, University of California, Berkeley, CA 94720; for the National Center for Computer Equity, contact PEER, 1413 K St., NW, Washington, DC 20005.

8. <u>Voyage of the Mimi</u> (New York: Holt, Rinehart and Winston, 1985.)

9. For information about Playing to Win, contact Antonia Stone, Director, 106 East 85 St., New York, NY 10028.

10. Holly Brady and Twila Slesnick, "Girls Don't Like Fluffware Either," <u>Classroom Computer Learning</u>, vol. 5, no. 8 (April/May 1985), pp. 22-27.

BIBLIOGRAPHY

Computer Equity Programs

Computer Equity Training Program, Jo Shuchat Sanders, Director. Women's Action Alliance, 370 Lexington Avenue, New York, NY 10017.

Providing training to teachers, administrators, and teacher trainers and seeking to increase girls' computer use at the middle-school level, this program emphasizes optional computer use during the school day or after school.

EQUALS in Computer Technology, Nancy Kreinberg, Director. Lawrence Hall of Science, University of California, Berkeley, CA 94720.

EQUALS provides inservice training for teachers and administrators throughout the country. The training includes both on-line and off-line activities with the intent of teaching important computer concepts and skills and encouraging equitable computer use.

Equity and Technology, Alice Fredman, Director. Educational Computer Consortium of Ohio, Teacher Center 271, 1130 S.O.M. Road, Cleveland, OH 44124.

Equity and Technology provides small grants for inschool equity projects, disseminates information about the projects and their results to interested educators nationally, and acts as a resource and clearinghouse for Ohio schools.

National Center for Computer Equity, Project on Equal Educational Rights (PEER). 1413 K Street, NW, 9th Floor, Washington, DC 20005.

Acting as a clearinghouse, the Center publishes a series of computer equity reports as well as computer equity action kits to help overcome student barriers to equal participation in computer education.

Office of Opportunities in Science (OOS), Shirley Malcom, Director. American Association for the Advancement of Science, 1333 H Street NW, Washington, DC 20005.

OOS has worked for more than 10 years to increase the

numbers of minority, female, and disabled scientists in the natural and applied sciences and also works to improve the science, math, and technology skills of minority females and disabled students. Reports of their projects and activities are available. They also publish newsletters on technology and disability and on linkages between scientists and engineers and community organizations.

Operation SMART, Ellen Wahl, Director. Girls Clubs of America, 205 Lexington Avenue, New York, NY 10016.

Using computers, local Girls Clubs work with girls from six to eighteen to encourage girls' interest and skills in science and mathematics and to increase their understanding of science as part of their everyday lives. An Operation SMART manual is available to enable other Girls Clubs to establish the program.

Playing to Win, Antonia Stone, Director. 106 East 85th Street, New York, NY 10028.

This program provides an opportunity for girls, boys, and adults from low-income inner city areas to use computers for fun and learning. Participants in Playing to Win range from day-care children to senior citizen groups; they work with computer-assisted instruction software, computer tool software, and programming.

Project MiCRO, Carol Edwards, Director. Southern Coalition for Educational Equity, 75 Marietta Street, NW, Suite 308, Atlanta, GA 30303.

Using extensive teacher training and parental involvement, Project MiCRO provides computer literacy and instructional computing through hands on experiences for 7th- and 8th-grade minority girls and boys throughout the South. Reports on the project and its impact are available.

SISCOM, Jane Schubert, Director. American Institutes for Research, Box 113, Palo Alto, CA 94302.

In order to balance female/male computer use, SISCOM places nine- to fourteen-year-old girls in a co-learning program with a "Big Sister." The sister pairs spend about two hours weekly at the computer, discussing activities, taking turns, and helping to solve problems. Materials describing SISCOM are available for use by Big Brothers/Big Sisters of America and other community agencies.

Teacher Resources

Center for Social Organizations of Schools. Instructional Uses of School Computers: Reports from the 1985 National Survey. Baltimore: Johns Hopkins University.
   This series of six newsletters summarizes the results of an extensive 1985 national survey of schools and their uses of computers. Issue 2 focuses on differences between girls and boys, low and high achieving students, and differences between cities, suburbs, and rural parts of the country. Issues 3-6 focus on specific uses of computers in a variety of curricular areas.

Dembo, Sheryl, ed. The Computer Explosion: Implications for Educational Equity. Washington, DC: Mid-Atlantic Centers for Race and Sex Equity, The American University, 1983.
   Bringing together a collection of articles from several magazines, this resource notebook includes an overview of computer equity issues, a discussion of instructional uses of computers, sample guidelines for evaluating software, a statistical overview of labor and education trends, sources of computer resources, and a glossary of terms. Available free of charge.

Erickson, Tim. Off and Running: The Computer Offline Activities Book. Berkeley: Lawrence Hall of Science, University of California, 1986.
   Off and Running introduces a variety of computer-related activities not needing a computer. Themes include the ideas of programming, problems people tend to have with computing, cooperation and computing, ethics, historical landmarks of computing, and equity. It can be used as a teacher resource book or used independently by advanced elementary and junior high students.

PEER Computer Equity Report. Sex Bias at the Computer Terminal--How Schools Program Girls. Washington, DC: NOW Legal Defense Fund, 1984.
   The first in a series, this report provides an introduction to computer equity issues for women and girls as well as roles teachers and software developers can play to encourage greater computer equity.

PEER Report. <u>Black Women in a High Tech World</u>. Washington, DC: NOW Legal Defense Fund, 1982.

One of the few publications focusing on women of color and computer equity, this report examines the employment and access statistics of black women in high tech, barriers to black women in high tech, and some things individuals can do.

Sanders, Jo S., and Antonia Stone. <u>The Neuter Computer: Computers for Girls and Boys</u>. New York: Neal-Schuman, 1986.

Designed to help educators, parents, students, teacher trainers, and policymakers solve the problem of computer equity, <u>The Neuter Computer</u> includes tested, effective activities and strategies for using computers equitably as well. Also includes guidelines for planning and evaluating a school computer equity program.

Schubert, Jane. <u>IDEAS for Equitable Computer Learning</u>. Palo Alto, CA: American Institutes for Research, 1985.

This kit focuses on providing educators a method to diagnose equity problems and choose the activities that are best suited to resolve the problem in a particular classroom environment. Includes practical strategies, a self-assessment checklist, a computer needs assessment survey, information on early childhood computers.

Wolfe, Leslie. <u>Programming Equity into Computer Education</u>. Washington, DC: PEER, 1413 K Street NW, Washington, DC: 1985.

Designed to help parents, educators, and community leaders overcome barriers that prevent females, minority, disabled, and low-income students from equal participation in computer education. The kit includes teacher and student needs assessment forms and procedures and suggests actions that community groups, local school districts, state governments, classroom teachers, and the federal government should take. Also included is an extensive annotated listing of existing computer equity resources and a glossary of computer terms.

Periodicals

Special Issues on Computer Equity

The Computing Teacher. Vol. II, No. 8, April 1984.   Theme
Issue: Computer Equity.
     Twenty-one short, readable articles give an overview of
the issues behind inequities in educational computer use and
provide many practical suggestions for making computer use
more equitable for minority, female, and disabled students.

Concerns from the Council of Chief State School Officers
Resource Center on Sex Equity, Issue XII, June 1984.   A
CONCERN About Computer Equity.
     Concerns focuses on roles administrators can play to
ensure computer equity. Covers such areas as the need for
equity, roles states can and should play in computer
education, suggestions for state policymakers, references,
and resources.

Equal Play. Vol. IV, Nos. 8 & 9, Spring/Fall 1983.   Computer
Equity.
     A resource magazine for adults who are guiding children
beyond stereotypes. This special issue provides articles and
resources including books, periodicals, bibliographies, and
information on programs and services related to equal
computer use.

Sex Roles: A Journal of Research. Vol. 13, No. 3/4, August
1985. Special Issues Women, Girls, and Computers.
     Covering the field with eleven research based articles,
this special issue presents data regarding adult use of
computers, children's use of computers, determinants of
differential computer use by females and males, and cognitive
consequences of computer use.

Educational Computing Periodicals: Computer Equity Articles

Classroom Computer Learning. Peter Li, Inc., 2451 East River
Road, Dayton, OH 45439.
     Aimed at the teacher with an emphasis on software

reviews and classroom activities, CCL has published equity-related articles such as "Girls Don't Like Fluffware Either" by Holly Brady and Twila Slesnick. (Vol. 5, No. 8, April/May 1985).

Computers in the Schools. The Haworth Press, Inc., 75 Griswold Street, Binghamton, NY 13904.
    Computers in the Schools, written for teachers and researchers, includes research reports, book reviews, trends, and general articles. Equity-related articles include "Computers in Education: A Question of Access" by Patricia B. Campbell and Sonia Gulardo (Vol. 1, No. 1, Spring 1984).

Educational Technology. 140 Sylvan Avenue, Englewood Cliffs, NJ 07632.
    Educational Technology addresses broader trends and implications of technology in education. Equity articles include "A Hard Look at Software: What to Examine and Evaluate (with an Evaluation Form)" by Joy Wallace and Raymond R. Rose (Vol. 24, No. 10, October 1984).

Electronic Learning. Scholastic, Inc., 902 Sylvan Avenue, Englewood Cliffs, NJ 07632.
    Provides features, columns, and departments in such areas as hardware, software, and administration and includes equity-related articles such as "The Social Effects of Computers in Education" by G. Fisher (Vol. 3, No. 6., March 1984).

Note: Computer equity articles also have been found in a wide range of other periodicals including: Educational Leadership, Family Computing, Glamour, Interracial Books for Children Bulletin, Personal Computing, Psychology Today.

Computer Packages and Programs

Russell, Susan Jo and Patricia B. Campbell. Pathways. Technical Education Resources Center, 1096 Massachusetts Avenue, Cambridge, MA 01238.
    Including five software packages, a slide/tape show, and a teacher and student guide, Pathways provides an application based approach to learning about computers for 4th to 7th

grades that emphasizes equity in computer education and use. The specific components include:

The World of Computers: Open to You: a ten-minute slide/tape presentation that introduces students to the many things adults and children can do with computers. The underlying message that computers are for everyone comes through as students view both women and men in all aspects of computing, including the building of computers.

NIM: an ancient strategy game that helps students consider questions about what computers know and how computers learn.

Magic City: a "word world" of adventure that emphasizes the playfulness of words and language.

How Many?: a tool that enables students to conduct their own surveys, type their results into the computer, and choose among different ways of seeing their data displayed.

3-D-Building: a tool that provides students the opportunity to explore the three-dimensional design capabilities of the computer.

Questions and Answers: a tool for designing guessing games or quizzes about favorite interests, hobbies, or school curriculum topics.

Rhiannon, 3717 Titan Drie, Richmond, VA 23225.
Currently marketing four adventure games for upper elementary/junior high school girls, Rhiannon designs slow paced, keyboard based software featuring girls as heroes. The software has received both praise and criticism for portraying the girl user in the traditional role of helper and nurturer. The specific games are:

Jenny of the Prairie: a pioneer girl facing winter alone must gather nature's provisions from a hazardous environment.

Chelsea of the South Seas: a nineteenth-century girl explores for native treasures and confronts tropical dangers on a small Pacific island.

Cave Girl Clair: a prehistoric girl must tend the fire and gather food and medicinal plants to survive.

Lauren of the 25th Century: a girl of the future must save the desert life forms she has pledged to protect.

Note: Jenny of the Prairie, Chelsea of the South Seas, and Cave Girl Clair are also available from The Family Software Catalog, Evanston Educators, Inc., 915 Elmwood Avenue, Evanston, IL 60202.

The Voyage of the Mimi. New York: Holt, Rinehart and Winston, 1985.
     Developed for use in grades 4-6 and applicable through grade 8, this science package was specifically designed to attract girls as well as boys. The complete unit includes twenty-six fifteen-minute videos, a book, teacher and student guide, and four computer-based learning modules that emphasize using computers as tools. (Components can be purchased separately.) The learning modules are:

Rescue Mission: Students learn and use map reading and navigation skills to successfully complete a rescue mission.

Whales and Their Environment: Students use computer-based probes to study heat transfer in whales and their environment.

Turtle Graphics Games: Using LOGO graphics, students begin to learn about computers and programming.

Endangered Species: Students use software to study the interrelationships of ecosystems.

Lawler's Best Sprite Logo Microworlds for Very Young Children. Robert Lawler, School of Education, Purdue University, Lafayette, IN 47907.

Tested extensively (and sometimes written) by the author's daughters and son, this series of 12 programs for young children presents "powerful ideas in ways that engage girls and help both girls and boys to better understand and do problem solving." The specific programs are:

Words: in four subprograms, ABC, BEACH, TRAIN, and PLAYA, children press letters and get drawings and type in words (in English or in one subprogram in Spanish) to create graph worlds on the computer.

Numbers: in two subprograms, BLOCKS and JUMP, children learn the relationships between number names and distances.

Drawings: in four subprograms, EEL, BLINKER, ZOOM, and SKYDIVER, children assemble figures from parts, do mosaic designs, and draw by programming.

Models of Every Day Objects: in two subprograms, CLOCK and CALENDAR, children set a clock with numbers and make their own calendar.

Note: In addition to these packages, two software publishers are headed by women who have spent many years working as advocates for girls' and women's computer use and access. Software published by HRM Software (Adeline Naiman, Director, HRM Software, 175 Tompkin Avenue, Pleasantville, NY 10570) and Micros for Micros (Micros for Micros, Lawrence Hall of Science, University of California, Berkeley, CA 94720) emphasizes cooperation and creativity rather than competition and cruelty.

Additional Software

While not designed primarily to encourage and interest girls, there is some excellent software that most students would like to use. Samples of this type of software include:

Writing/Language Arts:
Bank Street Writer III (Mindscape, Inc. Elementary-Junior High School).
Newsroom (Springboard Software. Elementary-Senior High School).

Science:
Experiments in Chemistry (HRM Software. Senior High School).
Rocky's Boots (The Learning Company. Junior-Senior High School).

Math:
Estimation (Lawrence Hall of Science. Elementary School).
Creative Play (Lawrence Hall of Science. Elementary School).

Social Studies:
Where in the World Is Carmen Sandiego? (Scholastic. Junior High-School).
The Other Side (Tom Snyder Products, Inc. Junior-Senior High School).

Guidelines for Evaluating Software

Campbell, Patricia B. "Preliminary Guidelines for Selecting Computer Software." Interracial Books for Children Bulletin. Vol. 15, No. 5, 1984.
    One of the few guidelines to focus extensively on equity issues, the ten areas covered provide a framework for general assessment as well. The areas include: Violence and Nonviolence, Passivity and Empowerment, Competition and Cooperation, Failure and Success.

"Evaluating Software," in <u>The Computer Explosion:</u> <u>Implications for Educational Equity</u>. Ed. Sheryl Dembo. Washington, DC: Mid-Atlantic Centers for Race and Sex Equity, The American University, 1983.

This section of a larger publication includes an article covering issues in evaluating software, sample evaluation forms that do not include equity concerns, and a series of five equity oriented evaluation questions that can be used in conjunction with other evaluation forms. Available free of charge.

Jones, Nancy B., and Larry Vaughn. <u>Evaluation of Educational</u> <u>Software: A Guide to Guides</u>. Austin, TX: Southwest Educational Development Laboratory, 1983.

Including ten different sets of guidelines for evaluating software, this "guide to guides" helps teachers determine what they are looking for in a piece of software. Also included are computer books, directories, clearinghouses and information centers, and periodicals related to computers in education.

Wallace, Joy, and Raymond R. Rose. "A Hard Look at Software: What to Examine and Evaluate (with an Evaluation Form)." <u>Educational Technology</u>, Vol. 24, No. 10, October 1984.

Practical advice for reviewing software from an equity perspective.

GUIDANCE COUNSELING

Melissa Keyes and Pamela J. Wilson

Equity and Developmental Guidance

Children and adolescents develop and grow in a reasonably sequential and therefore, somewhat predictable manner. School counselors can use this knowledge productively as they plan and shape K-12 nonsexist, multicultural, nondiscriminatory guidance and counseling programs. This type of program will respond to the needs of children in a meaningful and provocative manner, encouraging all children to achieve to their optimum ability.

Everything that we know about human development and learning points to the fact that events that occur or don't occur in a child's developmental pattern have an impact upon lifelong attitudes toward learning. They help or hinder the acquisition of skills, attainment of career goals, and the evolvement of satisfactory attitudes about self, society, family, and career. Much of what we know about equity issues points to factors that result in children growing up with very limited options: early socialization regarding specific roles or patterns of behavior, lack of opportunity to experience a broad range of stimuli, low exposure to adequate role models, differential treatment within the educational and the home setting, and the discrepancies still inherent in American culture and society regarding male/female roles. Given these two sides of the coin -- the need for positive, proactive, early attention to a child's developmental needs and society's somewhat "ambivalent" attitude toward equity issues -- one can readily see the need for a highly structured approach to ensuring that nonbiased guidance and counseling is a part of every child's educational experience.

The American School Counselor Association released a role statement in 1981 that includes the following:

The different educational levels (elementary, middle or junior high, secondary, and postsecondary) approximates the different steps of developmental growth from childhood through adolescence to adulthood. Therefore, the focus of

school counselors serving different school levels
is differentiated by the developmental tasks
necessary for the different stages of growth the
students confront going through school.

It is understood that schools in all societies are
concerned with transmission of cultural heritage
and socialization of the youth. Career
socialization is recognized as a very important
aspect of this process. In the United States,
schools are concerned about the individual
students, and it is through the concept of guidance
that efforts are directed toward personalizing the
school experience in a developmental way.

Counselors believe that students achieve and grow
in positive ways when competencies develop and the
home and school strive both separately and together
to establish supportive interpersonal relationships
and maintain healthy environments. Counseling and
guidance is an integral function in the school that
is maximized when counselors provide consultation
and in-service programs for staff regarding the
incorporation of developmental psychology into the
curriculum. They also provide parents with
additional understanding of child and adolescent
development in order to strengthen the role of
parents in the promotion of growth in children.
Individual and small group counseling is provided
to complement indirect helping through parents and
teachers. Important direct interaction with
students, however, is provided through a
developmentally-oriented guidance curriculum.
Counselor interventions, regardless of their
conceptual origin, aim to serve the needs of
students who are expected to function in school
settings in the various education, vocational, and
personal-social domains.

This approach to guidance and counseling provides the
structure necessary for schools to deal effectively with
gender and equity concerns. Because in the past, school
guidance and counseling all too often was a fragmented system
that reacted and responded to kids "in trouble," little could
be done to provide instruction and support for the healthy
development of all students. The traditional school
guidance services approach rarely organized itself around any
specific task, much less the promotion of unbiased

instruction and the deliberate support of opportunity for all regardless of sex, race, or disability.

The developmental approach is based on specific student competencies identified as areas that are key to a successful and productive maturation process. The effectiveness of developmental guidance lies with the deliberateness of the approach and the emphasis on prevention of problems rather than an attempt to remediate. The effectiveness of this deliberate attention to what is needed for healthy personal/social, career/vocational, and learning development is particularly germane to the many nuances and shadings that have an impact on equity.

Personal/Social Development

We know that many developmental tasks hinge upon an individual's self-concept or sense of self-worth. The confidence and assertiveness that often are needed to tackle society's less-than-equitable norms and mores are directly related to how well people have come to understand and appreciate their own strengths and weaknesses.

Something as important as the development of a strong self-concept cannot be left to chance, and the K-12 developmental guidance approach not only recognizes that fact, but buttresses that key area with companion instruction in decision-making, problem-solving, communication skills, and interpersonal relationships. Such instruction and guidance must, of course, be free of bias and facilitate optimum development for both genders, all cultures, and disabled and nondisabled students alike.

Career/Vocational Development

Guidance and counseling in the school has a particularly vital role to play when it comes to career/vocational development and the promotion of equity. In no other area of maturation is it so patently obvious that deliberate attention must be paid to providing students with information and assistance that will encourage them to expand their horizons regardless of sex, race, and physical, mental, or emotional ability. One of the greatest detriments to a student's pursuing a nontraditional career or an educational path never before taken by a family member or acquaintance is often, simply, a total lack of awareness concerning the options available.

We know that children and adolescents are socialized through family, school, church, television, peers, etc., to the specific set of beliefs, attitudes, behaviors, and roles that are present in their particular environment. This socialization process is especially potent in the area of career development, for the process may encourage differentiated experiences and treatment dependent upon sex, race, class, or disability. Changes that have occurred across cultures and within societies have made many of our socialization patterns out of date. Major changes are needed in the context, content, and concepts of career/vocational guidance and counseling that will help both the student and society.

In order that the K-12 career/vocational system might function more equitably, several objectives need to be present: (1) the definition of career needs to be expanded to include life patterns and roles, not just a discreet occupational experience, (2) students must be made aware of their own career socialization, the ways in which the sex-role system may have limited them, and ways in which they can transcend their socialization and conditioning to develop more fully their potential, (3) there needs to be increased emphasis on providing role models, exposure to nontraditional occupations, broadening the experience base, information on the changing world of work, impact of technology on jobs, and current labor market information, and (4) opportunities must be provided to participate in meaningful and unbiased assessment of abilities, aptitudes, interests, and values in order that realistic choices might be made.

Learning Development

The other area that is part of a comprehensive K-12 guidance program is support and instruction in the area of learning. Just as career development requires a high level of attention and reinforcement regarding equity concerns, so does the area of cognitive development. Some of the responses must center around paying deliberate attention to learning styles, attribution theory, and motivation issues when designing educational programs for children and adolescents.

Equity Issues

There is a wealth of current research on male/female learning styles, the differentiated reinforcement system that occurs in many classrooms, internal vs. external motivation, the importance of school success to career success, and the impact that math and science courses can have on scholastic success and subsequent career success. Conclusions reached concerning gender, race, culture, or disability relative to the above topics all point, once again, to the importance of paying deliberate attention to the issues whether it be in an individual counseling situation, a curriculum planning meeting, a career night, or an academic requirements planning session with a student.

Strategies for Change

1. Counselor education programs, usually at the master's degree level, which train individuals to be counselors in educational, private, community mental health, and other settings should put great emphasis upon sensitizing counselors to gender bias and other discrimination and to overcoming their negative effects.

2. Classes in child and adolescent development should form the core of a preparation program for school counselors. However, care should be taken to examine the work of all developmental theorists and to understand that criticism has been leveled for reliance upon the male population as the basis for the theoretical conclusions. Recent work features a more equitable sample, and the future should provide us with even more relevant data and conclusions regarding developmental patterns of all human beings.

3. School counselors should be well-equipped to provide equitable counseling by being bias free or, at the very least, aware of their own biases and compensate accordingly. Individuals who did not receive adequate training in equity issues in their graduate program should seek such training through inservice, workshops, and additional coursework.

4. The environment of the counseling office and the materials used by the counselor must be free of stereotypic language, pictures, and content.

5. Both genders, all races, and those with disabilities should be equitably served and provided access to all career

materials, assessment tests, financial aid information, college and vocational school applications, and other activities that provide a variety of options.

Conclusion

The crux of the counseling profession is belief in the ability of the individual to grow and change and, therefore, become empowered to solve problems, take action, make choices, and generally go about the business of improving the human condition. In a K-12 setting, the function of a school counselor is to provide instruction to all students so that they might be better prepared to improve their lot in life. The skills necessary for good problem-solving and decision-making are learned behaviors. As long as bias or discrimination is absent from or addressed in the teaching and counseling process, the student will be equipped to deal with maturation issues in a productive manner.

The K-12 guidance and counseling program is one of the optimum delivery points for information that can countermand some of the bias that still exists in our society. By challenging preconceived ideas and out-of-date notions, a structured approach to guidance based on the developmental needs of children is a strong way to ensure that the educational system can make inroads toward eliminating unequitable treatment based on gender, race, culture, or disability. Consistent and deliberate support for the maturing individual as she or he develops personally, socially, academically, and vocationally is the key to equitable opportunity for all.

In the bibliography, the classroom resources are divided into categories loosely based on the level of educational focus: <u>Elementary</u>, <u>Middle/Junior and Senior High School</u>, and <u>K-12</u>. These provide activities to expand awareness of choices, enhance skill building, and foster problem-solving in healthy personal/social, career/vocational, and learning development. The <u>Counselor/Teacher Resources</u> section contains materials designed to eliminate discrimination and the bias and stereotyping all too often found in guidance and counseling materials and practices.

The initial search for materials took place in the ERIC database, using the following descriptors: female(s), woman, women, racial, counseling, guidance, disability(ies), career, and sex equity, in various combinations. After collecting document numbers and abstracts in the search, the reviewer examined many of the materials on microfiche. In addition, the reviewer explored catalogs and materials in current use by equity professionals.

Criteria for selection included known success by equity professionals and educators, validation studies, attention to all equity factors in the materials, and practicality as perceived by the reviewer based on twenty years experience in public schools. Materials addressing career or guidance activities in specific discipline areas, such as mathematics and science, were not included in this chapter. Readers may be wary of materials published more than five years ago; however, most of the early training activities can still be very useful depending on the sophistication level of the audience. Note: Most materials address only one issue, such as sex equity, other issues may be infused.

Notes

1. American School Counselors Association, "The Practice of Guidance and Counseling by School Counselors," The School Counselor, 29, 1981, pp. 7-12.

BIBLIOGRAPHY

Elementary

Cain, Mary Alexander. Boys and Girls Together: Non-Sexist Activities for Elementary Schools. Holmes Beach: Learning Publications, Inc., 1980.
   Includes activities for elementary students on career education.

Educational Equity Center for the Pacific. Oceans of Options: Sex Equity Lessons for the Classroom. San Francisco: Far West Laboratory for Educational Research and Development, 1983.
   Includes activities for awareness of sex bias, equity, and bias-free career education; extensive equity background reading. Projects for administrators are included.

The Fable of He and She. Distributed by Learning Corporation of America, New York, 1974.
   This film raises awareness of the limitations of sex-role stereotyping for elementary students. 16mm, 11-minutes.

Kavanaugh, Michell. When I Grow Up. Atlanta: Humanics Unlimited, 1979.
   Career-awareness activities.

Middle/Junior and Senior High School

Bingham, Mindy, Judy Edmondson, and Sandy Stryker. Challenges: A Young Man's Journal for Self-Awareness and Personal Planning. Santa Barbara, CA: Advocacy Press, 1984.
   Provides written activities in journal style to help young men establish values and goals for their futures.

_____. Choices: A Teen Woman's Journal for Self-Awareness and Personal Planning. Santa Barbara, CA: Advocacy Press, 1983.
   Provides written activities in journal style to help young women establish values and goals for their futures.

Equal Goals in Occupations Project. <u>Rainbow, Shave Ice,</u> <u>Crackseed, and Other Ono Stuff: Sex Equity Goodies for the</u> <u>Classroom</u>. Honolulu: Office of the State Director of Vocational Education, 1984.

Compilation of classroom activities to enable students to reach sex-fair career goals.

General Foods Corporation. <u>Choosing to Succeed</u>. 1986. (For copies write to Choosing to Succeed, P.O. Box 4702-B, Kankakee, IL 60902. Free of charge.)

Handbook listing black colleges and universities and their programs.

Girl Scouts of the U.S.A. <u>From Dreams to Reality: A Career</u> <u>Exploration Program</u>. New York: Girl Scouts of the U.S.A., 1978.

Activity kit in career awareness and exploration containing 130 developmental and sequential activity cards focusing on general career topics in the five worlds of girl scouting.

Hopkins, Loma J., et al. <u>Career Guidance Materials for Use</u> <u>with Students with Disabilities. A Resource Catalogue</u>. Washington, DC: Department of Education, 1982.

More than 60 materials specifically useful for career guidance for community college students with disabilities. May be adapted for senior high.

Los Angeles Unified School District. <u>CAREERWAYS: A</u> <u>Multimedia Real-Life Career Education Program for Grades 7-</u> <u>12</u>. 1980. (Contact Sharon Seib, Project Disseminator, CAREERWAYS, Los Angeles Unified School District, 1320 W. Third Street, Los Angeles, CA 90017).

Designed to increase students' knowledge about the world of work and reduce the negative effects of stereotyping on course selection and career choice. Validated and disseminated by the National Diffusion Network (NDN).

Mitchell, Joyce Slayton. <u>See Me More Clearly: Career and</u> <u>Life Planning for Teens with Disabilities</u>. New York: Harcourt Brace Jovanovich, 1980.

A useful guide to thinking about and planning for a career. Tips for adolescents with disabilities on dealing

with teachers and counselors who may be unsympathetic or
naive about disability issues.

New York State Education Department. Guidance and
Counseling: Ensuring the Rights of Students. Albany: New
York State Education Department, 1985. ERIC 270 685.
(Available from Occupational Education Civil Rights Technical
Assistance Unit, New York State Education Department, Albany,
NY 12234.)
 Activities for counselors and students designed to help
students make informed career decisions and manage their own
lives, regardless of sex, race, disability, or national
origin.

Stein, Dorothy, et al. Thinking and Doing: Overcoming Sex
Role Stereotyping in Education. Honolulu: Hawaii Educational
Equity Program, University YWCA.
 Career awareness activities for students.

TABS: Organization for Equal Education of the Sexes. Stay in
School--Your Life Depends On it. New York: OEES, 438 Fourth
St., Brooklyn, NY 11215.
 A series of posters featuring young high school women,
including teenage mothers, and their stories about dropping
out of school.

Wisconsin Department of Public Instruction and Women's
Education Resources, University of Wisconsin-Madison.
Increasing Options Through Life/Work Planning. Madison:
Wisconsin Department of Public Instruction, 1986 (revised).
 Activities forming a process that helps students age 13-
18 examine skills, values, interests, and needs for gaining
and maintaining self-direction.

Women's Educational Equity Act Program. Choices/Changes: An
Investigation of Alternative Occupational Role Models.
Rochester, NY: Rochester City School District, 1982.
 Mini-biographies written largely by students to explain
why women and men from all walks of life choose to pursue
nontraditional careers.

_____. Connections: Women and Work and Skills for Good Jobs. Rochester, NY: Rochester City School District, 1982.
     Leader's guide, gamebook, and sound filmstrip help inform girls and boys in grades 6-9 about non-traditional occupations, interest girls in a broader range of careers, and encourage boys to support girls in pursuing such careers.

_____. Fair Play: Developing Self-Concept and Decision-Making Skills in the Middle School. Tallahassee: Florida State University, 1982.
     Includes units that can be integrated into classes; accompanying implementation handbook, plus model for introducing the program system-wide.

_____. Focus on the Future. Tallahassee: Florida State University, 1982.
     Students respond to pictures of adults in work and home situations, followed by discussion to explore how stereotyping limits opportunities.

_____. Options: A Career Development Curriculum for Rural High School Students. Hanover, NH: Dartmouth College, New Hampshire Department of Education, 1980.
     Uses role-playing, case studies, classroom discussions, activities, self-assessments to help students, especially young women, make decisions about their futures.

_____. Project Choice: Creating Her Options in Career Exploration. Cleveland: Case Western Reserve University, 1979.
     Outlines a 14-week career development program targeted to talented adolescent women.

_____. Steppin' Up and Moving On: A Career Education Program for the Urban, Noncollege-bound Student. Cleveland: Case Western Reserve University, 1982.
     Includes vocational interest assessments, resume analyses, and career game exercises designed to be used in the classroom.

_____. Whole Person Book, I and II. Toward Self-Discovery and Life Options. Lincoln, NE: Nonsexist Training for Future Counselors and Teachers Project, 1982.
     Guides students through activities as they examine

personal values, talents, and interests.   May be used as
complementary curriculum in classes.

K-12

Schneidewind, Nancy, and Davidson, Ellen.   Open Minds to
Equality: A Sourcebook of Learning Activities to Promote
Race, Sex, Class, and Age Equity.   Englewood Cliffs, NJ:
Prentice-Hall, 1983.
      Includes activities that teach about equality and
generate equality in elementary and secondary students, both
academically and interpersonally.

Wisconsin Department of Public Instruction.   Expanding
Horizons.   Madison: Wisconsin Department of Public
Instruction, 1980.
      Activities for counselors and teachers to use with K-12
students.

Counselor/Teacher Resources

Anderson, Tom, and Sheryl Barta.   Multicultural Nonsexist
Education in Iowa Schools: Guidance and Counseling.   Des
Moines: Iowa State Department of Public Instruction,
Educational Equity Section, 1983.   ERIC ED 236 524.
      Includes definitions; rationale; goals and objectives;
self-evaluation checklist divided into guidance program
structure, materials and strategies; plus bibliography.

Colorado Department of Education.   Counselors Use Title IX
for Sex Equity.   Denver: Colorado Department of Education,
1979.
      Trainer's manual with activities designed to help
counselors assess equity in practices and materials, with
opportunity to change.

Bliss, M., and A. Schwartz.   Exploring Attitudes Toward Women
with Disabilities: A Curriculum Guide for Employers and
Educators.   New York: McGraw-Hill, 1979.
      Helps personnel specialists and educators conduct
activities to promote positive attitudes towards women with
disabilities through recognition of: (1) similarities between
disabled and nondisabled in needs, aspirations, and

capabilities, (2) dual discrimination of disabled women, (3) individuality/uniqueness, and (4) the need to relate more effectively and productively to people with disabilities.

Barnard College Office for Disabled Students. Access to Equity: A Resource Manual for College Women with Disabilities. New York: Barnard College, 1988.

Information and materials directed at equalizing the educational opportunities for college women with disabilities. Suggestions for curricula on assertiveness training, sexuality, self-defense, employment, and other subjects of concern.

Carrillo, Ann Cupolo, Katherine Corbett, and Victoria Lewis. No More Stares. Berkeley: Disability Rights Education and Defense Fund, Inc., 1982.

Readers of No More Stares will become acquainted—through photographs and brief personal accounts—with more than 100 women and girls with disabilities. The book is a highly successful attempt to shatter stereotypes by depicting women and girls who are disabled on the job, at home, in school, and participating in sports—with children, colleagues, friends, and family.

Corbett, Katherine, and Merle Froschl, with Jennifer Luna Bregante and Leslie Levy. "Access to the Future: Serving Disabled Young Women," The Second Mile: Contemporary Approaches in Counseling Young Women, edited by Sue Davidson. Tucson, AZ: New Directions for Young Women, 1983.

This article documents the double discrimination experienced by women with disabilities—tripled if they are women of color—and analyzes sex bias and stereotyping as these affect services for female youth who are disabled. Major issues discussed are role models, education, independence, work, and interpersonal relationships.

Cruzic, K. Disabled? Yes. Defeated? No. Englewood Cliffs, NJ: Prentice-Hall, 1982.

Describes resources for people who are disabled, their families, friends, and therapists; includes brief biographies of people with disabilities in a variety of careers.

Diamond, Esther E., ed. Issues of Sex Bias and Sex Fairness in Career Interest Measurement. Washington, DC: Department of Health, Education and Welfare, National Institute of Education Career Education Program, 1975.

Examines the technical and social issues concerning vocational career interest surveys to create a greater understanding and to suggest some acceptable answers.

Greenwood, Charles R., et al. Minority Issues in the Education of Handicapped Children. Minority Issues Inservice Program (MIIP): Instructor's Manual. Washington, DC: Office of Special Education and Rehabilitative Services, U.S. Department of Education, 1982. ERIC ED 227 623.

Guidelines and course materials for teaching and inservice course for regular and special education teachers. Includes these topics: assessment issues, language and learning styles, multicultural curricula and many others.

Henderson, George, ed. Understanding and Counseling Ethnic Minorities. Springfield, IL: Charles C. Thomas, 1979.

Readings presented on historical, anthropological, psychological, sociological, and educational considerations in helping persons of African, Mexican, Puerto Rican, American Indian, Chinese, and Japanese descent in counseling situations.

Jenkins, MacDonald. Growing Up Equal. Englewood Cliff, NJ: Prentice-Hall, 1979.

Activities and resources for parents and teachers of young children.

Los Angeles County Office of Education. FREESTYLE. Downey, CA: Los Angeles County Office of Education, 1978.

Instructional and staff development program includes curricular material and thirteen 30-minute video cassettes.

Michigan State Department of Education Office for Sex Equity. A Sex Affirmative Model Program: Counseling and Guidance. Lansing, MI: Michigan State Department of Education, 1981. ERIC 266 377.

Addresses four program audiences: students, teachers, parents, and community. Goals and activities given for each group.

Networking Project for Disabled Women and Girls. Harilyn Rousso, Project Director. YWCA of New York City, 610 Lexington Ave., New York, NY 10022.

Several materials are available from this unique mentoring project whose purpose is to increase the educational, vocational, and social aspirations of adolescent girls with physical and sensory disabilities: videotape illustrating the role-model process, role-model book profiling the lives of ten women with disabilites, and a replication packet.

O'Toole, Corbett, J. "The Case of the Missing Role Model," Independent, Issue 2, 1979.

In this thought-provoking article, the author makes the connections between sex, race/ethnicity, and disability bias. The personal anecdotes help the reader to understand the discrimination experienced by women with disabilities. The article discusses the issues of housing, employment, poverty, health care, and family planning.

O'Toole, Corbett, and CeCe Weeks. What Happens After School? A Study of Disabled Women and Education. Women's Educational Equity Communication Network, 1978.

Through interviews with six women, the authors illuminate the educational and work experiences of women with disabilities. Additional chapters on early experiences with school and family, high school, college years, work, and summary suggestions for educators and parents. (Available from ERIC Document Reproduction Service, 3030 North Fairfax Drive, Arlington, VA 22201.)

Schmelter-Davis, L. Vocational Evaluation of Handicapped College Students: Hearing, Motor, and Visually Impaired. Lincroft, NJ: Brookdale Community College, 1984.

Covers evaluation adaption techniques, assessment measures for ability and aptitude tests, personality tests, interest inventories, and projective testing.

Resource Center on Educational Equity. Achieving Equity in Education Programs for Disabled Women and Girls: A Model Workshop Manual. Washington, DC: Council of Chief State School Officers, 1985.

Training materials for state educational agency staff.

Smith, Amanda J. <u>New Pioneers. The North Carolina Program to Eliminate Sex Bias in Occupational Education</u>. Raleigh, NC: North Carolina State Department of Public Instruction, 1977. ERIC 145 192.

Offers a strategic model for change in the educational system and an inservice program to eliminate sex bias in the curriculum.

Steigler, C.B. <u>How To...Strategies for Sex Equity. "The Role of the Counselor."</u> Frankfort, KY: Kentucky State Department of Education Bureau of Vocational Education. ERIC 189 457.

Monograph written to assist guidance counselors in fulfilling their role in achieving sex-fair vocational education. Discusses complying with the law, examining personal attitudes, screening tests, developing and collecting materials.

Verheyden-Hilliard, Mary Ellen. <u>Reducing Sex Stereotyping in Career Education: Some Promising Approaches to Persistent Problems</u>. Washington, DC: Department of Health, Education and Welfare Office of Career Education, 1979. ERIC 174 854.

Reports findings of a study undertaken to gather information about successful project approaches to the reduction of sex-role stereotyping in career education.

Wax, T.M., and M. Danek. "Deaf Women and Double Jeopardy," <u>Gallaudet Today</u>, 14(4), pp. 13-15, 1984.

Defines "double jeopardy" as a combination of prejudice (unfavorable feelings people harbor against others) and discrimination (unfavorable actions and behaviors directed against those others). Explores vocational, educational, and interpersonal inequities experienced by women who are disabled.

Wisconsin Department of Public Instruction. <u>School Counseling Programs: A Resource and Planning Guide</u>. Madison, WI: Wisconsin Department of Public Instruction, 1986.

Presentation of the Wisconsin Developmental Guidance Model. Provides a framework for building a school counseling model that addresses students' developmental needs and provides them with a more complete set of personal/social, learning, and career development skills.

_____. Sex Equity Activities Handbook for Counseling and Guidance. In press.

   Accompanies the DPI's School Counseling Programs and draws together activities to be used with students from kindergarten through senior high school. Develops personal/social, learning, and career developmental skills that are sex-fair and sex-affirmative.

Women's Educational Equity Act Program. Becoming Sex Fair: The Tredyffrin/Easttown Program: A Comprehensive Model for Public School Districts. Washington, DC: U.S. Department of Education, 1979.

   System-wide training program includes material for use with guidance counselors, including the "Counselor's Self-Evaluation of Non-Sexist Behavior."

_____. Born Free. Training Packet to Reduce Sex-Role Stereotyping in Career Development. Minneapolis: University of Minnesota, 1980.

   Activities useful for developing sex equity awareness with educators, parents, and other community members.

_____. Career Educational Resource Kit: An Annotated Bibliography of Nonsexist Resources.

   Helps counselors in rural areas develop an effective nonsexist career counseling program within limited budgets.

_____. The Catalyst Training Package: Increasing Options for Rural Youth. Montpelier, VT: Washington County Youth Service Bureau, 1982.

   Fifteen-week training program provides weekend retreats, self-assessments, and classroom activities to help students examine career options and eliminate sex stereotyping. Includes activities for parent and community involvement.

_____. Choosing Occupations and Life Roles. Charleston, WV: Appalachian Educational Lab, 1983.

   Guides and Teacher's Handbook to combat stereotyped thinking about career selection and help stimulate informed, unbiased choices.

_____. Expanding Options. Facilitator's Guide: Counselor Workshop, 1984.
Includes procedures and supporting materials for a series of sex equity workshops targeted at counselors: activity guides, handout materials, mini-lectures, and an optional session on assertiveness.

_____. Freedom for Individual Development: Counseling and Guidance. 1977.
Activities for counselors focusing on awareness and equity issues in career development.

_____. It's Her Future.
Video cassette, 17 min.

Note: Materials from the Women's Educational Equity Act Program may be obtained from the WEEA Publishing Center, Education Development Center, Inc., 55 Chapel Street, Newton, MA 02162.

HISTORY

Frances Arick Kolb

Background

Women's history was one of the first disciplines to arise out of the contemporary feminist movement. As early as 1969 historians began to examine women's lives and to discover that women had been active participants and leaders in history. From the first consciousness that women were missing from historical study, historians have created a major field in women's history that is challenging traditional historical concepts.

In the early 1970s, when historians assessed history and social studies textbooks to determine their content on women, they discovered that these textbooks ignored women either as a group or as individuals.[1] The first phase of women's history--"contribution history"--resurrected those women who were actors in major events. As a result, biographical dictionaries like <u>Notable American Women</u> and many biographies of women of achievement have been written.[2] Also, the number of individual women in texts has increased.

While it is important that these notable women now appear in the history textbooks, their addition did not change the way history was conceived or written. Since history was still being defined according to male norms, the text writers added women to the traditional periods and events of history. Frequently, achieving women were shown in such typical women's activities as caring for the sick and aiding the poor.[3] Some textbooks marginalized these women by setting them apart in a special or highlighted section. Textbook authors also tended to focus on women such as Dorothea Dix, Jane Addams, or Eleanor Roosevelt, whose achievements lay in traditional female pursuits and/or those who took on male roles, such as Molly Pitcher and Deborah Sampson. Contribution history has tended to show women on the home front in wars, in the colonial family, and in organizations.[4]

Creating a New Historical Perspective

Feminist historians began to move beyond contribution history. They asked new questions about women, questions associated especially with social history. They investigated ordinary women's lives to see what the majority of women were doing in any historic period, and they discovered not only the oppression of women but that women had valiantly struggled to overcome that oppression. Adrienne Rich has written, "As feminists, we need to be looking above all for the greatness and sanity of ordinary women and how these women have collectively waged resistance. In searching that territory we find something better than individual heroines: the astonishing continuity of women's imagination of survival, persisting through the great and little deaths of daily life."[5]

Within the oppression that forced women into a separate sphere--the private sphere of home and family--historians discovered that women created a positive and fulfilling culture by and for themselves. As one feminist writer has described it, "These writers in their different (and sometimes contradictory) ways emerged with an amorphous but clear sense of women forming distinct cultures within whatever society they lived--cultures that had in common at last some traits of nurturance, intuition and hardiness."[6]

Especially central to this new historical perspective was Carroll Smith-Rosenberg's "world of love and ritual," a nineteenth-century world created by women and for women in which deeply felt friendships provided support to women. Such a construction of male and female society suggested that a dichotomy exists between the private world of women and the public world that is men's. This theory has led to discussion concerning women's autonomous culture.[7]

As feminist historians dig into the buried roles of women in various historic periods, they have been led to ask if the very conceptualization and periodization of history might be wrong. According to historian Gerda Lerner, "The search for a better conceptual framework for the history of women begins at that stage. One is led, step by step to new definitions, to the search for more appropriate concepts, to dissatisfaction with periodization in traditional history. One searches for appropriate comparisons of 'women' with other groups in society. One tries to find new models, borrowing concepts and tools from other disciplines. Women's History, at this stage, is no longer only a 'field,' rather it is a methodology, a stance, an angle of vision."[8]

For example, if the Renaissance did not bring women the benefits it brought to men, can it still be called a renaissance? In the mid-1970s, Joan Kelly first posed this question in her essay, "Did Women Have a Renaissance?" She concluded, "The startling fact is that women as a group, especially among the classes that dominated Italian urban life, experienced a contraction of social and personal options that men of their classes either did not, as was the case with the bourgeoisie, or did not experience as markedly, as was the case with the nobility.[9] Similarly, as the bicentennial of the U.S. Constitution is being celebrated, historians need to ask: If women and all black Americans, more than one-half the population, were not considered in either the development or actual writing of the constitution, did this document establish a democracy for America?

In the process of investigating these new constructs and theories, feminist historians have found that class, race, and ethnicity are factors that affect women's and men's histories differently. Since any history that does not take this diversity into account is incomplete, such a diversification leads to a greatly expanded definition of what is historically important. Because traditional history has been focused on white, male, northern Europeans, contemporary historians are looking to new sources to account for the lives of people of color and of different ethnic backgrounds and classes. Diaries, legal writs, myths and legends, and statistics are alternative means to understanding people who have not ordinarily left written records. An example of the imaginative use of unusual historic sources is Laura Ulrich's study of colonial New England in which she analyzes tombstones, genealogies, embroidery, private papers of sons and husbands, court records, and probate inventories to find the evidence of female life.[10]

As feminist historians bring forth these new ideas, history as a discipline changes. Women's history has become a means of transforming historical thought.

Institutionalizing Women's History

As recently as 1977, women's history was virtually unknown as a study topic in the K-12 curriculum. To remedy this situation, the Education Task Force of the Sonoma County

Commission on the Status of Women proposed to the County Office of Education that a "Women's History Week" be designated incorporating International Women's Day, March 8th. The Commission and the Office of Education worked together for the next several years to develop programming and curriculum materials for local teachers to use in exploring the many contributions women of all races, cultures, ethnic backgrounds, and life styles have made to the building of this nation. They also worked with the participants of the Women's History Institute at Sarah Lawrence College toward getting an official Congressional Resolution declaring National Women's History Week. The effort was successful in 1981 when Sen. Orin Hatch (R-UT) and Rep. Barbara Mikulski (D-MD) co-sponsored the first Joint Congressional Resolution for National Women's History Week.

As the idea of celebrating Women's History Week began to spread across the nation, the National Women's History Project was created to serve as an information clearinghouse, to provide technical assistance to educators and community organizers, and to produce and distribute multicultural women's history materials.[11] Since that time, public schools, universities, state governments, municipalities, other institutions, and thousands of people throughout the country actively work to promote the multicultural study of women's history. Due to the enormous success of National Women's History Week and the growing availability of information on women's history, in 1987, Congress passed a resolution designating March as National Women's History Month.

Another catalyst for the institutionalization of women's history is the women's studies movement with programs on 450 campuses across the country. In the last ten years, 50 women's research centers have been set up that foster a wide range of research, writing, and programs about women.[12] A number of magazines that publish women's studies research have been founded. Among those that especially feature history are Women's Studies Quarterly, Frontiers, Feminist Studies, and Signs.[13] Paralleling the growth of women's studies has been the development of the National Women's Studies Association, which had 2,000 members in 1983.

Women's history caucuses and organizations also have arisen at the regional and national levels. These organizations provide advocacy for women in the profession, promote women's history scholarship, and publish women's history materials. As examples, the Berkshire Conference of

Women Historians holds a major conference every three years,
and the Coordinating Committee on Women in the Historical
Profession serves as an advocate for women and women's
history in the professional associations.[14]

Because of this institutional growth, local
universities, women's centers, and state departments of
education have become excellent resources for women's
history. Many states now issue materials especially on
women's history and offer conferences, workshops, and
seminars for public school teachers. In addition,
Desegregation Assistance Centers throughout the country often
have women's history resources for borrowing and can provide
speakers and technical assistance to school districts.[15]

With the growth and institutionalization of women's
history, a wealth of new materials have been developed.
Because of the extent of the materials, this bibliography
only includes items published after 1980. The older texts,
anthologies, and research books that should be a part of
every teacher's repertoire can be found in a number of the
bibliographies and biographical guides that are included.
European studies of women in history and texts have been
slower in coming, so that the bibliography includes only a
few items on European and other cultures. The increasing
scholarly research in these areas should lead to new
classroom materials in the near future.

The bibliography is organized as follows: **Elementary**,
Secondary, **Media**, and **Teacher Resources**. The **Elementary**
section features curriculum guides and classroom resouces as
well as a few anthologies for classroom readings. Also
included are works on celebrating Women's History Month.
Since much of the history material for the elementary
classroom is biographical, please refer to the Biography
section of the Libraries and Media Centers bibliography for
additional sources. Teachers also can investigate
biographies further through the National Women's History
Project catalogue and in the new books section of **Social**
Education.[16]

In the **Secondary** section, two types of works are
presented. The first section is on anthologies and texts
that have been published since 1980. (Again, some good
classic texts and anthologies that are still available have

not been included here.) The second section features curriculum materials published since 1980 that are useful in developing lesson plans, units, and activities for women's inclusion in history course or for the development of a separate high school women's history course.

Because of the large number of written materials, only a few nonprint materials have been highlighted in the Media section. The newly-revised Feminist Resources for Schools and Colleges provides descriptions of films, videotapes, and other resources as does the resource article in the recent women's history special issue of Social Education.[17]

Teacher Resources also includes two sections: biographical and bibliographic tools and current books by feminist historians that provide teachers with the classic works in women's history and some of the most recent research in the field. Many of the books are exciting reading because of the new ideas about women, new ways of looking at history, and new resources for finding women.

Throughout the bibliography, the items that are available from the National Women's History Project are so noted. The address is Box 3716, Santa Rosa, CA 95402.

Notes

1. Janice Trecker, "Women in American History: High School Textbooks," Social Education, XXXV (1971), pp. 248-355; see the update by Mary Kay Tetreault, "The Treatment of Women in U.S. History High School Textbooks: Decade's Progress," Women's Studies Quarterly, X, no. 3 (Fall 1982).

2. Edward James and Janet T. James, eds., Notable American Women 1607-1950: A Biographical Dictionary (Cambridge, MA: Harvard/Belknap Press, 1971).

3. Mary Kay Tetreault, "Rethinking Women, Gender and the Social Studies," Social Education, LI, no. 3 (March 1987), p. 171.

4. Tetreault, "Rethinking Women."

5. Adrienne Rich, "Resisting Amnesia: History and Personal Life," Ms. Magazine (March 1987), pp. 66-67.

6. Karen Lindsay, "Women's Culture and the Humanities,"

<u>Humanities</u> (October 1986), p. 3.

7. Carroll Smith-Rosenberg, "The Female World of Love and
Ritual: Relations Between Women in Nineteenth-Century
America," in <u>Disorderly Conduct: Visions of Gender in
Victorian America</u> (New York: Oxford University Press, 1986).
For a further discussion of these ideas, see also "Hearing
Women's Words: A Feminist Reconstruction of History," pp.
41–42.

8. Gerda Lerner, <u>The Majority Finds Its Past: Placing Women
in History</u> (New York: Oxford University Press, 1979), p.
xiv.

9. Joan Kelly, <u>Women, History, and Theory: The Essays of
Joan Kelly</u> (Chicago: University of Chicago Press, 1984), p.
20.

10. Laura Ulrich, <u>Good Wives: Image and Reality in the
Lives of Women in Northern New England, 1650–1750</u> (New York:
Alfred Knopf, 1982), p. 5.

11. See catalogue from National Women's History Project, Box
3716, Santa Rosa, CA 95402.

12. Catharine R. Stimpson, <u>Women's Studies in the United
States</u> (New York: Ford Foundation, 1986), pp. 21, 24.

13. <u>Women's Studies Quarterly</u>:   at $25.00 per year from
Feminist Press, City University of NY, 311 East 94th Street,
New York, NY 10128; <u>Frontiers: A Journal of Women Studies</u>:
three issues at $16.00 a year, from Box 325, Women Studies,
University of Colorado, Boulder, CO 80309; <u>Signs</u>:   quarterly
at $27.50 per year, from University of Chicago Press,
Journals Division, Box 37005, Chicago, IL 60637; <u>Feminist
Studies</u>:   quarterly at $19.50 per year: from Women's Studies
Program, University of Maryland, College Park, MD 20742.

14. You can find out more about the organizations of women
in the historical profession by writing to Nupur Chandhuri,
1737 Vaughan Drive, Manhattan, KS 66502.

15. See Gloria Contreras, "A Gender Balancing Resource
List," <u>Social Education</u>, LI, no. 3 (March 1987), pp. 200–205,
for some of the programs and state departments that have been
most active in the promotion of women's history, and the
Libraries and Media Centers chapter for a listing of the
Desegregation Assistance Centers.

16. See National Women's History Project catalogue, Box 3716, Santa Rose, CA 95402, and yearly listings of "Notable Children's Trade Books in the Social Studies," Social Education, a publication of National Council for the Social Studies that is available as part of NCSS membership.

17. Anne Chapman, ed., Feminist Resources for Schools and Colleges: A Guide to Curricular Materials, 3rd ed. (New York: The Feminist Press, 1986). Social Education, LI, no. 3 (March 1987).

BIBLIOGRAPHY

Elementary

Abrams, Eileen. <u>A Curriculum Guide for Women's Studies for the Middle School Grades</u>. Old Westbury, NY: The Feminist Press, 1981.
    To show the achievements of women in history, the four lessons on women's history use birthdays, book reports, and creative writing around biographies. The last lesson is on oral history.

Banfield, Beryle. <u>Winning "Justice for All"</u>. New York: Council on Interracial Books for Children, 1980.
    For upper elementary students, this book explores social justice issues through lessons that feature a wide variety of skills. Lessons in the three modules on stereotypes, how racism and sexism operate, and how to fight racism and sexism involve biographies, surveys, sentence completion, statistics, and stories. Student workbook and teacher edition available.

Cain, Mary Alexander. <u>Boys and Girls Together: Non-Sexist Activities for Elementary Schools</u>. Holmes Beach, FL: Learning Publications, Inc., 1980. (Order from Learning Publications, Box 1326, Holmes Beach, FL 33509).
    A variety of suggested lessons and units are provided in social studies to develop some of the following concepts: women have always worked; women contributed to our history; the feminist movement has a long history; childrearing and gender roles vary across cultures and history.

"Disabled Women: Hidden from History." (Distributed by Anne Finger, 324 Market St., Venice, CA 90291.)
    A 22" x 17" hand-printed poster featuring Helen Keller, Frida Kahlo, Dorothea Lange, and Harriet Ross Tubman.

Eisenberg, Bonnie, and Mary Ruthsdotter. <u>101 Wonderful Ways to Celebrate Women's History</u>. Santa Rosa, CA: National Women's History Project, 1986
    Many ideas for school and community programs along with

an extensive resource section of books, posters, performers, and traveling exhibits.

Equity Lessons for Elementary School. Newton, MA: EDC/Women's Educational Equity Act Publishing Center, 1982.
Developed by teachers in the Philadelphia Public Schools, this book includes two lessons on women's history for grades 4-6: one lesson on the Women's Hall of Fame involves students in biographical study to decide which women belong in the Hall of Fame. A second lesson on Women of the American Revolution in which students learn about women's roles in that period.

Meyers, Ruth, and Beryle Banfield, eds. Embers: Stories for a Changing World. New York: Council on Interracial Books for Children.
For upper-elementary students, there are historical units on women working, famous firsts, and freedom fighters. These stories tell about a highly diverse group of achieving women (including women of color and women with disabilities) such as Sojourner Truth, Harriet Tubman, Elizabeth Blackwell, and Alicia Alonso. Student and teacher edition available.

Morgan, Betty. Eleanor Roosevelt Curriculum Kit K-6. Santa Rosa, CA: National Women's History Project, 1983.
In honor of Roosevelt's centennial, the booklet includes a biography, chronology, puzzles, and other activities.

Mujeres de La Raza. Oakland, CA: National Hispanic University, n.d. (Order from National Women's History Project.)
Biographies of a small number of Hispanic women, especially those who have worked for the liberation of their people. In Spanish and English, it also has biographies and pictures that could be displayed or used for coloring.

Phillips, Elizabeth. Women and Girls with Disability: An Introductory Teaching Packet. New York: Organization for Equal Education of the Sexes, Inc., 1978.
Includes lesson plans and a poster for incorporating information about women and girls with disability into the curriculum, K-12.

_____. Women in American History: An Introductory Teaching
Packet. New York: Organization for Equal Education of the
Sexes, 1978.
    Multicultural lesson plans and a poster to help teach
about women's role in American history, K-12.

Pogrebin, Letty Cottin. Stories for Free Children. New
York: McGraw-Hill, 1982.
    One part of this book of stories from Ms. Magazine
concerns "Famous Women, Found Women" and includes stories
about famous women like Amelia Bloomer, Sibyl Ludington, and
Deborah Sampson but also about some unknown women who led
interesting lives.

Stallone, Carol. The Faces and Phases of Women. Seneca
Falls, NY: The National Women's Hall of Fame, 1983. (Order
from National Women's History Project.)
    For upper elementary students, this gives brief
biographies of 31 women organized by areas such as education,
government, etc. However, it is somewhat lacking in minority
and ethnic women.

Tomin, Barbara, and Carol Burgoa. Teaching Women's History
in the Elementary Grades: A Biographical Approach. Unit 1:
Susan B. Anthony. Santa Rosa, CA: Tomin-Burgoa Productions,
1983. (Order from National Women's History Project.)
    Minibiography in booklet form, with tests and varied
activities, including a puppet, all of which can be
reproduced for the classroom.

Women in History and in Contemporary America - Grades K
Through 6. Los Angeles: Los Angeles Unified School District,
Commission on Sex Equity, 1982. (Free from the Commission,
450 North Grand Avenue, Room H256, Los Angeles, CA 91112.)
    For all elementary levels, the lessons are on such women
as Shirley Chisholm and Mary McLeod Bethune, women in the
work force, and great women in politics. Besides an
extensive bibliography, the book has biographies of thirteen
achieving women from heterogeneous backgrounds.

Women's History Curriculum Units - Grades K Through 3. Santa
Rosa, CA: National Women's History Project, 1984.
    Each unit includes biographies of six different women

representing five major ethnic groups and women with disabilities. Includes such women as Maria Tallchief, Chien-Shiung Wu, Nancy Lopez, Annie Wauneka, and Shirley Chisholm. The units have classroom and individual activities including language and math exercises, oral history, and flannel board copymasters.

Women's History Posters. New York: Organization for Equal Education of the Sexes, Inc.

More than forty posters are available that feature a variety of historical and contemporary women. A new Rights and Justice series focuses on Helen Keller, Delores Huerta, Mother Jones, Rachel Carlson, and Holly Near. A series of posters featuring women with disabilities also is available. Each poster includes a biography. Write for a catalog (438 Fourth St., Brooklyn, NY 11215.)

Secondary

Texts and Anthologies

Bridenthal, Renate, et al. Becoming Visible: Women in European History. 2nd ed. New York: Houghton Mifflin, 1987.

Each chapter by different contributors addresses the major issues and areas in the periods covered by European history survey courses. Some of the topics are women in the Renaissance, the Russian Revolution, and Nazi Germany. The book can be used as a supplementary text or as the major text in a women's history course.

Gross, Susan Hill, and Marjorie Wall Bingham. Women in World Area Studies. Multivolume set. St. Louis Park, MN: Glenhurst Publications, Inc., 1983, 1985.

These thirteen books are available individually or in sets. Particularly useful for history are: Women in Ancient Greece and Rome (1983), Women in Medieval/Renaissance Europe (1983), and Women in Latin America, (1985), 2 vols. Each text has a teacher's guide with tests. Also available separately are nine accompanying sound filmstrip sets.

Kava, Beth Millstein, and Jeanne Bodin. We, the American Women: A Documentary History. Rev. ed. Chicago: Science Research Associates, 1983.

Each chapter covers a period of American history and has

an essay on the history of the period, a variety of short documents, and an extensive bibliography. The documents range from poems by Anne Bradstreet to laws on property rights to Margaret Sanger's description of the opening of a birth control clinic.

Reimer, Eleanor S., and John C. Fout, eds. European Women: A Documentary History, 1789-1945. New York: Schocken Books, 1980.

Women in modern Europe are shown at work, in politics, and dealing with health issues. Documents come from a variety of European countries and include topics such as organizing women workers, suffrage, socialism, Nazism, changing attitudes toward marriage, and views of abortion and contraception.

Riley, Glenda. Inventing the American Woman: A Perspective on Women's History. 2 vols. Arlington Heights, IL: Harlan Davidson, 1986.

Using their recent scholarship in women's history, Riley provides an introductory text that especially looks at women's work, roles, activities, and cultural values. The author focuses on the proscribed vs. actual roles of women in various time periods. The book has an excellent bibliography and is highly heterogeneous in its treatment of women.

Seller, Maxine, ed. Immigrant Women. Philadelphia: Temple University Press, 1981.

These reminiscences are organized by topics and areas of life, such as family, education, work, surviving in a new land. The immigrants are from all continents and from various past and present times.

Stephenson, June. Women's Roots: Status and Achievements in Western Civilization. Napa, CA: Diemer, Smith, 1981. (Order from National Women's History Project.)

Beginning with prehistory, this book documents women's roles and lives through antiquity, medieval, Renaissance, and modern periods. It includes an extensive bibliography.

Curriculum Guides

Boethel, Martha, and Melissa Hield. The Women's West

Teaching Guide: Women's Lives in the 19th Century American West. Sun Valley, ID: Coalition for Western Women's History, 1985. (Order from: National Women's History Project.)

Lessons about women in the West using diaries, stories, letters, autobiographies, and reminiscences to help students learn about the lives of Native American, Hispanic, Chinese, black, and white women in the West. As these lessons show women who were community builders, workers, healers, and suffragists, students will find that stereotypes about women on the frontier evaporate.

Cirksena, J. Diane, and Valijia Rasmussen. Women in United States History. St. Louis Park, MN: Glenhurst Publications, Inc., n.d.

Each manual (nine in total) is organized around a central theme such as "Is There a History of Women?" (For the introductory unit, "Republican Mothers," for the Revolutionary period, "Deferring Domesticity".) They could be integrated into American History or used as texts for Women's History. Each unit includes biographies, photographs, diaries, and other selections from primary sources. Teacher guides have objectives and masters for worksheets.

Groves, Susan. In Search of Our Past: Units in Women's History. Newton, MA: EDC/Women's Educational Equity Act Publishing Center, 1980.

Teacher and student guides to U.S. and world history with units that compare feudalism in Europe and China, describe the lives of a black female slave and the slave owner's wife, show the multiple and surprising roles of Native American women, and describe various events about immigrant women, women in the Industrial Revolution, and women and political change in the Third World. The many excellent classroom activities use such techniques as oral history, essay and story writing, and the development of graphs and charts.

Kolb, Frances. Portraits of Our Mothers. Boston: The NETWORK, Inc., 1982.

This book features a community celebration and classroom units that arose out of oral interviews of mothers by students from fourth to twelfth grade. Many lesson plans and suggested activities, especially on how to use the oral history data students have collected.

Mazey, Mary Ellen, and David R. Lee. Her Space, Her Place:
A Geography of Women. Washington, DC: Association of
American Geographers, 1983. (Order from National Women's
History Project.)
       Geography lessons that ask where is she, where does she
go, what does she think, and what roles does she play in
changing the face of the earth. The answers lie in such
topics as ERA voting patterns, distribution of population by
sex, gendered spatial activities, and women's living spaces.

Women in History and in Contemporary America. Grades 7-12.
Los Angeles: Los Angeles Unified School District, Commission
on Sex Equity, 1982. (Free from the Commission, 450 North
Grand Avenue, Room H256, Los Angeles, CA 91112.)
       A variety of lessons on history, social issues, and
contemporary American problems whose goals are to provide a
syllabus on women that can be integrated into U.S. history,
to show the contributions of women to American history, and
to illustrate the sexism that women have encountered. It
also includes biographies of a heterogeneous group of
achieving women, a chronology of women's milestones, and a
bibliography.

Women's History Lesson Plan Sets. Santa Rosa, CA: National
Women's History Project, n.d.
       Lesson sets for three key years in U.S. history, 1776,
1849, and 1920, that feature activities, chronologies, and
recommended print and nonprint resources.

Media

FUNDI: The Story of Ella Baker. 60 mins., color.
Distributor: First Run Features.
       A history of the civil rights movement through the
personal history of Ella Baker, known affectionately as
Fundi. A friend and advisor of Martin Luther King, she was
instrumental in the organization of the civil rights movement
of the 1960s.

The Life and Times of Rosie the Riveter. 60 mins., color.
Distributor: New Day Films.
       Four women of heterogenous backgrounds tell about
working in war industries during the Second World War. The
film also shows advertising, songs, and other propaganda

created to encourage women into the factories and then out of them after the war. Highly useful as a description of women's nontraditional work in the war, discussion on propaganda, and on women's roles at home and work.

<u>Lucretia Mott</u>. 59 mins., color; available in either 16 mm or video. Distributor: Philadelphia Area Cultural Consortium.

A dramatization of Lucretia Mott's work as an abolitionist and women's rights activist in the pre-Civil War period. It also provides background on Quakers, the Underground Railroad, and women's role in the abolitionist movement.

<u>Lucy Covington: Native American Indian</u>. 16 mins., color. Distributor: Encyclopedia Britannica Education Corporation.

Lucy Covington is a contemporary Native American leader. Using both historic footage about her tribe and oral history interviews, the film tells the story of her work and that of her tribe as they struggle to regain their tribal rights.

<u>One Fine Day</u>. 6 mins., color; available in 16 mm or video. Distributor: National Women's History Project.

A beautiful film that uses music and pictures to portray the images and history of women in the nineteenth and twentieth centuries. More than 60 black-and-white still photos as well as more contemporary film of women from Julia Ward Howe to Sally Ride and Geraldine Ferraro.

<u>Sewing Women</u>. 14 mins., black and white. Distributor: Deepfocus Productions.

Through the story of a Chinese-American woman, the history and social conditions of Chinese immigrants in the United States is depicted. Because <u>Sewing Woman</u> is an oral history that is both personal and universal, it is highly appealing to students.

<u>She's Nobody's Baby</u>. 55 mins., color. Distributor: ABC Films.

A history of women in the twentieth century narrated by Alan Alda and Marlo Thomas and produced by <u>Ms. Magazine</u>. Using historic footage and contemporary ideas, it traces women's struggle to be heard, to redefine their roles and prove that they are "nobody's baby."

<u>Union Maids</u>. 48 mins., color. Distributor: New Day Films.
    <u>Union Maids</u> is the story of three women who lived
through the union history of the 1930s. It shows sitdowns,
scabs, hunger marches, and the birth of the CIO, all events
that these women participated in as workers, union members,
and organizers.

<u>With Babies and Banners</u>. 45 mins., color. Distributor: New
Day Films.
    The story of the women who actively participated in the
1937 sitdown strike at General Motors as they gather for a
reunion held just a few years ago. Women became the backbone
of this strike because the male workers were in the factory.
Women found themselves maintaining their families, preparing
food, picketing outside the factory, and publicizing the
strike. The strike was a key event in the beginnings of the
CIO.

Teacher Resources

<u>Bibliographies and Biographical Guides</u>

Chapman, Anne, ed. <u>Feminist Resources for Schools and</u>
<u>Colleges: A Guide to Curricular Materials</u>. 3rd ed. New
York: The Feminist Press at CUNY, 1986.
    A well-annotated compendium of up-to-date materials for
teaching both U.S. and European history as well as the
history of women resources and on interdisciplinary works.

Davis, Marianna W., ed. <u>Contributions of Black Women to</u>
<u>America</u>. 2 vols. Columbia, SC: Kenday Press, 1981.
    The first volume covers the arts, business, law, and
sports; the second social sciences, sciences and civil
rights. The author's purpose is to provide black role models
that are historically important and thereby pay tribute to
black women who are the object of double jeopardy.

Duley, Margot I., and Mary I. Edwards. <u>The Cross-Cultural</u>
<u>Study of Women: A Comprehensive Guide</u>. New York: The
Feminist Press at CUNY, 1986.
    The authors focus first on the theoretical perspectives
that cut across cultures and then cover area studies for
India, China, Oceania, Sub-Saharan Africa, Latin America, and
Islamic Middle East and North Africa. As a comprehensive

guide, it includes historiography, pedagogical suggestions, lecture topics, and reading lists for students and teachers.

Frey, Linda, Marsha Frey, and Joanna Schneider, ed. Women in Western European History: A Select Chronological, Geographical, and Topical Bibliography from Antiquity to the French Revolution. Westport, CT: Greenwood Press, 1982.
   A massive work organized by traditional time divisions that are subdivided by geographical area, genre and topic. Seven thousand entries are included as well as a subject and author index.

Green, Reyna. Native American Women: A Contextual Bibliography. Bloomington, IN: Indiana University Press, 1983.
   Along with its many entries that are critically annotated, the book has an excellent introductory historical essay and indices by time period and subjects.

Lerner, Gerda. Teaching Women's History. Washington, DC: American Historical Association, 1981.
   Brief essays and bibliography on a variety of concepts and strategies for teaching women's history and the history of racial and ethnic minority women.

_____. Women Are History: A Bibliography in the History of American Women. Madison, WI: University of Wisconsin Graduate Program on Women's History and Department of History, 1986.
   A bibliography that has recently been updated, it includes method and theory, and the history of women both by period and by topics such as motherhood, women of color, and lesbians. A cross-referenced index is included.

McHenry, Robert, ed. Famous American Women: A Biographical Dictionary from Colonial Times to the Present. New York: Dover Publications, 1980.
   Shorter biographical sketches of more than 1,000 women indexed by field and also by women's organizations.

Selected Bibliography of Social Science Readings on Women of Color. Memphis, TN: Center for Research on Women, Memphis

State University, 1985. (Order from the Center, Clement Hall, Memphis State University, Memphis, TN 38152.)

Extensive bibliography of Afro-American, Asian American, Latina, and Native American women. Many of the references are historical items.

Sicherman, Barbara, et al. <u>Recent U.S. Scholarship on the History of Women</u>. Washington, DC: American Historical Association, 1980.

Through an essay format, the authors review a large number of books and articles that provide a brief but excellent introduction to American and European history of women.

Sicherman, Barbara, and Carol Hurd Green, eds. <u>Notable American Women: The Modern Period</u>. Cambridge, MA: Belknap/Harvard University Press, 1980.

The fourth volume of <u>Notable American Women</u>, it features the biographies of American women who died between 1951 and 1975. It should be in every teacher's and school's library.

Uglow, Jennifer S., ed. <u>The International Dictionary of Women's Biography</u>. New York: Continuum, 1983.

Biographical guide to more than 1,500 women from America and Europe. The book also provides some references and has a comprehensive subject index.

Current Works

Banner, Lois W., Gloria F. Orenstein, and Elinor Accampo. <u>Manual for Teaching Gender Roles in Western Civilization</u>. Los Angeles: University of Southern California, n.d. (Order from Study of Women and Men in Society, 331 Taper Hall, University of Southern California, Los Angeles, CA 90089-0034.)

Brief essays on a variety of themes that include images of women, ideology and its impact on women, women and work, women and family, women and reform, and women and Victorianism.

Degler, Carl. <u>At Odds: Women and the Family in America from the Revolution to the Present</u>. New York: Oxford University Press, 1980.

A history of women within the family using statistical and personal documents to show how the interaction has shaped the family and women's lives. Degler believes that the family depends upon women's subordination and that a woman within the family is often "at odds" with her attempts to move outside of it.

Friedman, Jean, and William Shade, eds. Our American Sisters: Women in American Life and Thoughts. 3rd edition. Lexington, MA: DC Heath, 1982.
Excellent anthology of essays on a variety of topics including the intersection of race and sex, divorce in the eighteenth century, working women in the Gilded Age, how movies and household appliances impact women's lives. Divided into four chronological periods, this book, which includes many of the classic works on women's history, might also be read by advanced high school classes.

"Getting Women and Gender into the Curriculum Mainstream," Social Education, LI, no. 3 (March 1987).
Articles on phases in women's history and how they have changed, a description of the new feminist pedagogy, an interactive process curriculum on women and family history, cross cultural learnings on women's history, and description of supplementary resources to integrate gender, race, and class issues into the social studies classroom.

Giddings, Paula. When and Where I Enter: The Impact of Black Women on Race and Sex in America. New York: Bantam Books, 1984.
History of black women from the seventeenth century to the contemporary period that shows the intersection of racism and sexism and how black women have transcended double discrimination.

Hartmann, Susan M. The Home Front and Beyond: American Women in the 1940s. Boston: Twayne, 1982.
From the vantage point of 1950 it is possible to discern how women's lives were permanently reshaped by the war and the economic regeneration. Hartmann begins with a chapter on the status of women on the eve of war, then covers women in the military, labor force, government, popular culture and family, and their education and legal status.

Hooks, Bell. <u>Ain't I a Woman? Black Women and Feminism</u>.
Boston: South End Press, 1981.
    Examination of the impact of sexism on black women from
slavery to the contemporary period. She insists that sex,
race, and class are all immutable facts of human existence
that must be considered for all groups of women.

Hull, Gloria. <u>All the Women Are White, All the Blacks Are
Men, But Some of Us Are Brave: Black Women's Studies</u>. Old
Westbury, NY: The Feminist Press, 1981.
    An excellent reference and pedagogical tool that also
has essays on such topics as racism, black feminism, and
black women in the social sciences. It features six
bibliographical essays, an audiovisual listing, and course
syllabi.

Jones, Jacqueline. <u>Labor of Love, Labor of Sorrow: Black
Women, Work and the Family from Slavery to the Present</u>. New
York: Basic Books, 1985.
    Black working women, North and South, are chronicled as
they worked outside the home, sustained family lives, and
preserved their group culture. It shows black women's role
in agriculture, their exploitation in slavery, and after
slavery their continuing work outside of the capitalist
industrialist system.

Kerber, Linda. <u>Women of the Republic: Intellect and
Ideology in Revolutionary America</u>. Chapel Hill, NC:
University of North Carolina Press, 1980.
    Study of women in the Revolutionary period that details
how women developed a new role as Republican mothers as a way
of bridging the public/private dichotomy of women's lives.

Kessler-Harris, Alice. <u>Out to Work: A History of Wage-
Earning Women in the United States</u>. New York: Oxford
University Press, 1982.
    An exploration of the formation of women's work into
wage labor and its consequences for women as workers and
women's self-image from the Colonies to the present. The
author looks at the relationship between wage labor and
family roles and tries to show different class, ethnic, and
racial patterns of both.

Norton, Mary Beth. <u>Liberty's Daughters: The Revolutionary</u>
<u>Experience of American Women, 1750-1800</u>. Boston: Little
Brown, 1980.

In the first half on Colonial women in the family,
Norton shows that women were not the equals of men but lived
and worked within proscribed roles. In the second half on
the American Revolution, she shows the Revolution's impact on
women and women's activities in the Revolution.

Smith-Rosenberg, Carroll. <u>Disorderly Conduct: Visions of</u>
<u>Gender in Victorian America</u>. New York: Oxford University
Press, 1986.

Collection of essays that presents new constructions
concerning women's lives in the nineteenth century. The
introductory essay is on the development of women's history
and its connection to and impact on social history. The
other selections look at women's changing roles in terms of
sexuality, social groups, popular and women's culture.

Ulrich, Laurel Thatcher. <u>Good Wives: Image and Reality in</u>
<u>the Lives of Women in Northern New England, 1650-1750</u>. New
York: Alfred A. Knopf, 1982.

To delineate the multiple roles of Colonial women that
ranged from housewife to deputy husband, from consort to
neighbor, the author has used ingenious sources such as
diaries, letters, wills, legal writs, church papers, and even
embroidery.

Ware, Susan. <u>Holding Their Own: American Women in the</u>
<u>1930's</u>. Boston: Twayne Publishers, 1982.

An overview of women's roles and lives in the 1930s
using the new scholarship. It has chapters on such diverse
areas as popular culture and fine arts, employment, and
social reform.

Thanks to Molly MacGregor, Executive Director of the National
Women's History Project, for help in compiling this material.

LANGUAGE ARTS AND LITERATURE

Frances Arick Kolb

Research on Bias and Stereotyping

In 1969 and 1970, groups of feminists in New Jersey and
New York surveyed children's literature and reported that a
dismal portrayal of females, from childhood to old age, was
found in children's books and texts. The research of
Feminists on Children's Media revealed that Newbery Award
books featured few women heroes; boys outnumbered girls three
to one. So, too, when Women on Words and Images surveyed the
most commonly used elementary reading books, they found that
women were few in number and shown in limited roles.
Seventy-five percent of the textbook stories focused on male
characters. The few females in the texts were passive,
domestic, and dependent. Their report concluded, "Books
designed to teach reading skills also were teaching young
children to have stereotyped expectations about the lives of
men and women, boys and girls."[1]

Another area of the language arts that feminists
challenged in the early 1970s was language usage.[2] Research
has shown that when male generic language is used, students
produce images that are overwhelmingly male. If both gender
unspecified and gender specific language are used, they
elicit from students more gender balanced images and
understanding of both sexes.[3]

Because of the publicity and feminist lobbying,
publishers began to review their procedures and their
publications. By the mid-1970s, most publishers had issued
guidelines to ensure that authors would depict images of
women and men that encompassed a broader range of
characteristics and were closer to the realities of
contemporary life. For example, "Guidelines for Creating
Positive Sexual and Racial Images in Educational Materials,"
issued by Macmillan Publishing Company in 1975, stated,
"Remember that half of the human population is female and
should be represented appropriately in our textbooks." As
one of its recommendations, the guidelines suggested that
"emphasis should be placed frequently on portrayals of girls
and women participating actively and positively in exciting,

worthwhile pursuits, while males should be permitted often to
observe and lend support." [4]

Throughout the 1970s, a multitude of studies and reviews
followed. Feminists reviewed the literature taught in
classrooms, the definitions found in dictionaries, the
classifications used in library catalogs, fairy tales, Mother
Goose rhymes and other traditional children's literature,
language usage, and foreign languages. [5] As they assessed the
image of women in the media, advertising, television, and
other areas of popular culture, the same patterns of absence
and poor image were discovered. A study of television in
1973-74 concluded, "The prime-time message of the television
screen is that there are more men around, and that they are
dominant, authoritative and competent. While neither sex
displays a majority of positive behaviors, women come off
showing even more negative behaviors than men." [6]

In the 1980s, scholars continue to conduct research on
bias in children's literature and texts, and they still find
problem areas, even after the feminist critiques of the
1970s. For example, Gwyneth Britton and Margaret Lumpkin
looked at 77 books in seven reading series published between
1980 and 1982. While the percentage of females and people of
color had risen, females continued to be underrepresented.
Not only were white males still portrayed in more careers and
in greater total numbers, but the careers for both sexes were
still stereotyped and unrealistic. [7] Two recent articles that
discussed the image of women in children's picture books
echoed this assessment. Women continued to be
underrepresented, and those that were shown seemed to be
engaged in the same household tasks as always. In a review
of Caldecott Medal winners from 1976 to 1980, the author
concluded that the books showed "an abundance of traditional
stereotypes" and "male dominance." [8]

A recent survey of college and introductory American
literature courses found a similarly dismal picture of number
of women authors taught. When the researcher counted the
number of times writers appeared in the syllabi of fifty such
courses from twenty-five representative universities and
colleges across the United States in 1980-81, he found that
only one white woman, Emily Dickinson, and no blacks, male or
female, were among the twenty writers most often taught.
Among the fifty writers most often taught were six white
women and two black men. He concluded, "Such facts reflect,
in my view, that the racist and sexist assumptions about
literary values which helped shape the canon continue to

influence curricula."[9]

Positive Trends

While progress on literature and texts is occurring, albeit slowly, vigilance is needed because new issues and problems continue to arise. For example, the recent flood of romance novels for teenagers has reintroduced the sexist, racist world that feminists hoped had disappeared.[10]

Some positive recent trends, however, are evident in the number of new literature anthologies and activity guides for the elementary grades designed to remediate the narrow images found in most texts. The new anthologies for the elementary classroom provide teachers with supplements to their stereotyped reading texts.[11]

For the high school level, there are new collections of literature for and about women of color and collections by and about women with disabilities. These can give high school literature a broader, more multiethnic and inclusive perspective on the world. (Both the Secondary and the Teacher Resource Sections of this bibliography provide sources for these new collections.) In using the new literature for and about women of color, Gloria T. Hull's essay, "Reading Literature by U.S. Women of Color," is an excellent background piece. As a black woman, she records her experience in studying the literature of other ethnic women. In three months of reading the works of Native American, Chicana, Puerto Rican, and Asian American women, she found herself discovering many new issues and ideas.[12]

Bibliographies and collections of literature by and of Third World women for college-level courses and the first major anthology of literature by women for the university also are evidence of progress. With the publication of the Norton Anthology, teachers now have a one-volume source for women's literature for American and British literature courses.[13]

New Views of Women's Lives

As feminist scholars have moved from the study of bias and the negative images of women to the more positive view that highlights the contributions of women to literature, they have begun to explore new views of women's lives and women's spheres. In the 1970s, feminist literary criticism concentrated on the exposure of stereotyping, the search for forgotten women writers, and proof that women had always been discontented. Moving beyond these important first steps, feminists have begun to examine literature to see "how literature comprehends, transmits, and shapes female experience and is, in turn, shaped by it." Feminist critics are now looking at how women made space for themselves in a basically masculine world, how they have created women's communities, and how they have defined themselves.[14]

Feminist scholars also have broadened the very definition of literature through the introduction of nontraditional sources such as autobiographies, oral interviews, and diaries. Because the full range of women's lives is not usually found in traditional literary sources, teachers may want to seek out these unusual sources. In an article by Marianne Whelchel, she describes a course she developed in which she not only used unusual sources but had the students use oral interviews to create their own literature. As she said, "Women without the blocks of time and the rooms of their own needed for writing in the traditional genres have spoken in these forms. In them we hear the voices of overworked housewives and mothers, of working-class and pioneer women, even of illiterate women."[15]

Integrating Women into the Curriculum

For high school literature teachers, a number of questions arise when they attempt to integrate women into high school literature: How many women writers or works that present positive, accurate images of women are in the reading list in the high school literature course? Does "great literature" mean literature without women or without women authors? Should high schools have a special course on women writers, and if so, what would be the curriculum of such a course? Should the high school concentrate on the infusion of women into the regular curriculum?

Aid in answering these questions can be found in the work of feminist scholars who have engaged in projects to "mainstream" the new women's scholarship into the college-level liberal arts curriculum. From the recent publications that chronicle these projects, high school English teachers will be able to learn both the theory and the practice of the integration of women's literature and women's research into liberal arts courses of study in colleges and universities.[16]

The bibliography is divided into three major sections: Elementary, Secondary, and Teacher Resources. The Elementary and Secondary sections list activities, units, and curricula for the language arts, K-12. These sections also include print and nonprint media of fairy tales, stories, plays, and poetry for use in the classroom. Teacher Resources has been subdivided into three areas: Bibliographies, including a number of bibliographical guides to children's reading, multiethnic sources, and media; Research Studies, including literary criticism and current studies of content and language; and Curriculum Guides and Teacher Materials, including guidelines, general theory, and background material for curriculum.

Neither individual works of literature nor individual writers have been included. The bibliography section of Teacher Resources provides sources to find these. While the emphasis is on materials since 1979-80, some "classics" for which no recent substitutes exist are included.

Notes

1. Women on Words and Images, Dick and Jane as Victims: Sex Stereotyping in Children's Readers (Princeton, NJ: WWI, 1975), and Feminists on Children's Media, Little Miss Muffet Fights Back (New York, rev. ed., 1974). See also Lenore Weitzman, et al., "Sex Role Socialization in Picture Books for Preschool Children," and Suzanne Caplinski, "Sexism in Award Winning Picture Books," in Sexism in Children's Books: Facts, Figures and Guidelines (London: Writers and Readers Publishers Corp., 1976).

2. Casey Miller and Kate Swift, Words and Women (New York: Anchor, 1976) and Alleen Pace Nilsen, et al., Sexism and Language (Urbana, IL: NCTE, 1976).

3. Kathryn B. Scott and Candace Garrett Schau, "Sex Equity and Sex Bias in Instructional Materials," in Handbook for Achieving Sex Equity Through Education, ed. Susan Klein. (Baltimore: Johns Hopkins Press, 1985), p. 220.

4. Guidelines for Creating Positive Sexual and Racial Images in Educational Materials (New York: Macmillan and Co., 1975); see also McGraw-Hill Guidelines in Sexism in Children's Books: Facts, Figures and Guidelines.

5. On fairy tales and nursery rhymes, see Marcia Lieberman,

"Some Day My Prince Will Come: Female Acculturation Through the Fairy Tale," College English (December 1972), pp. 303-395 and Dan Donlan, "The Negative Image of Women in Children's Literature," Elementary English (April 1972), pp. 217-227. On foreign languages, see Barbara Drygulski Wright, "Feminist Transformation of Foreign Language Instruction: Progress and Challenges," Working Paper #117 (Wellesley, MA: Wellesley College Center for Research on Women, 1983). On dictionaries, see Lucy Picco Simpson, "Is 'Sexism' in the Dictionary?" Interracial Books for Children Bulletin, X (1979), pp. 15-17. See also chapters on dictionaries, children's books and elementary reading, and literature in Alleen P. Nilsen, et al., Sexism and Language (Urbana, IL: National Council of Teachers of English, 1977).

6. Women on Words and Images, p. 30; see also Journal of Communication, XXIV, no. 2 (Spring 1974) and XXVIII, no. 1 (Winter 1978), in which the entire issue was devoted to research studies on women and the media. See also George Gerbner and Nancy Signorielli, "Women and Minorities in Television Drama, 1969-1978," paper from University of Pennsylvania, Annenberg School of Communications, 1979.

7. Gwyneth Britton and Margaret Lumpkin, "Basal Readers: Paltry Progress Pervades," Interracial Books for Children Bulletin, XIV, no. 6 (1983), pp. 4-7.

8. Rosalind E. Engle, "Is Unequal Treatment of Females Disappearing in Children's Picture Books?" Reading Teacher, XXXIV (March 1981), pp. 647-652; Joe B. Hurst, "Images in Children's Picture Books," Social Education, XLV, no. 2 (February 1981), pp. 138-143.

9. Paul Lauter, "A Small Survey of Introductory Courses in American Literature," Women's Studies Quarterly, IX, no. 4 (Winter 1981), p. 12; see also his article, "Reconstructing American Literature: A Strategy for Change," in Bonnie Spanier, et al., Towards Balanced Curriculum: Sourcebook for Initiating Gender Integration Projects (Cambridge, MA: Schenckman, 1984), pp. 142-154.

10. "Romance Series for Young Readers," Interracial Books for Children Bulletin, XII (1981).

11. Examples are Ruth Myers and Beryle Banfield, Embers: Stories for a Changing World (New York: Council on Interracial Books for Children, 1983), and Letty C. Pogrebin, Stories for Free Children (New York: McGraw-Hill, 1982).

12. Gloria T. Hull, "Reading Literature by U.S. Third World Women," Working Paper #114 (Wellesley, MA: Wellesley College Center for Women on Research, 1984).

13. Sandra M. Gilbert and Susan Grubar, The Norton Anthology of Literature by Women: The Tradition in English (New York: W.W. Norton and Co., 1985).

14. Cheri Register, "Review Essay: Literary Criticism," Signs, VLI, no. 2 (Winter 1980), pp. 268-282.

15. Marianne Whelchel, "Transforming the Canon with Nontraditional Literature by Women," College English, XLVI, no. 6 (October 1984), p. 587.

16. Marilyn Schuster and Susan R. Van Dyne, Women's Place in the Academy: Transforming the Liberal Arts (Littlefield, NJ: Rowman and Allanheld, 1985), and Spanier, et al., Towards a Balanced Curriculum (Cambridge, MA: Schenckman, 1984).

BIBLIOGRAPHY

Elementary

Cain, Mary A. Boys and Girls Together: Nonsexist Activities for Elementary Schools. Holmes Beach, FL: Learning Publications, 1980.
    Organized by subject areas, two chapters are on reading texts and reading/language arts curriculum. These cover analysis of basal readers for sexism and many suggestions and activities on stereotyping and language arts, such as nonsexist story starters, scrambled words, and work puzzles.

Equity Lessons for the Elementary School. Newton, MA: EDC/WEEA Publishing Center, 1982.
    Ten lessons for grades K-8 curriculum in which several are for language arts. Some examples are lessons on feelings, toys, fairy tales, bias in textbooks. The book also includes guidelines for the selection of materials.

The Fable of He and She. New York: Learning Corporation of America, 1974.
    Animated 16mm film of eleven minutes about a mythical place where work is divided between men and women until the characters learn that what is best suits the individual, regardless of gender.

Free To Be, You and Me. Videotape and record (order from: Lady Slipper Records, Box 3130, Durham, NC 27705). Book (New York: McGraw-Hill, 1974).
    Landmark video (44 minutes), record, and book version of nonsexist stories for children. Video won much attention and an Emmy award as the best Children's Special of the Year. Fairy tales, poems, songs and stories on a wide variety of themes around sex roles are found in this collection.

Free To Be...a Family. New York: Bantam Books, 1987.
    A collection of stories that expands upon original Free To Be concept, focusing on how to live with a community of different kinds of people. Stories are nonsexist, multicultural, and include people with disabilities.

Hunter, Lisa, ed. <u>Oceans of Options: Sex Equity Lessons for the Classroom</u>. San Francisco: Far West Laboratory for Educational Research and Development, 1983.

Among the many lessons are language arts activities for grades K-8 that cover bias in instructional materials, identification of stereotyping, reading aloud, biographies, and the creation of a bias-free newspaper.

<u>"Hurray for Captain Jane!" and Other Liberated Stories for Children</u>. New York: Caedmon Records, 1975.

Reading of stories that help children both to identify with others and develop their own specialness.

"Identifying Sexism and Racism in Children's Books." New York: Council on Interracial Books for Children, n.d.

Two filmstrips and tape cassettes plus background readings that demonstrate how children's books transmit sexist and racist messages. These filmstrips will help children to recognize the bias in the literature they read.

Kavanaugh, Michelle. <u>When I Grow Up</u>. Vol. 1. Atlanta: Humanis Limited, 1979.

Series of exercises to help children acquire self-confidence free of negative values imposed by gender stereotypes and to enlarge their thinking about opportunities. For grades pre K-8.

King, Edith. <u>Teaching Ethnic Awareness: Methods and Materials for the Elementary Classroom.</u> New York: Scott Foresman, 1980.

Activities for elementary pupils to help instill more ethnic awareness. The book features specific language arts activities such as the creation of ethnic stories, dramatic role playing, and puppet shows.

Kolb, Francis. <u>Portraits of Our Mothers</u>. Andover, MA: The NETWORK, Inc., 1983.

Many activities around oral interviews that give students skills in writing family histories, biographies of family members, descriptions of events, and interviews.

Kumagai, Gloria L. America's Women of Color: Integrating Cultural Diversity into Non-Sex-Biased Curricula: Elementary Curriculum Guide. Newton, MA: WEEA Publishing Center, 1982.

Lessons and activities developed by elementary teachers on America's women of color; included are activities on vocabulary, reading aloud, and biographies.

Lurie, Allison. Clever Gretchen and Other Forgotten Folktales. New York: Thomas Crowell, 1980.

An anthology of short folk tales in which heroines distinguish themselves by bravery and wit. For grades 4-6.

Myers, Ruth, and Beryle Banfield, eds. Embers: Stories for a Changing World. New York: Council on Interracial Books for Children, 1983.

Anthology of fiction, biography, poetry, and oral history about people who overcame barriers of sex, race, and disability. Topics are friendship, families, famous women, school, working, and breaking barriers. For ages 8-12. Teacher's guide also available.

Once upon a Choice. Franklin Lakes, NJ: New Day Films, 1983. 16 mm film.

A humorous fairy tale film (16 mm) of fifteen minutes in length that deals with sex-role stereotyping. The plot concerns a princess who is offered three prospective spouses and makes a surprising choice.

People and Places U.S.A. Newton, MA: EDC/WEEA Publishing Center, 1981.

Elementary reading text about three girls and three boys who travel around the United States. Its goal is to present nonsexist materials to students in grades 3-5 and help them develop a positive self-image. Supplementary activities and vocabulary are found in the Teacher's Guide.

Phelps, Ethel Johnston. Tatterhood and Other Tales. Old Westbury, NY: Feminist Press, 1978.

A collection of international folk and fairy tales retold by women storytellers. Good to use for reading aloud to elementary students.

_____. The Maid of the North: Feminist Folk Tales from
Around the World. New York: Holt, Rinehart & Winston, 1981.
    A collection of twenty-one tales from Finland, Pakistan,
South Africa, England, the American Southwest, and Russia,
all chosen for their nontraditional female heroes.

Pogrebin, Letty C., ed. Stories for Free Children. New
York: McGraw-Hill, 1982.
    Taken from a monthly column in Ms. Magazine, this
anthology contains fables, fairy tales, stories about
emotions, and biographies of famous women, all emphasizing
nonsexist, multiracial, and multicultural themes.

Sexism in Media and Language. Palatine, IL: The Learning
Seed Company, 1977.
    A collection of teaching materials that includes a
filmstrip on "Sexism in Media," a silent filmstrip titled
"Images for Evaluation," student worksheets, and television
and news monitoring forms.

Shapiro, June, Sylvia Kramer, and Catherine Hunenberg. Equal
Their Chances: Children's Activities for Non-Sexist Learning.
Englewood Cliffs, NJ: Prentice Hall, 1980.
    In order to break down the forms of sexism in the
elementary classroom, this teacher's guide has chapters on
various subject areas. The language arts chapter provides
many suggestions for learning activities for creative
writing, written and oral language skills, and letter and
newspaper writing.

The Yellow, Red, and Blue Book. Seattle: Project Equality,
Highline Public Schools, 1976. (Order from: Highline Public
Schools, 15675 Ambaum Blvd. SW, Seattle, WA 98166.)
    To expand students' awareness of traditional sex-role
stereotyping, this book presents short-term classroom
activities developed for and by teachers of grades K-6.

Secondary

Becoming Sex Fair: Stage Three Manual: Revising the
Curriculum. Newton, MA: EDC/WEEA Publishing Center, 1979.
    Two sections of the many lessons and ideas for the
secondary classroom are pertinent: Foreign Languages, which

provides ideas and strategies for countering sexism in the study of foreign languages, and Literature, which provides strategies for presenting a more balanced view of women in literature, including sample activities and a bibliography.

Baird, Joseph L., and Deborah S. Workman, eds. <u>Toward Soloman's Mountain: The Experience of Disability in Poetry</u>. Philadelphia: Temple University Press, 1986.
   This unique anthology is a collection of "serious, tough-minded, nonsentimental" poems about disability. They appear here for the first time and describe victories, frustrations, and a full range of life experiences.

Browne, Susan E., Debra Conners, and Nancy Stern, eds. <u>With the Power of Each Breath</u>. San Francisco: Cleis Press, 1985.
   This anthology is written for, by, and about women with disabilities. All of the 54 women who contributed are disabled. The editors state that, "These pages are a journey into our lives as we survive in an inaccessible society, express our anger, grow up in our families, live in our bodies, find our own identity, parent our children, and find our friends and each other."

Campling, Jo. <u>Images of Ourselves: Women with Disabilities Talking</u>. Boston: Routledge & Kegan Paul, 1981.
   Campling presents stories through the words of women with disabilities. The women differ in age, disabilities, politics, and lifestyles. (Available on cassette from Recording for the Blind.) A companion 3/4 inch videotape is available. (Contact Rehabfilm, 1123 Broadway, New York, NY 10010.)

<u>Fair Play: Developing Self-Concept and Decision Making Skills in the Middle School: Student and Teacher Books on Decisions on Language</u>. Newton, MA: EDC/WEAA Publishing Center, 1983.
   A series of lessons for students in which such topics as the messages of language, oral speech, and the differences in male and female communication are covered. Teacher and student guide available.

Fisher, Dexter. <u>The Third Woman: Minority Women Writers in the United States</u>. New York: Houghton Mifflin, 1980.
   An extensive anthology of literature by black, Chicana,

Asian American, and Native American women writers in which
folklore, legends, interviews, essays, poetry, and short
stories are presented.

Hoffman, Nancy, and Florence Howe. <u>Women Working: An
Anthology of Stories and Poems</u>. Old Westbury, NY: The
Feminist Press and McGraw Hill, 1979.
     An anthology of works mainly by women writers from the
nineteenth and twentieth centuries, in which the sections are
organized around work as oppressive, satisfying, familial,
and transforming. Authors range from Adrienne Rich to Sarah
Orne Jewett and Mary Wilkes Freeman, including a number of
black and ethnic writers. Teacher Guide also available.

Katz, Jane B., ed. <u>I Am the Fire of Time: The Voices of
Native American Women</u>. New York: E.P. Dutton, 1977.
     Anthology of Native American women's poetry, oral
histories, and literature. Included are anthropological and
autobiographical narratives, songs, prayers.

<u>Killing Us Softly</u>. Boston: Cambridge Films, 1979.
     Thirty-minute 16mm film and videotape that shows how
advertising that seems harmless and funny on an individual
basis can add up to a powerful form of cultural conditioning
that is damaging, especially to women.

Kumagai, Gloria L. <u>America's Women of Color: Integrating
Cultural Diversity into Non-Sex-Biased Curricula: Secondary
Curriculum Guide</u>. Newton, MA: EDC/WEEA Publishing Center,
1982.
     Teacher-developed lesson plans on the similarities and
differences, stereotyping, and discrimination of the four
major groups of women of color in the United States: Asian,
black, Hispanic, and Native American. Especially useful to
help Anglo students learn about women of color. The lessons,
which are labeled by grade level and subject area, could be
integrated into reading, language arts, and literature.

"Language and Textbooks." Newton, MA: EDC/WEEA Publishing
Center, n.d.
     Half-hour videotape of a lecture/discussion on sexism in
language and textbooks featuring well-known experts in the
field as well as teachers and students.

Lyons, Mary. <u>A Story of Her Own: A Resource Guide to Teaching Literature by Women</u>. <u>Grades 7-9</u>. Charlottesville, VA: Heartwood Books, 1985. (Available from National Women's History Project, Box 3716, Santa Rosa, CA 95402.)
    A compilation of a variety of tools for teaching: a bibliography of fifty short stories by women, a thematic division of the stories, a list of fifty works of fiction by women, a film list, and several student activities, including a play, authors' board game, and a roll call of writers.

Moffatt, Mary Jane, and Charlotte Painter, ed. <u>Revelations: Diaries of Women</u>. New York: Vintage Books, 1975.
    Nineteenth- and twentieth-century diary selections by thirty-two women from seven to eighty years old and from many countries. Topics include love, work, and power by writers such as Anne Frank, Louisa May Alcott, George Sand, and Virginia Woolf.

Moraga, Cherrie and Gloria Anzaldua, eds. <u>This Bridge Called My Back: Writings by Radical Women of Color</u>. New York: Kitchen Table Press, 1984.
    This anthology of writings by Third World women of color includes poems, transcripts, conversations and letters, public addresses, and stories about youth, racism,, and the lives and culture of the writers.

Nilsen, Alleen P. <u>Changing Words in a Changing World</u>. 2 vols. Newton, MA: EDC/WEEA Publishing Center, 1980.
    A course of study with an instructor's guide and curriculum book to help students and teachers understand language as a complex tool of communication that has an impact on and reflects gender differences in our society. It includes a glossary of terms, further readings, and student activities for research, analysis, and discussion.

Pearlman, Deborah. <u>Breaking the Silence, Seven Courses in Women's Studies</u>. Newton, MA: EDC/WEEA Publishing Center, 1979.
    Of these women's studies courses developed especially for women who are from the Third World, poor, working class, or institutionalized, two are on literature. "Literature and Black Writers" focuses on poetry and short stories on self-images, images of family, work, and living in a hostile society. The course on "Reading and Writing" begins with

poetry by and about women and leads to writing by the
students. Because the courses are designed for women only,
they would need some revision for coeducational classes.

Reese, Lyn, Jean Wilkinson, and Phyllis Sheon Koppelman. I'm
on My Way Running: Women Speak on Coming of Age. New York:
Avon Books, 1983.
   Anthology of dramatic personal accounts of coming of age
so that female students can see that their concerns and
experiences have been shared by girls from everywhere and
throughout time. Selections come from around the world with
authors from India, Africa, China, and France as well as
Americans and Native Americans, who talk about taking risks,
mother-daughter relationships, sexuality, and puberty.

Saxton, Marsha, and Florence Howe, eds. With Wings: An
Anthology of Literature By and About Women with Disabilities.
New York: The Feminist Press at CUNY, 1987.
   Through personal accounts, fiction, and poetry, women
describe the physical and emotional experience of disability.
The selections dispell myths and stereotypes and celebrate
the strengths and talents of women and girls with
disabilities.

Schniedewind, Nancy, and Ellen Davidson. Open Minds to
Equality. A Sourcebook of Learning Activities to Promote
Race, Sex, Class, and Age Equity. Englewood Cliffs, NJ:
Prentice-Hall, 1983.
   Resource book designed both to teach students about
equality and generate more equality among students.
Activities cover all forms of bias, from racism to ageism to
sexism. Many activities involve reading, writing, creative
writing, research, and thinking skills. The lessons help
students to know, think, and feel the "isms" of our society
and then make changes.

See What I Say. (Distributed by Filmmakers Library, 133 E.
58th St., New York, NY 10022.)
   In this 16mm, 24-minute film, Holly Near, a feminist
folk singer, breaks through the barrier that separates the
hearing and the deaf communities. She shares her concert
stage with Susan Freundlich, recognized American Sign
Language interpreter, who incorporates mime and dance in the
translation of the lyrics. Their synchronized performance

heightens the impact of her vision of a better world. The powerful stories of four women and their experience with deafness are told in the film.

<u>Tell Them I'm a Mermaid</u>. (Distributed by Embassy Telecommunications, 1901 Avenue of the Stars, Los Angeles, CA 90067.)

First aired on network television in December 1983, this unique 23-minute musical-theater documents the lives of seven women with physical disabilities. With an original music score and choreography, the women use their personal experiences to refute society's stigmas and stereotypes about disability. (Available as a 16mm film and in 3/4" and 1/2 " videotape.)

<u>To Be a Woman and a Writer</u>. Filmstrip set. New York: Guidance Associates, 1976.

Two filmstrips and tapes on women writers. The first on the nineteenth century describes the special lives of these women and their creation of literary "women of spirit." Part Two looks at twentieth-century writers, their special problems as women, and their art and status.

Washington, Mary Helen, ed. <u>Midnight Birds: Stories of Contemporary Black Women Writers</u>. Garden City, NY: Anchor Books/Doubleday, 1980.

A collection of short stories by writers such as Alice Walker, Ntozake Shange, and Toni Morrison. The editor has described this volume as "a sturdier collection, more open to adventure, prouder, more strong-minded, more defiant" than her earlier collection. These stories concern relationships between women of color and between black and white women, women who are heroic, and women seeking their heritage.

"Women in Literature: Historical Images of Work," <u>Title IX Line</u>, V. no. 2 (Spring/Summer 1985). (Free from Center for Sex Equity in Schools, University of Michigan, School of Education, Ann Arbor, MI 48109.)

Excerpts from nineteenth- and twentieth-century American literature on women at sea, in wartime, at Macy's, on the frontier, in the factory, and in the schoolroom. Writers include Sinclair Lewis, Harriet Arnow, and Shirley Jackson.

Teacher Resources

Bibliographies

Adell, Judith, and Hilary D. Klein, ed. A Guide to Non-
Sexist Children's Books. Chicago: Academy Press Limited,
1976.
     An annotated bibliography for both sexes of nonsexist
books, both fiction and nonfiction, that is divided into
three sections by grade level. While some of the books may
be out of print, most will be found in libraries.

Alarcon, Norma, and Sylvia Kossnar. Bibliography of Hispanic
Women Writers. Bloomington, IN: Chicano-Riqueno Studies,
1980.
     Bibliography of individual authors including their
writings, criticism, and biographies. The book also has a
section on Women Authors-General and Portrayal of Women in
Hispanic Literature and provides an index of authors by time
period.

Bracken, Jeanne, and Sharon Wigutoff. Books for Today's
Young Readers: An Annotated Bibliography of Recommended
Fiction for Ages 10-14. Old Westbury, NY: Feminist Press,
1981.
     After the authors reviewed a large number of books to
find the best novels that challenged traditional sex roles
and presented positive images of a pluralistic society, they
chose 73 books to annotate. Still neglected, say the
authors, are many areas of a pluralistic world, such as
nonstereotyped images of parents, sensitive boys, or poor
families.

"'Common Differences' Between Black and White Women: Changing
the Ways We Think about and Teach Women's Experiences and the
Humanities: Bibliography." (Order from Duke-UNC Women's
Studies Research Center, 207 E. Duke Building, Duke
University, Durham, NC 27708.)
     Divided into fiction, nonfiction, juvenile literature,
and films, this bibliography provides many sources for
analysis of relationships, including readings, biographies,
media, and literature on black and white women together.

Cotera, Martha. <u>Multicultural Women's Sourcebook: Materials</u>
<u>Guide for Use in Women's Studies and Bilingual Multicultural</u>
<u>Programs</u>. Newton, MA: EDC/WEEA Publishing Center, 1982.
     First section on Multicultural/Multiethnic Materials is
followed by sections on particular ethnic groups, such as
Cuban, Jewish, and white ethnic women. Within each of these
subdivisions the materials are classified according to
reference, background reading, and student materials.

Davis, Enid. <u>The Liberty Cap</u>. Chicago: Academy Press
Limited, 1978.
     Articles from 1974-76 that appeared in a journal called
<u>The Liberty Cap</u>, whose purpose was to seek out nonsexist
reading books for children. Since many classics of
children's literature were reviewed here, most of the books
are still found in libraries and read by children.

Feminist Collections: "Women's Studies Library Resources in
Wisconsin"; "New Books on Women and Feminism"; "Feminist
Periodicals: A Current Listing of Contents"; "Wisconsin
Bibliography in Women's Studies." (Individual and
institutional subscriptions available from: Women's Studies
Librarian-at-Large, 112 A Memorial Library, University of
Wisconsin, 728 State St., Madison, WI 53706.)
     These periodical publications are all available for the
one fee. Also write for a listing of free bibliographies.
Examples of recent ones on literature are: "Films and
Videotapes about Women, 1984," "North American Indian Women:
Selected Sources," "Lesbian Literature 1980-1983: A Select
Bibliography."

Green, Rayna. <u>Native American Women: A Bibliography</u>.
Bloomington, IN: Indiana University Press, 1983.
     An indexed bibliography that includes literature and
films by and about Native American women. An introductory
essay on Native American women gives a good critical overview
of the history, literature, and research on Native American
women.

Kumagai, Gloria. <u>America's Women of Color. Minority Women:</u>
<u>An Annotated Bibliography</u>. Newton, MA: EDC/WEEA Publishing
Center, 1982.
     Five sections of resources on elementary-secondary,
postsecondary, teacher, elementary audiovisual and secondary

audiovisual. Each of these sections is divided into Asian,
Indian, Black, Hispanic, and Multicultural. Especially
detailed annotations are given for the postsecondary and
teacher resources.

Newman, Joan. <u>Girls Are People Too! A Bibliography of
Nontraditional Female Roles in Children's Books</u>. Metuchen,
NJ: Scarecrow Press, 1982.
    Fiction and nonfiction books that have nontraditional
female characters are annotated and divided into primary
(preschool to Grade 3) and Intermediate (Grades 4-9)
categories. Within these categories are subject areas:
General, black, Native American, Handicapped and Other
Minorities. A chronology of notable women is included.

Northwest Regional Educational Laboratory, Center for Sex
Equity. <u>Bibliography of Non-Sexist Supplementary Books K-12</u>.
Tucson: Oryx Press, 1984.
    Books are categorized by reading level, with subject
area listing. These lists include a number of novels and
biographies, old and new, that would provide students with
nonsexist, nonracist readings on women writers and women's
writings.

Sullivan, Kaye. <u>Films for, by and about Women</u>. Metuchen,
NJ: Scarecrow Press, 1980.
    Useful source of films on individual women writers or
literary works. A subject and filmmaker index, a well as a
list of places to rent or purchase the films is also
provided.

Research Studies

Britton, Gwyneth, and Margaret Lumpkin. "Basal Readers:
Paltry Progress Pervades." <u>Interracial Books for Children
Bulletin</u> 14 (1983): pp. 4-7.
    In an update of their earlier study of bias in reading
texts, the authors have surveyed the careers of women, men,
and minorities as portrayed in reading texts. Their research
showed that minorities are overrepresented while women are
underrepresented. Both sexes continue to be presented with
unrealistic career options.

Haber, Barbara. Women's Annual: 1980, 1981, 1982-83.
Boston: G.K. Hall and Co.
     Each volume has two pertinent chapters: "Women,
Scholarship and the Humanities," and "Popular Culture."
These cover literary criticism, popular novels and films, new
literary theory, and new biographies of writers. Extensive
bibliographies of new writing are included.

Klein, Susan, ed. Handbook for Achieving Sex Equity Through
Education. Baltimore: Johns Hopkins Press, 1985.
     Excellent guide to current research in sex equity in
education. Two chapters relevant to language arts and
literature are Kathryn P. Scott and Candace Garrett Schau,
"Sex Equity and Sex Bias in Instructional Materials," and
Kathryn P. Scott, et al., "Sex Equity in Reading and
Communication Skills."

McConnell-Ginet, Sally, Ruth Borker, and Nelly Furman. Women
and Language in Literature and Society. New York: Praeger
Publishers, 1980.
     Anthology of review articles on such topics as men's and
women's language, language in women's lives, literary
criticism of women writers, and language from a cross-
cultural perspective.

Nilsen, Alleen Pace, et al. Sexism and Language. Urbana,
IL: National Council of Teachers of English, 1977.
     Classic anthology of research articles on language from
the early 1970s. The articles discuss linguistic sexism in
various areas such as legislation and courts, literature,
marriage, dictionaries and texts, and elementary schools.

Sheridan, Marcia E., ed. Sex Stereotypes and Reading:
Research and Strategies. Newark, DE: International Reading
Association, 1982. (Available from 800 Barksdale Rd., Box
8139, Newark, DE 19714.)
     Essays that review research on sex differences in
reading, attitudes on reading, and reading interests.
Articles question long-held myths about sex-linked reading
behavior and interests. Other articles are a history of the
content of reading books, a review of current reading books,
plus strategies for nonsexist teaching.

Women and Language. (Published three times a year; University of Illinois at Urbana-Champaign, 244 Lincoln Hall, 702 S. Wright Street, Urbana, IL 61801).

Periodical that reports on research, publications, conferences, and curriculum development in the area of language and gender.

Curriculum Guides and Teacher Materials

Asch, Adrienne, and Michelle Fine. Disabled Women: Psychology from the Margins. Philadelphia: Temple University Press, 1988.

An interdisciplinary set of manuscripts that explore the lives and experiences of women with disabilities from a feminist perspective. The essays combine ethnographic research, policy studies, and in-depth interviews.

Bilklen, Douglas, and Robert Bogdan. "Media Portrayals of Disabled People: A Study in Stereotypes," Council on Interracial Books for Children, Bulletin, Vol. 8, No. 6-7, 1977.

The authors confront the stereotypes that society attributes to people with disabilities. "Handicapist" (similar to "sexist" and "racist") language and stereotypes are described. Using examples from familiar books, movies, television, magazines and songs, the authors make the reader aware of the negative light in which people with disabilities are depicted.

Butler, Matilda, and William Paisley. Women and the Mass Media. Sourcebook for Resources and Action. New York: Human Sciences Press, 1980.

Course guide on media and women. Some of the topics covered are content analysis of the media, sexism in language, institutional sexism, sexism and its impact on the audience and on children.

Carpenter, Carol. "Exercise to Combat Sexist Reading and Writing." College English 43, no. 3 (March 1981): pp. 293-300.

Essay assignments and class activities for composition on sexism in language and in fairy tales.

Cotera, Martha P. Checklists for Counteracting Race and Sex Bias in Educational Materials. Newton, MA: EDC/WEEA Publishing Center, 1982.

    Guidelines and checklists for selecting and evaluating materials that provide instruments to review fiction, readers, and bilingual materials. A bibliography of other tools and guides for selection of materials are included.

Gilbert, Sandra M., and Susan Grubar. The Norton Anthology of Literature by Women: The Tradition in English. New York: W.W. Norton and Co., 1985.

    The first major anthology of literature by women has writings by 150 authors from the English speaking countries of England, the United States, and Canada. Three novels, Jane Eyre, The Awakening, and The Bluest Eye are presented in their entirety. An introduction to each historical period, biographical notations, and a biographical introduction to each author are included.

Guidelines for Selecting Bias-Free Textbooks and Storybooks. New York: Council on Interracial Books for Children, 1980.

    Evaluation of sex, race, and disability bias in textbooks and children's storybooks along with instruments to assess basal readers, literature anthologies, dictionaries, and biographies.

Hull, Gloria T., Patricia Bell Scott, and Barbara Smith. All the Women Are White, All the Blacks Are Men, But Some of Us Are Brave: Black Women's Studies. Old Westbury, NY: The Feminist Press, 1982.

    Two sections in this wide-ranging book focus on literature. They feature essays on teaching black women writers and bibliographical essays on black women novelists, poets, and playwrights.

International Association of Business Communication. Without Bias: A Guidebook for Nondiscriminatory Communication. San Francisco: IABC, 1977.

    Detailed discussion and instruction on language revision.

Lauter, Paul, ed. Reconstructing American Literature: Courses, Syllabi, Issues. Old Westbury, NY: The Feminist Press, 1983.

Sixty-seven American literature syllabi for college courses, many of which are integrated approaches to the introductory survey that are designed to open the literature curriculum to the works of women and people of color. High school teachers should find these useful suggestions for their own curriculum revision.

Miller, Casey, and Kate Swift. The Handbook of Nonsexist Writing. New York: Harper and Row, 1980.

A guide to eliminating semantic bias. Contains information on how sexist language evolved and practical suggestions for avoiding gender bias in speaking and writing.

"Multicultural Nonsexist Education in Iowa: Language Arts." (Available at no cost from Department of Public Instruction, Educational Equity Section, Grimes State Office Building, Des Moines, IA 50319.)

An aid to teachers for assessment of curriculum for sex and race bias. Provides definitions, goals, and a rationale for nonsexist, multicultural education in the language arts as well as a checklist review for curriculum, content and materials, and teaching strategies.

National Council for Teachers of English. "Guidelines for Nonsexist Use of Language in NCTE Publications." (One copy free from National Council for Teachers of English, 1111 Kenyon Rd., Urbana, IL 61801.)

Probably the best general guide. Not only does it provide specific rules teachers can use in their writing and speech, but it also can be used as a teaching tool.

Phillips, Elizabeth. Equality Intropacket: Women and Girls with Disabilities. Organization for Equal Education of the Sexes, Inc., 438 Fourth St., Brooklyn, NY 11215.

An outstanding and comprehensive packet of materials, most appropriate for educators interested in changing attitudes and curricula around issues of disability and gender. Complete with resource list and bibliographies for children, adolescents, and adults.

Pico, Isabel, and Idsa Algria. <u>El Texto Libre De Prejuicios Sexuales y Raciales</u>. San Piedres, PR: University of Puerto Rico, n.d. (Available from Consortium for Educational Equity, Rutgers, The State University of New Jersey, Kilmer Campus, New Brunswick, NJ 08903.)
  In Spanish, this booklet looks at sexism in the Spanish language and how to make the sexes equal in Spain.

Sadker, Myra, and David Sadker. <u>Sex Equity Handbook for Schools</u>. New York: Longman, Inc., 1982.
  Excellent guide to sex equity. Has a major segment on bias in instructional materials that features exercises and case studies. The section on nonsexist teaching includes lesson plans for language arts classes.

Sadker, Myra, David Sadker, and Joyce Kaser. <u>The Communication Gender Gap</u>. Washington, DC: The Mid-Atlantic Center for Sex Equity, n.d. (Available from The Mid-Atlantic Center, The Network, Inc., 5010 Wisconsin Ave. N.W., Washington, DC 20016.)
  Pamphlet that includes a quiz, research material, and classroom observation forms to inform people on the differences in the communication patterns of women and men.

Schuster, Marilyn, and Susan R. Van Dyne. <u>Women's Place in the Academy: Transforming the Liberal Arts</u>. Littlefield, NJ: Rowman and Allanheld, 1985.
  Theory and practice to transform liberal arts courses and curricula, so that they are more inclusive of women and minorities. Two excellent resources are the "Syllabus Redesign Guidelines" and "Selected Bibliography for Integrating Research on Women's Experience into the Liberal Arts Curriculum."

Spanier, Bonnie, Alexander Bloom, and Darlene Boroviak. <u>Toward a Balanced Curriculum: A Sourcebook for Initiating Gender Integration Projects</u>. Cambridge, MA: Schenckman Publishing Co., Inc., 1984.
  A how-to book for the development of more inclusive college curricula that describes a wide variety of projects, strategies for change, and resources.

Women and Disability Awareness Project. <u>Building Community:</u>
<u>A Manual Exploring Issues of Women and Disability</u>. New York:
Educational Equity Concepts, Inc., 1984.

Examines the connections between discrimination based on
gender and discrimination based on disability. Contains
background information on disability rights and on women and
girls with disabilities; workshop formats that allow
activists, educators, and staff trainers to explore
disability issues; an annotated bibliography; and selected
readings.

**Stephen Frazer, The Network, Inc. aided in the annotation of
the Elementary Curriculum and Materials sections.**

MATHEMATICS

Joy M. Wallace

The Equity Issues

Almost all good-paying jobs require a solid understanding of mathematics. High school women who do not take advanced mathematics are shutting themselves off from 90 percent of these jobs.[1]

Mathematics is a critical key to the job market, and its influence is increasing. The Occupational Outlook Quarterly reports that students with a good math background qualify for more jobs than students with minimum math. Not only do people qualify for more jobs with more math, but the jobs for which they qualify can be performed with added success.[2]

Unfortunately, many females are filtered away from these well-paid jobs because they lack the necessary mathematics skills. This "closed circle" of underrepresentation of females in mathematics has its roots in elementary schools when factors such as differential teacher and parent treatment of boys and girls begins to influence unequal participation in mathematics. The end result is differential preparation for the world of work, with females being least prepared.

In the 1985 publication, Mathematics and Science: Critical Filters for the Future of Minority Students, DeAnna Banks Beane identifies cognitive and affective factors influencing student participation in mathematics and science and provides important data on the participation and performance of female students and students of color.[3] In summary:

o Far fewer black, Hispanic, and Native American students enroll in high school mathematics courses than white students.

o Fewer female students enroll in high school mathematics than male students.

o SAT mathematics scores are lower for female,

black, Native American, and Hispanic
students than for white male students.

o Black and Hispanic students score lower than
white students at all age levels on the
National Mathematics Assessment in
knowledge, skills, understanding, and
application.

o At ages 13 and 17, female students score
lower than male students on the National
Mathematics Assessment in applications and
understanding.

While there are no comparable data on students with
disabilities, one can infer that the situation is similar and
that females and students of color who are disabled
experience double and triple layers of discrimination.

Why Students "Drop Out" of Mathematics

The evidence is conclusive. In the mathematics
classroom, the experience of girls and young women, and
especially girls and young women of color, does not
facilitate enjoyment, confidence, and competence in
mathematics. These students receive little encouragement
from teachers and work with little positive reinforcement.
It is not surprising, therefore, that females select
themselves out of mathematics experiences.

Research indicates that the strongest predictors of
continued student participation in math are: 1) enjoyment
and confidence in math, 2) perceived need and usefulness of
math, and 3) parental and teacher encouragement. The typical
mathematics classroom setting frequently provides
differential experiences for male and female students on all
three of these predictors. Students in observed geometry
classes experienced differential treatment in level of
challenge posed in questions, remediation attempts for an
incorrect answer, and the amount of individual help given.
All the differences favored male students.[4]

Substantial evidence supports the fact that mathematics
education in schools does not meet the needs of female
students nor students of color. This situation places female
students of color in double jeopardy. The Third National
Mathematics Assessment by the National Assessment of

Educational Progress speculates that one explanation for
differences in white and minority student test scores is that
minority students drop out of mathematics earlier than white
students. For instance, the NAEP report shows that by the
Algebra I level, significant enrollment differences exist,
with 75 percent of all whites taking Algebra I and only 57
percent of blacks. The NAEP report also shows that while
whites performed above the national level at ages 9, 13, and
17, blacks were performing eleven to fifteen percentage
points below the norm, and Hispanics were nine to eleven
points below the norm.[5]

Explanations of why young women drop out of secondary
mathematics are numerous. Most revolve around social and
environmental issues that result in math avoidance. Many
studies focusing on the participation rate of females,
including black, Hispanic, and Native American females, in
mathematics and science courses, identify teacher
expectations and differential treatment, lack of role models,
lack of career education, and perceived lack of value of the
subject matter as reasons for low participation.[6]

A recent Educational Testing Service study explains why
some females continue to take mathematics and science courses
in high school and college. Female science majors report
having been influenced by teachers in making high school
plans and having positive attitudes toward mathematics.[7]
Unfortunately, this is not the norm for most young women.
Typically, young women do not have a positive attitude about
mathematics nor are they encouraged by parents, teachers, and
counselors to take more mathematics.

Role of Teachers

Students' experiences in schools are teacher-dependent.
Cognitive and affective factors passed on to students are
orchestrated by teacher preparation, attitudes, teaching
strategies, and sensitivity. In relation to mathematics,
elementary and secondary teachers each have characteristics
as groups that influence their impact on students.

Since the teacher training preparation of elementary
school teachers contains little mathematics, elementary
teachers enter the classroom ill-prepared in this area. As a
result, many elementary teachers are math anxious, most
mathematics in elementary school is routine drill and
practice of computation skills, more than 90 percent of

teachers are textbook-dependent for mathematics, and mathematics and science are the least favorite subject matters to teach for most elementary teachers.[8]

The consequence of these factors can result in a hidden curriculum that decreases enthusiasm for mathematics in students and does not develop creative problem-solving or understanding of mathematics concepts. Furthermore, since the majority of elementary teachers are women, these role models subtly socialize students to believe that females are not good in math and do not like math.

While certainly there are teachers who make the teaching of mathematics an exciting and positive experience, for the most part, the secondary school situation is not much better. Secondary teachers do not see themselves as role models for students and frequently use teaching techniques that generate anxiety about mathematics: emphasis on the right answer, time pressure, student isolation, humiliation, and competitiveness. Information about the connections between mathematics and future career choices is not shared in typical classrooms and the focus for secondary teachers is on content, not teaching methodology.[9]

The result of these factors is increased student dislike or anxiety about mathematics, and subsequent withdrawal from mathematics courses. Also, since the majority of high school mathematics teachers are men, they reinforce the "hidden curriculum" that mathematics is a male domain.

Strategies

Many of the major reasons why students continue taking mathematics, or drop out, are human issues. If the overall goal of mathematics education is to increase student preparation, these human factors must be addressed. The current national focus on curriculum improvement and increasing effectiveness in mathematics education has resulted in both positive and negative strategies being implemented. In many states and school districts, the easy solution has been to increase graduation requirements in mathematics, forcing all students to take larger doses of what already exists. What exists is not equitable or necessarily quality education. In some cities, new textbooks are being purchased or curriculum is being revised. However, there appears to be little focus on providing equitable learning environments that meet the learning needs of all students.

In order to increase the effectiveness of the teaching of mathematics, as much attention must be paid to teacher-delivery techniques as to curriculum or textbook revision. Teacher interactions with students is deserving of as much attention as mathematics content.

Emphasize Cooperation

Research indicates that the competition associated with the traditional teaching of mathematics generates anxiety about mathematics in many students. Mathematics can present a conflict in values especially for students who value cooperative social interaction, rather than competition. As a result, some students choose to avoid the subject whenever possible. Creative problem-solving is not an experience that requires competition with others. It is possible to present mathematics content for small group problem-solving while emphasizing cooperation and relying more on social interaction. This strategy does not suggest that all problem-solving be cooperative, but that cooperative experiences be integrated with the existing curriculum. "Cooperative Logic" problems developed by the EQUALS project at the Lawrence Hall of Science, University of California in Berkeley, California, provide positive, successful experiences for students. These activities add a dimension of fun to mathematics, and rely on small groups for problem-solving, rather than promoting competition among individuals.[10]

Teachers and curriculum coordinators can revise most mathematics content to include cooperative experiences. Doing so acknowledges divergent learning styles, accommodates cultural values, and increases interaction within the mathematics classroom. Cooperative experiences in the mathematics classroom result in a sharing of approaches to solving problems. Students learn new approaches from their peers, thus increasing their own repertoire of problem-solving strategies.

Provide Role Models

All students need to see someone like themselves who is successful in the field of mathematics. Since the majority of high school mathematics teachers are white males, high school mathematics departments reinforce the attitude that math is a white male domain. Obviously, teacher hiring practices can promote more diversity within mathematics departments. However, females, people of color, and people with disabilities who are working in math and science related careers also can offer valuable career information and serve as role models for all students. The Expanding Your Horizons in Science and Mathematics conference model, developed by the Math/Science Network, provides such experiences. It encourages students to pursue mathematics, disseminates career information, and establishes links between students and role models in science and math related careers.[11]

Review and Supplement Textbooks

Even though textbook companies are attempting to eliminate bias, examples of stereotyping are still found in mathematics textbooks. Textbooks should be reviewed for stereotypic photographs and text and supplemented with materials that promote more options for more students.

Provide Equitable Attention

Current research shows that teachers have biases based on gender, race/ethnicity, and disability and that their interactions with students are influenced by these biased expectations. All teacher interaction, such as discipline, physical proximity to students, grading, etc., are influenced by these attitudes.[12] Teachers also must attend to interactions that are especially instrumental to effective mathematics instruction, such as questioning techniques, high-level questioning, classroom discussions, and teacher responses to student questions. Classroom monitoring reveals that teachers at all grade levels spend more time interacting with white male students than with others. White male students also receive more questioning and high-level questions than other students.[13] It is very important for educators first to be sensitive to disparities in the classroom and then to provide staff development to help the teachers become aware of how classroom management and unconscious attitudes can contribute to inequities. The Gender/Ethnic Expectation, Student Achievement (GESA) model and staff training, available from the Los Angeles County Schools in Los Angeles, California, is a highly effective program that enables educators to provide more equitable attention to students.[14]

Connect Mathematics with the Real World

Too many students fail to see the connection between their mathematics lessons and the real world. A common question in classrooms is, "When am I going to need this?" Teachers can give practical examples of how calculators, geometry, algebra, or calculus are used as part of jobs in order to connect mathematics content with reality. EQUALS classroom activities, such as "Math Used in Jobs," show students what percentage of workers from 100 different occupations use mathematics skills such as decimals, statistics, and percentages.[15] Classroom speakers from a broad range of careers that utilize mathematics skills also can help students understand the connection between classroom mathematics experiences and future career experience.

Manipulatives for Concept Development

Classrooms are full of students who can memorize a formula or rule, but who do not fully understand the mathematics concept being taught. These students receive high or adequate test scores until it is time to apply the concept in a new situation, like a standardized test.

Moving from the concrete to the abstract increases learning for all students in all tested areas of mathematics: knowledge, skills, understanding and applications. Thus, mathematics concepts are best learned and retained when students have concrete and visual explanations and experiences for each concept.

If manipulatives are used, they usually appear only at the elementary level. The teaching of secondary mathematics concepts, too, can benefit from a concrete, manipulative approach. Infusing strategies such as EQUALS into the mathematics curriculum for concept development promotes understanding of mathematical concepts rather than memorizing.

Involve Parents

Few parents know how to help their children in mathematics. Many parents are math anxious, feel unable to help develop mathematics skills at home, or limit themselves to flash cards or drill and practice mathematics activities. Parents also tend to have lower mathematics expectations for

their daughters than for their sons. Both mothers and
fathers see mathematics as being more difficult for girls,
and not as valuable as for boys. They reinforce, therefore,
the existing stereotypes about mathematics and girls and
strengthen the messages being received in school.

The involvement of parents in education can be very
positive, especially if educators provide ways for parents to
assist with skill development at home. For example, the
Family Math program, developed by EQUALS, gives schools a way
to reach parents. Parents who participate in family math
learn developing problem-solving, spatial and measurement
skills at home.[16]

Address Math Anxiety Issues

Anxiety about any subject area can arrest skill
development and student involvement in that subject. To
constructively address math anxiety, both teacher and student
awareness of the problem must increase. Teachers need to
become aware of their own classroom practices that might
develop and promote anxiety. Knowing the potential results
of these behaviors can lead to a positive behavior change.
Teachers need to learn classroom practices that nurture
positive attitudes about mathematics and develop comfort and
confidence in mathematics for all their students.

All students can benefit from discussions about math
anxiety that include strategies for increasing confidence and
comfort and techniques to use to reduce anxiety when taking
tests.   High school students find it beneficial to form
support groups with math-anxious peers to recognize feelings,
share confidence-building strategies, and study together.

Have Students Speak the Language of Mathematics

Vocabulary and language fluency promote empowerment in
any arena. In mathematics, however, only the teacher and
perhaps a few top students, have the benefit of being fluent
in the language. Since language allows people to translate
and share experiences, all students need the mastery of the
language of mathematics in order to express the subject
matter, experiences, and problems. Teachers need to discuss
language meaning with students, and have students speak the
language of mathematics to describe their experiences and
problems.

Conclusion

The strategies mentioned are only a beginning. These and other approaches can facilitate more effective teaching in mathematics. For positive changes to occur that will ensure educational equity in mathematics, strategies must be constructed from multiple perspectives in the education community. Parents, individual classroom teachers, schools, districts, regional service agencies, state departments of education, and institutions of higher education all can play an important role.

Unfortunately, even in the late 1980s, after fifteen years of the current feminist movement, there are not a great many resources available in the area of math equity. The selections in this bibliography include materials that can be infused into the ongoing curriculum and, except for the "classics," materials that have been published since 1980. It is divided into three sections: Elementary, Secondary, and Teacher Resources.

Notes

1. Bringing Women to Science: The Research News, University of Michigan, Vol. XXXIII, No. 9-10, Sept./Oct. 1982.

2. Occupational Outlook Quarterly (Summer 1983).

3. DeAnna Banks Beane, Mathematics and Science: Critical Filters for the Future of Minority Students (Washington, DC: The Mid-Atlantic Center for Race Equity, The American University, 1985).

4. J. Becker, "Differential Treatment of Girls and Boys in Math Classes," Journal for Research in Mathematics (January 1981).

5. Third National Mathematics Assessment (National Assessment of Educational Progress, 1983).

6. Westina Matthews, "Influences on the Learning and Participation of Minorities in Mathematics," Journal for Research on Mathematics Education, Vol. 15, No. 2, 1984. Claudette Bradley, "Issues in Mathematics Education for

Native Americans and Directions for Research," *Journal for Research on Mathematics Education*, Vol. 15, 1984. Joan Skolnick, Carol Langbort, and Lucille Day, *How To Encourage Girls in Math and Science* (New York: Prentice Hall, Inc., 1982). Holly Knox, "Math, Science Improvements Must Involve Female and Minority Students," *Education Week*, May 11, 1985, p. 24. *Closing the Skills Gap: Maximizing Options for Females and Minorities*, Connecticut Project for Equal Education Rights Report (January 1984).

7. Marlaine Lockheed, Margaret Thorpe, J. Brooks-Gunn, Patricia Casserly, and Ann McAloon, *Sex and Ethnic Differences in Middle School Mathematics, Science and Computer Science: What Do We Know?* A Report Submitted to the Ford Foundation, Educational Testing Service (May 1985).

8. These generalizations are drawn from data collected by Northeast EQUALS from more than 2,000 teachers throughout New England.

9. *Ibid*.

10. Sue Diane Downie, Twila Slesnick, and Jean Kerr Stenmark, *Math for Girls and Other Problem Solvers* (Berkeley: Lawrence Hall of Science, University of California, 1981).

11. For information about Expanding Your Horizons conferences, contact Math/Science Network, c/o Mills College, 5000 MacArthur Blvd., Oakland, CA 94613.

12. Dolores A. Grayson, *Gender/Ethnic Expectations and Student Achievement* (GESA), Los Angeles County Office of Education, Downey, CA 90242.

13. *Ibid*.

14. *Ibid*.

15. Sherry Fraser, *SPACES: Solving Problems of Access to Careers in Engineering and Science* (Palo Alto, CA: Dale Seymour Publications, 1982).

16. Jean Kerr Stenmark, Virginia Thompson, and Ruth Cossey, *Family Math* (Berkeley: Lawrence Hall of Science, University of California, 1986).

BIBLIOGRAPHY

Elementary

Chapline, Elaine, and Claire Newman. <u>Teacher Education and Mathematics (TEAM): A Course to Reduce Math Anxiety and Sex Role Stereotyping in Elementary Education</u>. New York: Women's Educational Equity Act Program, Queens College of the University of New York, 1984.

This package consists of eight components: Approximation and Estimation; Sex-Role Stereotyping in Mathematics Education; Choice and Chance; Metric Measurement; Women as Mathematicians; Demystifying Math; Patterns; and Instructor's Handbook. Materials are appropriate to reproduce as lessons to infuse into existing curriculums.

Downie, Diane, Twila Slesnick, and Jean Kerr Stenmark. <u>Math for Girls and Other Problem Solvers</u>. Berkeley: Lawrence Hall of Science, University of California, 1981.

The numerous activities included in this book resulted from a series of workshops held for girls ages 6-14 to provide hands-on experiences in logical thinking and problem solving. Activities are also geared to develop positive attitudes about mathematics.

Perl, Teri Hoch, and Joan M. Manning. <u>Women, Numbers and Dreams</u>. Available from The National Women's History Project, P.O. Box 3716, Santa Rosa, CA 95402.

Math puzzles and activities accompany each of the thirteen biographies of nineteenth- and twentieth-century women mathematicians. Demonstrates how mathematics can be fun and lead to a variety of interesting careers. A teacher's manual accompanies the book. Suitable for grades 3-6.

Skolnick, Joan, Carol Langbort, and Lucille Day. <u>How To Encourage Girls in Math and Science</u>. Englewood Cliffs, NJ: Prentice-Hall, Inc., 1982.

Geared to parents and teachers, this book provides theoretical answers and practical methods for encouraging girls in mathematics and science.

Stenmark, Jean Kerr, Virginia Thompson, and Ruth Cossey.
<u>Family Math</u>. Berkeley: Lawrence Hall of Science, University
of California, 1986.
    These hands-on, creative activities may be used by
teachers or parents with children. Word problems and logical
reasoning, measurement, numbers and operations, probability
and statistics, time and money, geometry and spatial
thinking, patterns, calculators, and careers are the focus of
activities.

Secondary

Afflack, Ruth. <u>Beyond EQUALS: To Encourage the
Participation of Women in Mathematics</u>. Oakland, CA:
Math/Science Network, 1982.
    The emphasis of the activities in this book are on
problem solving, concrete representations, and spatial and
logical reasoning. Activities are designed to develop
comfort and confidence, while developing mathematical skills.

Askew, Judy. <u>The Sky's the Limit in Math-Related Careers</u>.
Newton, MA: EDC/Women's Educational Equity Act Publishing
Center, 1980.
    This booklet is a collection of information about the
careers of numerous female role models. Careers include
computers, engineering, finance, math education, research
mathematics, and statistics.

Fraser, Sherry. <u>SPACES: Solving Problems of Access to
Careers in Engineering and Science</u>. Palo Alto, CA: Dale
Seymour Publications, 1982.
    Geared to middle school students, these activities are
designed to stimulate students' thinking about scientific
careers, develop problem-solving skills, promote positive
attitudes toward the study of mathematics, increase interest
and knowledge about scientific work, strengthen spatial
visualization skills, and introduce language. The book
format is geared to easy teacher utilization and integration
into existing mathematics curriculum.

Kreinberg, Nancy. <u>I'm Madly in Love with Electricity</u>.
Berkeley: Lawrence Hall of Science, University of California,
1977.
    This booklet includes descriptions of scientific and

mathematical careers and comments written by women in those careers. Also included are resource people, and publications and organizations related to science and math.

Operation SMART: A Program to Encourage Every Girl in Science, Math, and Relevant Technology. New York: Girls Clubs of America, Inc., 1986.
    A notebook of activities designed to increase the participation of girls in mathematics, science, and technology.

Osen, Lynn M. Women in Mathematics. Cambridge, MA: Massachusetts Institute of Technology, 1974.
    From antiquity to the 20th century, the author effectively traces the impact women have had on the development of mathematics. Also includes profiles of individual lives and the social context in which each woman worked. Grades 9-12.

Perl, Teri. Math Equals: Biographies of Women Mathematicians + Related Activities. Menlo Park, CA: Addison-Wesley Publishing Co., 1976.
    This book contains biographies about the lives of ten female mathematicians. Each chapter includes activities related to the special focus of each woman's mathematical work.

TABS: Organization for Equal Education of the Sexes. Math/Science Posters. New York: OEES, 438 Fourth St., Brooklyn, NY 11215.
    A series of posters of contemporary and historical women working in fields of math and science. Multicultural; each includes a biography.

Teacher Resources

Anick, Constance Martin, and Thomas P. Carpenter. "Minorities and Mathematics: Results from the National Assessment of Educational Progress." Mathematics Teacher, vol. 74 (October 1981): pp. 561-566.
    This article uses data from the National Assessment of Educational Progress to document inequities in the mathematics education of black and Hispanic students.

<u>Association for Women in Mathematics: Newsletter</u>. P.O. Box 178, Wellesley College, 828 Washington St., Wellesley, MA 02181.
  This newsletter contains articles on women's progress (or lack of it) in mathematics teaching and research; includes biographies of famous women mathematicians; contains book reviews and employment information.

Beane, DeAnna. <u>Mathematics and Science: Critical Filters for the Future of Minority Students</u>. Washington, DC: The Mid-Atlantic Center for Race Equity, The American University, 1985.
  This comprehensive booklet includes test score and enrollment data; outlines the scope of the problem of minority students in mathematics and science; and provides strategies for addressing the problem.

Becker, J. "Differential Treatment of Girls and Boys in Math Classes." <u>Journal for Research in Mathematics</u>, January 1981.
  This article details the results of research conducted with ten high school geometry teachers to determine how students' gender influences treatment by teachers.

Bradley, Claudette. "Issues in Mathematics Education for Native Americans and Directions for Research." <u>Journal for Research in Mathematics Education</u>, vol. 15, no. 2 (1984): pp 96-106.
  Factors contributing to the problem of inadequate education of Native American students in mathematics are described as well as strategies for change.

Brush, Lorelei R. <u>Encouraging Girls in Mathematics: The Problem and the Solution</u>. Cambridge, MA: Abt Books, 1980
  This book describes a longitudinal study that tracked female students' opinions about mathematics, decisions regarding advanced mathematics courses, and career plans in sixth, ninth, and twelfth grade levels. Also included are strategies for helping girls to develop more positive attitudes about mathematics.

Campbell, Patricia B. "What's a Nice Girl Like You Doing in a Math Class?" <u>Phi Delta Kappan</u>, March 1986, pp. 516-520.
  A thorough overview of the equity issues that contribute

to the underrepresentation of girls and black and Hispanic students in higher level math classes. The article concludes with many practical strategies for change.

Center for Early Adolescence. Issues in Middle-Grade Education: Girls, Math, and Science: Research & Resources. University of North Carolina at Chapel Hill, Summer 1984.

A summary of research about girls in mathematics and science education and a list of resources are included in this eight-page pamphlet.

Cheek, Helen Neeley, ed. Handbook for Conducting Equity Activities in Mathematics Education. Reston, VA: National Council of Teachers of Mathematics, 1984.

Describes intervention programs and workshops on strategies for promoting equity plus a chapter on the state of the art including papers on minority and female issues in mathematics.

Closing the Skills Gap: Maximizing Options for Females and Minorities. Connecticut Project for Equal Education Rights Report, January 1984.

This six-page report includes Connecticut high school enrollment data and analysis for mathematics, science, and computer courses of white and minority males and females.

Davis, Barbara Gross, and Sheila Humphreys. Evaluation Counts: A Guide to Evaluating Math & Science Programs for Women. Math/Science Network, 1983.

This book explains data collection techniques to assess the effects of educational activities and practices on females. One chapter highlights how these techniques were used to analyze the impact of Expanding Your Horizons in Science and Mathematics conferences on girls who attended.

Fauth, Gloria C., and Judith E. Jacobs. "Equity in Mathematics Education: The Educational Leader's Role." Educational Leadership, March 1980, pp. 485-490.

This article addresses math equity from the perspective of administrators, and contains practical suggestions for working with teachers and parents, providing role models, selecting bias-free materials, and assessing progress.

Fennema, Elizabeth. Multiplying Options and Subtracting Bias. Reston, VA: National Council of Teachers of Mathematics, 1981.
A workshop manual for addressing issues of equity in mathematics, this is geared to presenting workshops to teachers, parents, and students. A video is also available.

Fox, Lynn H. The Problem of Women and Mathematics. Report to the Ford Foundation. New York, 1981.
Sex differences in mathematics, factors influencing the study and learning of mathematics, and factors influencing career interest and choices are discussed in this booklet. The author also includes directions for research and strategies for change.

Green, Rayna. Math Avoidance: A Barrier to American Indian Science Education and Science Careers. Washington, DC: Project on Native Americans in Science, American Association for the Advancement of Science, 1977.
This paper includes reasons given by Native American students explaining why they avoid taking mathematics courses and ways to change existing situations.

Lockheed, Marlaine, Margaret Thorpe, J. Brooks-Gunn, Patricia Casserly, and Ann McAloon. Sex & Ethnic Differences in Middle School Mathematics, Science and Computer Science: What Do We Know? A Report Submitted to the Ford Foundation. New York: Educational Testing Service, 1985.
This book summarizes results from research about sex and ethnic differences in middle school, describes exciting intervention programs, and makes recommendations. Also included are a table and list of meta-analysis, a directory of intervention programs and a bibliography.

Malcom, Shirley, Yolanda S. George, and Marsha Lakes Matyas. Summary of Research Studies on Women and Minorities in Science, Mathematics and Technology. A Report to the National Science Foundation. Washington, DC: American Association for the Advancement of Science, 1985.
This report from a two-day meeting summarizes existing research and identifies gaps in the research on women and minorities as a guide for future work.

Matthews, Westina. "Influences on the Learning and Participation of Minorities in Mathematics." Journal for Research on Mathematics Education, vol. 15, no. 2, 1984.
This article reviews research on minorities and mathematics since 1975. Influences on participation and performance include factors related to parents, students, and school.

National Council on Teachers of Mathematics. Mathematics Education of Girls and Women: Guidelines for Schools.
An equity assessment tool for schools. Includes a survey form, an overview of issues, and a brief list of resource organizations.

Scott-Jones, Diane, and Maxine L. Clark. "The School Experience of Black Girls: The Interaction of Gender, Race, and Socioeconomic Status." Phi Delta Kappan, March 1986, pp. 520-525.
This article documents the discrimination at several levels experienced by black female students. The authors outline the research and look at discrimination comprehensively from the perspective of gender, race, and class.

Tobias, Sheila. Overcoming Math Anxiety. Boston: Houghton Mifflin, 1980.
Reasons why people develop fear learning mathematics are discussed in this classic book. Also included are a math anxiety scale and information about programs for math-anxious people.

Valverde, Leonard A. Hispanic Students and Mathematics. Austin, TX: Office of Equal Education Opportunities, 1984.
Five probable factors affecting mathematics achievement of Hispanics in mathematics education are described: language, cognitive learning styles, instructional methods, curricular materials, and teacher adequacy. Intervention strategies and current research implications are described.

Wallace, Joy. "Nurturing an 'I Can' Attitude in Mathematics." Equity and Choice (Winter 1986), pp. 35-40.
Presents general strategies for increasing equity in elementary and secondary mathematics classrooms.

"Why Do Students Major in Science or Mathematics?"   <u>On Campus</u>
<u>with Women</u>.   Project on the Status and Education of Women,
vol. 16, no. 1, Summer 1986.
   This report analyzes data from women in science and
mathematics careers and training programs to determine
reasons for pursuing majors in science or mathematics.

<u>Women and Mathematics Education</u>.   c/o Judith Jacobs, George
Mason University, Education Department, 4400 University Dr.,
Fairfax, VA 22032.
   This newsletter serves as a general communications link
among all educators working in the field of women and girls
in mathematics; includes resources and news of innovative
programs.

<u>Women and Minorities in Science and Engineering</u>.   Washington,
DC: National Science Foundation, 1986.
   This book is an overview of the literature and research
about women in science and engineering, and minorities in
science and engineering.   Included are employment levels and
trends, career patterns, and labor market indicators.

Marylin A. Hulme and Walter S. Smith

Inequities in Science Education: The Data

Although several encouraging changes have occurred over the past two decades, women still remain underrepresented in science careers, especially in the physical sciences and engineering. The proportion of women receiving first professional science degrees has grown enormously between 1960 and 1985. For example, the percentage of women earning M.D. degrees went from 5.9 to 30.1; in all science doctorates (Physical Sciences, Mathematics, Life Sciences, Social Sciences) the percentages escalated from 8.8 to 30.12; and the percentages of women earning B.S. degrees in engineering grew from a miniscule .3 to 13.35.[1] These encouraging increases, however, must be tempered with several notes of caution which, when taken together, indicate that equitable participation of women in science has certainly not yet been achieved. Nor can it be achieved in the near future without conscientious, positive intervention on the part of educators and others.

The lack of equitable participation is illustrated by the data on engineering, by far the largest science career area. Despite the impressive gains that have been made by women in the field, in 1983 male engineering degree recipients still outnumbered female recipients 6.5 to 1. More importantly, the increasing percentage of first-year female college students entering engineering has leveled off in the 1980s relative both to men and to earlier groups of women students.[2]

Turning from engineering to science in general, the research clearly shows that women who study science in college have been and remain concentrated in the social and life sciences. Among current college graduates, women now constitute 20 percent of dentists, 30 percent of medical doctors and life scientists, 40 percent of veterinarians and social scientists, and 50 percent of pharmacists; but the proportion of women completing physical science and mathematics doctorates closely parallels the figures for engineering.[3]

When one considers enrollment patterns in high school science courses, the disparity between women's and men's career pursuits is not surprising. Among 1980 and 1982 high school graduates, approximately three quarters of both females and males had taken introductory biology. Sadly, only one quarter of female and male graduates in the same period had completed chemistry. An enormous disparity, however, existed in physics where 14.5 percent of males, but only 8.4 percent of females had completed that course. The problem is even greater for students of color (with the striking exception of Asian-Americans) where the percentages of blacks, Hispanics, and Native Americans completing physics were 5.5, 4.9, and 7.1, respectively.[4]

Given the disparity, achievement in science among nine-, thirteen-, and seventeen-year-olds is remarkably comparable for males and females. Although the 1982 National Assessment of Educational Progress science scores show that at all ages males outperformed females, the greatest difference in the three areas that were measured (Inquiry, Science/Technology/ Society, Content) occurred among seventeen-year-olds in science content, and that difference was less than ten percent.[5] Although science achievement is comparable for females and males, a rather large sex difference does exist when one looks at the science activities of students. In an article, "The Myth of Equality in Science Classrooms," Jane Butler Kahle and Marsha K. Lakes reported that young girls and boys had comparable experience in life science, e.g., cared for an animal, but many more boys than girls had had physical science experience, e.g., fixed something electrical.[6]

What emerges from the data is a picture of somewhat different but rather comparable achievement in science and attitude in science among girls and boys in elementary, middle, and early high school. However, as students approach the physical sciences in their junior year of high school and as they proceed into college, two clear trends appear. First, the majority of American students, both male and female, drop out of science; and second, the dropout rate for females far exceeds the rate for males except in the social and life sciences. While differences in science course-taking occur in senior high school and beyond, many strands of evidence indicate that the roots of the problem can be found at much younger ages. Thus, educators must initiate intervention programs by the middle school years or preferably before, so that lack of preparation does not become a barrier to keep females and students of color from entering science-related careers. Although there is yet no comparable research on science achievement of students with disabilities, one can assume that similar disparities appear in this population as well.

Strategies for Increasing Equity

Given the terribly large science dropout problem for both males and females, one obvious point of attack is to increase science enrollment for all students, regardless of their sex, race, or disability. A great number of strategies, all beyond the scope of this essay but included in many of the items in the bibliography, have been suggested to address such an important and complex problem as science equity. The interested reader should consult documents such as What Research Says to the Science Teacher, Science Teaching: A Profession Speaks, and Educating Americans for the 21st Century.

To increase the participation of women in science, some intervention strategies have been aimed at an entire school system. For example, some state education agencies or local districts have increased their science graduation requirements, thus assuring that all students will pursue high school science beyond the introductory level. Others have reviewed their textbooks, testing programs, and course enrollment process to provide across-the-board equitable treatment of the sexes and races. Opening courses to both sexes, however, has not always resulted in a balanced enrollment, and evidence shows that specific, targeted strategies are necessary to encourage science course enrollment by both sexes, but particularly by females.

Most strategies have been initiated at the classroom level on a one-to-one basis between students and their teachers or counselors. At the classroom level, interventions for single-sex groups have been designed to address the special needs of females uninhibited by a male presence. Some notable examples of single-sex interventions that have been conducted include the Futures Unlimited conferences for girls in grades 7-12, sponsored by the Consortium for Educational Equity of Rutgers University; the From Dreams to Reality program of the Girl Scouts of America, which encourages their members in science through career exploration; and Operation S.M.A.R.T., a science and computer program sponsored by the Girls Clubs of America. (See the bibliography for references to publications from each of these programs.)

Addressing the Major Problems

Various interventions have addressed one or a combination of the following problems, which can be posed from the individual girl's or woman's point of view, but are just as applicable for students of color and students with disabilities:

> Liking Science: Is science fun? Do I get a kick out of it?

> Science Skills: Do I have what it takes? Do I lack key skills and/or do I feel that I lack the skills?

> Science as Male Domain: Is science for men only? If I pursue science, will I experience a loss of femininity and/or role conflict?

> Science's Utility: Will I ever need to use science even if I study it in school?

Liking Science

People in science careers frequently report pleasurable childhood science experiences which led them to want more. They took a radio apart to fix it; they made a volcano of vinegar and baking soda; they spent time in the woods or under the stars and learned to use some simple scientific tools; or under a teacher's guidance they explored fossiliferous rocks. As mentioned previously, Kahle and Lakes found that fewer girls than boys have had these experiences, so many interventions have attempted to make sure that girls, too, are exposed to the pleasures of scientific inquiry. For example, COMETS (Career Oriented Modules to Explore Topics in Science) describes over 100 gee-whiz science activities—keyed both to school-based science topics and to a multitude of science-related possibilities.

Science Skills

Researchers have consistently found little (albeit sometimes statistically significant) gender-related differences in science abilities. Nonetheless, some sex differences have been singled out for special attention to rectify what some see as possible impediments to women's pursuit of science. For example, SPACES (Solving Problems of Access to Careers in Engineering and Science) contains numerous activities to improve early adolescent girls' spatial and problem-solving abilities.[9]

Whether or not females as compared to males lack certain skills, they are more frequently anxious about their ability to perform in science. To address this innate problem, which is akin to math anxiety, Jeffrey Mallow has developed science anxiety clinics for college-aged students, mostly women; but this strategy has not yet been applied in the K-12 setting.[10]

Science as a Male Domain

Perhaps the greatest number of published materials in the area of women in science address these dual problems: that (a) science is seen as a masculine preserve; and (b) women are thought to experience role conflict (as scientist, spouse, and parent) and/or loss of femininity when pursuing scientific careers. Books and audiovisual materials have been produced to present both female and male students with female role models, which contradict the notion of science being for men only and which show women enjoying science. There also are materials that address the issue of diversity in scientific role models in terms of race, ethnicity, and disability. Examples include Mary Ellen Verheyden-Hilliard's American Women in Science series for the primary grades; S. Phyllis Starner's Able Scientists-Disabled Persons for high school students; and audiovisuals such as Science: Women's Work from the National Science Foundation, the Women in Science series from the University of Michigan, and two excellent science films for elementary students, You Can Be a Scientist, Too from the Equity Institute and I'm Going To Be...an Engineer from the University of California Extension Media Center. In addition, Ciba-Geigy's attractive Exceptional Black Scientists poster series are available free to schools. (See bibliography for complete references.)

Another strategy is to bring students into contact with actual women scientist role models from varied racial and ethnic backgrounds as well as women with disabilities. For example, with scientists from their own locale, COMETS' activities are designed to be led personally by a community resource person who uses science on the job and who can talk with students about her career and family life, addressing the role conflict issue.

Science Utility

Many students view science as a prevocational subject to be studied only if they are considering careers in research, medicine, engineering, and the like. If students think they are heading toward a career in business, art, social work, journalism, or in the liberal arts, then dropping out of science study may seem to make sense. With that reasoning, more than 90 percent of high school students never take physics, the most fundamental science. By choosing not to study science, they do not develop required skills in that area and effectively are blocked out of science careers. Thus, the self-fulfilling prophesy of "I'm not going into science" comes to pass.

However, although science may not be central to careers such as lawyer or secretary, all jobs at some time apply science. And, women and men certainly apply science at home and in the community and need scientific understanding in order to make informed decisions as citizens. Science educators, as reported in Educating Americans for the 21st Century, support the acquisition of scientific literacy by all people.[11] Nevertheless, most materials developed to encourage women in science present science as used by women specifically in the lab or at the biological field station or construction site. Notable exceptions can be found in the videotape, Futures Unlimited, which includes a woman generating-plant technician, and the book, COMETS Profiles, which includes stories of a woman phone installer, elementary school teacher (with the emphasis on how she needs science for her work), and basketball coach.[12] However, more print and visual materials are needed to demonstrate that science is used in a variety of careers by women, as well as men.

The bibliography is divided into four sections: Elementary, Secondary, Teacher Resources, and Career Information.

The Elementary section includes supplementary materials that encourage both girls and boys to pursue and enjoy scientific activities from star-gazing to caring for crickets. An attempt has been made to include those books which show girls and boys cooperating together and which illustrate girls handling bugs, insects, and small animals (not simply puppies and kittens)--for example, See What I Caught. Activity books, such as This Book Is About Time and Let's Play Science, provide avenues for young children to explore the world around them and encourage them to indulge their curiosity. Also included are some sample biographies of women in exciting science careers. The reader is referred to the Biography section of the Libraries and Media Centers bibliography for additional sources on women in science.

The Secondary section continues to provide information and biographical materials at a more sophisticated level and includes books to motivate and encourage students to consider science not merely as an academic subject but as an exciting adventure. The Career Information section also is for high school students who will find a wealth of inexpensive information about many different careers in science.

Resources for teachers and guidance counselors are found in the fourth section, Teacher Resources, including research on sex differences in science; strategies and activities to encourage females, people of color, and people with disabilities to continue studying science; and statistical information on participation by students and workers in science, usually available by sex, race, and ethnicity. Several items address the issue of people with disabilities learning and working in science, particularly in the lab.

Notes

1. Betty M. Vetter and Eleanor L. Babco, Professional Women and Minorities, 6th ed. (Washington, DC: Commission on Professionals in Science and Technology [formerly Scientific Manpower Commission], 1986).

2. Vetter and Babco, p. 17.

3. Vetter and Babco, p. 36, 57, and 168.

4. Vetter and Babco, p. 12.

5. National Assessment of Educational Progress, 1982 Science Achievement Scores for nine-, thirteen-, and seventeen-year-old females and males.

6. Jane Butler Kahle and Marsha K. Lakes, "The Myth of

Equality in Science Classrooms," Journal of Research in Science Teaching, 20, (February 1983), pp. 131-140.

7. Norris C. Harms and Robert E. Yager, eds., What Research Says to the Science Teacher, vol. 3 (Washington, DC: National Science Teachers Association, 1983); Faith K. Brown and David P. Butts, eds., Science Teaching: A Professional Speaks (National Science Teachers Association, 1983); and Educating Americans for the 21st Century (National Science Board Commission on Precollege Education in Mathematics, Science, and Technology, Washington, DC: National Science Foundation, 1983).

8. Walter Smith, COMETS Science (Career Oriented Modules to Explore Topics in Science) (Washington, DC: National Science Teachers Association, 1984).

9. Sherry Fraser and others, SPACES (Solving Problems of Access to Careers in Engineering and Sciences) (Berkeley: EQUALS, Lawrence Hall of Science, University of California, 1982).

10. Jeffrey V. Mallow, Science Anxiety: Fear of Science and How to Overcome It (Clearwater, FL: H & H Publishing, 1986).

11. Report of the National Science Board's Commission of Precollege Education in Mathematics, Science and Technology, Educating Americans for the 21st Century (Washington, DC: National Science Foundation, 1983), p. v.

12. Futures Unlimited I: Expanding Your Horizons in Mathematics and Science(New Brunswick, NJ: Consortium for Educational Equity and Rutgers University Office of TV and Radio, 1984); and Walter Smith, COMETS Profiles (Washington, DC: National Science Teachers Association, 1984).

BIBLIOGRAPHY

Elementary

Allison, Linda. <u>Blood and Guts: A Working Guide to Your Insides</u>. Boston: Little Brown, 1976.
Explains human anatomy and physiology with the use of diagrams and cartoon-like drawings.

Behrens, June. <u>I Can Be an Astronaut</u>. Chicago: Children's Press, 1984.
Explains the training astronauts go through before they make their space flights.

Bowman, Kathleen. <u>New Women in Medicine</u>. Mankato, MN: Creative Education, 1976.
Brief biographies of seven notable women in the medical field, including a neurologist, a midwife, a birth control advocate, and an endocrinologist.

Burns, Marilyn. <u>The Book of Think, or, How to Solve a Problem Twice Your Size</u>. Boston: Little Brown, 1976.
A manual on problem solving and logic; to do when you are puzzled or perplexed.

_____. <u>This Book Is About Time</u>. Boston: Little Brown, 1978.
Describes different ways to look at, think about, and explore time; includes activities.

Davidson, Patricia S., and Robert E. Willcutt. <u>Spatial Problem Solving with Cuisenaire Rods</u>. New Rochelle, NY: Cuisenaire Company of America, 1983.
Provides activities and puzzles to encourage spatial problem solving and experimentation, including rotation and reflection problems to be done with a set of Cuisenaire rods.

Dolan, Edward F., and Richard B. Lyttle. <u>Janet Guthrie: First Woman Driver at Indianapolis</u>. Garden City, NY: Doubleday, 1978.

Account of a physicist who became the first woman driver in Grand Prix racing.

Emberlin, Diane. Contributions of Women: Science. Minneapolis, MN: Dillon Press, 1977.
    Brief biographies of women who have made outstanding contributions to science: Annie Cannon, Lillian Gilbreth, Margaret Mead, Rachel Carson, Ruth Patrick, and Eugenie Clark.

Genett, Anne. Contributions of Women: Aviation. Minneapolis, MN: Dillon Press, 1977.
    Brief biographies of six American aviators: Amelia Earhart, Anne Lindbergh, Jacqueline Cochran, Jerrie Mock, Geraldyn Cobb, Emily Howell.

Goldreich, Gloria, and Esther Goldreich. What Can She Be? 8 vols. New York: Lothrop, Lee and Shepard, 1974.
    Each book in this series describes a day in the life of a woman in a nontraditional profession. Science-related topics include an architect, a farmer, a geologist, and a veterinarian.

Greene, Carol. Marie Curie: Pioneer Physicist. Chicago: Children's Press, 1984.
    A biography of the extraordinary scientist who discovered radioactive elements and was the only woman to win two Nobel prizes.

Hoban, Tana. Circles, Triangles, and Squares and Count and See. New York: Macmillan, 1974.
    Both books for the preschooler contain photographs of shapes as they are found in everyday objects.

I'm Going To Be... Berkeley: University of California Extension Media Center, 1977.
    With a bit of magic, a girl and a boy find out all about different types of engineers—both female and male, including people of color. This 20-minute, 16-mm film is useful for career education, the elementary classroom, and staff development.

Lenthal, Patricia Riley. <u>Carlotta and the Scientist</u>. Chapel Hill, NC: Lollipop Power, 1973.

An early publication from a small feminist press tells the story of a very curious penguin, who, while her husband looks after their egg, becomes involved with a female scientist from an Antarctic weather station.

<u>Let's Look at Logic</u>. New York: Guidance Associates, 1977.

Two 20-minute filmstrips with cassette tapes present children with basic concepts of logic, introducing formal deductive logic and the use of Venn diagrams. Addresses the proposition that "girls can't understand logic." Set includes logic cards for student use.

Poynter, Margaret. <u>The Zoo Lady</u>. Minneapolis, MN: Dillon Press, 1980.

Biography of the woman who began work as the San Diego Zoo's bookkeeper, became the director, and gradually developed it into the premier breeding zoo it is today.

Pringle, Laurence. <u>Dinosaurs and People: Fossils, Facts and Fantasies</u>. New York: Harcourt Brace Jovanovich, 1978.

Traces the history of the discovery of dinosaur fossils and presents recent research, including the contributions of women.

<u>Science and Children</u>. Washington, DC: National Science Teachers Association).

A science education magazine for teachers of grades K-8.

Skolnick, Joan and others. <u>How to Encourage Girls in Math and Science</u>. Englewood Cliffs, NJ: Prentice-Hall, 1982.

Examines the effects of sex-role socialization on girls from childhood through high school. Provides strategies for helping students improve their math and science skills.

Sprung, Barbara, Patricia B. Campbell, and Merle Froschl. <u>What Will Happen If...Young Children and the Scientific Method</u>. New York: Educational Equity Concepts, Inc., 1985.

A guide to help teachers incorporate math, science, and technology-related activities into the daily life of the classroom. Provides activities and resources to ensure that all children, regardless of sex, race, or disability, develop essential math and science skills.

Srivastava, Jane Jonas. Weighing and Balancing. New York: Thomas Y. Crowell, 1970.
     Activities for young children for weighing and measuring, using both standard and unusual units of measure. Part of a series including Computers (1972), Number Families (1979), Spaces, Shapes and Sizes (1980), and Statistics (1980).

Stetten, Mary. Let's Play Science. New York: Harper and Row, 1979.
     Easy projects for young children to do at home or at school, such as growing things, using the five senses, and exploring the mechanics of water, air, light, and simple machines.

TABS Posters: Aids for Equal Education. Brooklyn, NY: Organization for Equal Education of the Sexes, 1978.
     Posters with lesson plans about women's achievements, nontraditional careers, and changing roles. Features such notable women as Marie Curie, Amelia Earhart, and Lucy Hobbs Taylor, first woman dentist. Also depicts women in the trades, in science jobs, and in medicine.

Verheyden-Hilliard, Mary Ellen. American Women in Science. 10 vols. Bethesda, MD: The Equity Institute, 1985.
     Brief biographies of ten American scientists: Shirley Mathis McBay, Sally Ride, Elma Gonzalez, Ru Chih Cheo Huang, Agnes Naranjo Stroud-Lee, Maria Cordero Hardy, Nancy Wallace, Antoinette Rodez Schiesler, Dixy Lee Ray, Constance Tom Noguchi. An accompanying 13-minute videotape, You Can Be a Scientist Too, demonstrates that everyday questioning and perseverance can be the start of a science career.

Zaslavsky, Claudia. Count on Your Fingers African Style. New York: Thomas Y. Crowell, 1980.
     Describes how finger counting is used to communicate price and quantity in an East African marketplace.

_____. Tic Tac Toe and Other Three-in-a-Row Games from Ancient Egypt to the Modern Computer. New York: Thomas Y. Crowell, 1982.

Traces the development of the three-in-a-row game and its variations through a number of cultures. Includes some mathematical problems.

Secondary

Blackwell, Peggy. Spatial Encounters: Exercises in Spatial Awareness. Newton, MA: EDC/Women's Educational Equity Act Publishing Center, 1982.

A series of activities designed to help acquire spatial visualization and orientation skills; especially appropriate for girls and women.

Black Women: Achievements Against the Odds. Washington, DC: Smithsonian Institution Traveling Exhibition Service, 1982.

Each of the twenty 24" x 36" posters pictures approximately six black women, well-recognized in their respective fields--business, religion, medicine, science, and math.

Careers Related to Science. New York: Denoyer-Geppert Audio-Visuals, 1977.

Three filmstrips with cassettes and guide include interviews with men and women working in science-based professions regarding how they got started, their day-to-day activities on the job, and what they think about their work.

Earhart, Amelia. The Fun of It: Random Records of My Own Flying and of Women in Aviation. Chicago: Academy Press, 1977.

The famous woman pilot describes her career and the role women played in the early days of aviation.

Exceptional Black Scientists: A Series. Ardsley, NY: Ciba-Geigy, 1982.

Eight posters picture contemporary black scientists at work with a brief description of their careers. Includes Jewel Plummer Cobb, Shirley Jackson, Jane Wright, and Jennie Patrick.

Facklam, Margery. <u>Wild Animals, Gentle Women</u>. New York: Harcourt, Brace Jovanovich, 1978.
Relates the experiences of women who have become successful ethologists. Offers tips for observing animals in their own habitats.

Fins, Alice. <u>Women in Science</u>. Skokie, IL: National Textbook Company, 1979.
Interviews with ten women scientists from a variety of disciplines, preceded by a general description about a particular scientific field. Also includes information about education, training, financial aid, and job opportunities.

Fraser, Sherry, and others. <u>SPACES</u> (<u>S</u>olving <u>P</u>roblems of <u>A</u>ccess to <u>C</u>areers in <u>E</u>ngineering and <u>S</u>ciences). Berkeley: EQUALS, Lawrence Hall of Science, University of California, 1982.
Provides math and career classroom activities for developing problem-solving skills while learning about math-based fields of study and work.

<u>From Dreams to Reality: Adventures in Careers</u>. New York: Girl Scouts of America, 1978.
Kit consists of cards, activities booklet, and teacher's guide for increasing awareness of career options, including science-based professions. <u>Careers to Explore: Brownie and Junior Leader's Guide for Brownie and Junior Girl Scouts</u> (1979) also available.

<u>Futures Unlimited I: Expanding Your Horizons in Mathematics and Science</u> and <u>Futures Unlimited II: Expanding Your Horizons in Technical and Vocational Education</u>. New Brunswick, NJ: Consortium for Educational Equity and Rutgers University Office of TV and Radio, 1984 & 1985.
Derived from the <u>Futures Unlimited</u> conferences, these 29-minute videotapes demonstrate the critical connection between mathematics and future careers. Role models discuss their jobs, education, and training, and also their lives and career goals.

Gleasner, Diana. <u>Breakthrough: Women in Science</u>. New York: Walker, 1983.
Reviews women's role in science and delineates the work,

motivation, and personal life of several women scientists: marine biologist Sylvia Earle Mead, Nobel prize astronomer Zera Rubin, economist Muriel Siebert, and structural engineer Bille Campbell.

Goodfield, June. An Imagined World: A Story of Scientific Discovery. New York: Penguin Books, 1982.
     A story of scientific research shows through the work of a young immunologist, her initial concepts, day-to-day experimentations, and findings.

Gornick, Vivian. Women in Science: Portraits from a World in Transition. New York: Simon and Schuster, 1983.
     Examines the position of women in the world of scientific research and what it is that attracts women and men to science.

Greenfield, Joan and Joyce Baldwin. Is Science in Your Future? Roslyn, NY: Roslyn High School, 1982.
     A booklet designed to provide high school biology students with information about jobs in their discipline. Includes activities, projects, reports from scientists, and resource materials.

Haber, Louis. Black Pioneers of Science and Invention (1970) and Women Pioneers of Science (1979). New York: Harcourt, Brace Jovanovich.
     Two books that provide descriptions of women and people of color who have made outstanding contributions to science.

Herzenberg, Caroline L. Women Scientists from Antiquity to the Present: an Index. West Cornwall, CT: Locust Hill Press, 1986.
     An international reference listing and biographical directory of some notable women scientists from ancient to modern times; an excellent primary resource.

Hodgman, Ann, and Rudy Djabbaroff. Skystars: The History of Women in Aviation. New York: Atheneum, 1981.
     Discusses the activities and roles of women in aviation from the earliest balloon flights to the contemporary space age, including women pilots in the military and in stunt flying exhibitions.

Intern: A Long Year. Chicago: Encyclopedia Britannica
Educational Corporation, 1972.
Twenty-minute, 16mm film shows a woman intern in an
inner city hospital, rotating through different departments
and experiencing everyday occurences. Attention also paid to
her home and social life.

Kammer, Ann E., and others. Science, Sex, and Society.
Newton, MA: EDC/Women's Educational Equity Act Publishing
Center, 1979.
Supplementary materials and readings to promote
scientific career options for high school girls.

Keep the Door Open Albuquerque, NM: Sandia Laboratories,
Motion Picture Division.
In this 16mm film, thirteen women discuss the problems
and joys of pursuing careers in chemistry, zoology, and
engineering; for mature junior high and older students.

Keller, Mollie. Marie Curie. New York: Watts, 1982.
Biography of the famed scientist with a straightforward
account of her childhood and career.

Kreinberg, Nancy. I'm Madly in Love with Electricity.
Berkeley: Lawrence Hall of Science, University of California,
1977.
Weaves together comments by women scientists and
engineers regarding their work. A list of women resource
people in the San Francisco Bay area is included, but does
not detract from the book's general usefulness.

Land, Barbara. The New Explorers: Women in Antarctica. New
York: Dodd Mead, 1981.
Describes women scientists working in Antarctica--their
research, the environment, and their relationship to their
male colleagues given difficult circumstances.

The Math/Science Connection. San Francisco: Math/Science
Network, Mills College, 1979.
An excellent 25-minute 16mm film offering strategies to
encourage girls and women to learn and enjoy science and
mathematics.

Menard, Sharon. <u>How High the Sky? How High the Moon? Women Scientists Today</u>. Newton, MA: EDC/Women's Educational Equity Act Publishing Center, n.d.

Packet of resource materials (4 cassette tapes with script and book) to assist girls in learning and preparing for scientific and technical jobs. Includes interviews with women scientists about their work and personal lives.

<u>Occupational Outlook Handbook, 1986-1987 Edition</u>. Washington, DC: U.S. Department of Labor and Bureau of Labor Statistics, biennial.

Updated every two years, this handbook provides copious information (job descriptions, salaries, education and training requirements, and employment outlook) about numerous careers including engineering, the natural sciences, the social sciences, technical and electronic fields, mechanics, and medicine.

<u>Operation SMART: A Program to Encourage Every Girl in Science, Math, and Relevant Technology</u>. New York: Girls Clubs of America, Inc., 1986.

A notebook of activities designed to increase the participation of girls in mathematics, science, and technology.

Opfell, Olga S. <u>The Lady Laureates: Women Who Have Won the Nobel Prize</u>. Metuchen, NJ: Scarecrow Press, 1978.

Biographies of women who have won the Nobel prize in peace, literature, and science. Also includes a short history of the Nobel prize.

<u>Opportunities in Science and Engineering</u>. Washington, DC: Scientific Manpower Commission, 1980.

Eighty slides, cassette tape, and booklets contain information on scientific and engineering careers for use with high school and undergraduate students.

<u>Putting It All Together: A Model Program for Women Entering Engineering</u>. Newton, MA: EDC/Women's Educational Equity Act Publishing Center, 1982.

A fifteen-minute slide show, tape, and booklet featuring a Purdue University program for encouraging young women in engineering and promoting interaction with role models.

Reid, Robert. <u>Marie Curie</u>. New York: New American Library, 1974. (O.P.)
    Excellent biography of Marie Curie, Nobel prize winner, scientist, mother, and wife.

<u>Sandra, Claire, Dee and Zella: Four Women in Science</u>. Newton, MA: EDC/Women's Educational Equity Act Publishing Center, 1980.
    In this 19-minute 16-mm film, an astronomer, a veterinarian, a physicist, and a membrane systems engineer discuss their work and their family life. An excellent portrayal of women working in nontraditional jobs.

<u>Sarah the Welder</u>. Boston: Massachusetts Educational Television, 1983.
    Thirty-minute videotape depicts a high school student overcoming the prejudices of her boyfriend, teachers, parents, and school administrators to enroll in a welding class.

Sayre, Anne. <u>Rosalind Franklin and DNA</u>. New York: Norton, 1975.
    Biography of English research chemist Rosalind Franklin describes her struggle to obtain recognition for her work in biochemistry, particularly with DNA.

<u>Science Abled</u>. Ann Arbor, MI: University of Michigan, School of Dentistry, 1987.
    These two 30-minute videotapes, one for students and one for "influential others," are designed to encourage students with physical and/or sensory disabilities to pursue careers in science and technology.

<u>Science: Woman's Work</u>. Washington, DC: National Science Foundation, 1982.
    Twenty-five minute, 16-mm film presents six women scientists both at work and at home: a marine biologist, an astronomer, a geologist, a science writer, a psychologist, and a computer specialist. Includes women of color and provides good role models.

Siegel, Patricia Joan, and Kay Thoams Finley. <u>Women in the</u>

Scientific Search: An American Bibliography. Metuchen, NJ: Scarecrow Press, 1985.

Introduction on general biographical information on women is followed by individual entries arranged by scientific subject (e.g., astronomers). Each entry consists of brief biographical notes on the individual scientist followed by books and articles on her.

Smith, Elizabeth Simpson. Breakthrough: Women in Aviation. New York: Walker, 1981.

Profiles of contemporary women with careers in aviation, including a boom operator, cargo pilot, aviation inspector, corporation pilot, aeronautical engineer, astronaut, and flight engineer.

Smith, Walter. COMETS Science and COMETS Profiles (Career Oriented Modules to Explore Topics in Science). 2 vols. Washington, DC: National Science Teachers Association, 1984.

Science provides 24 science modules (over 100 activities) for teachers in grades 5-9 to bring community resource people, especially women, into the classroom to teach science, describe their profession, and serve as role models. Profiles, which can be used independently or with the science materials, presents 24 biographical sketches of women in science plus activities to develop critical reading and writing skills.

_____, and Kala M. Stroup. Science Career Exploration for Women. Washington, DC: National Science Teachers Association, 1978.

Activities with supplementary resource lists, which easily can be integrated into the curriculum and are designed to encourage girls to consider science careers.

Space for Women. Washington, DC: National Audiovisual Center, 1981.

Twenty-seven minute, 16-mm film showing women working in a variety of jobs on the space program. Includes astronauts in training, electrical and computer engineers, psychophysiologists, and others. Produced by NASA.

Stearner, Phyllis S. Able Scientists--Disabled Persons: Careers in the Sciences. Clarendon Hills, IL: Foundation for

Science and the Handicapped, 1984.

Illustrates the lives and achievements of 27 scientists and students of science with disabilities, including women, who are overcoming obstacles and maintaining careers/studies in their chosen fields.

Sweeney, M.A., ed. Surveying Your Future: Nontraditional Careers for Young Women. Albuquerque, NM: New Mexico Network for Women in Science and Engineering, University of New Mexico, 1984.

Published to acquaint young women, their parents, teachers, and advisors with the opportunities available to women in nontraditional fields such as science.

Wanted: More Women in Science and Technology. New York: American Physical Society, Committee on the Status of Women in Physics, 1981.

A packet of information and suggestions for junior and high school counselors and teachers explaining the importance of a strong background in mathematics, chemistry, and physics.

Weiss, Iris R. Exploring Careers in Science and Engineering. Research Triangle Park, NC: Research Triangle Institute, 1982.

A multimedia kit designed to raise awareness about the reasons for the low participation of women and people of color in science-related careers. Also contains strategies for encouraging female students and students of color in these areas; for integrating science career exploration activities into the existing curriculum; and an annotated bibliography of additional resources. Filmstrip, cassette tape, posters, and teacher/student activity/resource books.

Williams, Barbara. Breakthrough: Women in Archeology. New York: Walker, 1981.

The personal and professional lives of six contemporary women archeologists, including information about their educational backgrounds, motivations, and the prejudices they encountered as women in this field. A list of schools and museums which furnish information on archeology education is provided.

A Winning Formula. New York: New York City Board of Education, Office of Equal Opportunity, 1986.

This videotape, with guide, interviews six Westinghouse science winners from the New York City high schools and shows them working at their science projects and talking to middle school students. Provides excellent multiracial role models for younger students.

Women in Science. Ann Arbor, MI: University of Michigan, School of Dentistry, 1984.

Seven 30-minute videotapes depicting women in biomedicine, chemistry, computer science, dentistry, engineering, geology, physics, and astronomy. A composite video entitled Scientific Careers for Women: Doors to the Future discusses barriers to women's increased participation in science. Includes teacher's guides and brochures.

Women's Work: Engineering. Newton, MA: EDC/Women's Educational Equity Act Publishing Center, 1977.

Twenty-six minute, 16-mm film showing women civil, materials, and chemical engineers, interviewed at work and at home, discussing the education and training necessary to become an engineer. Provides excellent role models.

Teacher Resources

AWIS Newsletter. Washington, DC: Association for Women in Science.

This publication includes some short biographies, interviews with women working in science, as well as current events and employment information.

Beanne, DeAnna Banks. Mathematics and Science: Critical Filters for the Future of Minority Students. Washington, DC: The Mid-Atlantic Center for Race Equity, The American University, 1985.

This resource manual reviews the role of the principal in effecting change; provides elementary educators with background information about factors underlying the underrepresentation of blacks, Hispanics, and Native Americans in math and science courses; and describes successful intervention programs that address this underrepresentation.

Berryman, Sue E. Who Will Do Science? New York: Rockefeller
Foundation, 1983.
     Examines the statistical underrepresentation of women
and minorities in science up to the Ph.D. level, and
identifies probable causes for this underrepresentation.

Bertram, Sheila. Women in Pure and Applied Science:
Bibliography. Edmonton, Alberta, Canada: Faculty of Library
Science, University of Alberta, 1987.
     Frequently updated, the July 1987 version contains 2,475
citations culled from journals, books, proceedings, and so
forth, addressing the full range of women and science. This
rich resource should be the place to commence a literature
search.

Bleier, Ruth. Science and Gender: A Critique of Biology and
Its Theories on Women. New York: Pergamon Press, 1984.
     A step-by-step approach to planning and conducting a
Futures Unlimited conference for 7-12 graders, particularly
females, to encourage them to continue studying math and
science. Illustrated with photos of actual conference.

The Brighton Women and Science Group. Alice Through the
Microscope: The Power of Science over Women's Lives.
London: Virago, 1980.
     One of the first books to address some of the problems
and issues of women and science. It begins with a
concentration on science education and the lack of
accessibility of science to women and then focuses on how
science reinforces traditional sex roles.

Chasek, Arlene S. Futures Unlimited: Expanding Choices in
Nontraditional Careers. New Brunswick, NJ: Consortium for
Educational Equity, Rutgers, The State University, 1985.
     A step-by-step approach to planning and conducting a
Futures Unlimited conference for 7-12 graders, particularly
females, to encourage them to continue studying math and
science. Illustrated with photographs of actual conferences.

Cremer, Christine. Women Moving Up: A Resource Directory
Focusing on Careers in Science, Engineering, and Technology.
Berkeley, CA: University of California, Lawrence Hall of
Science, 1980.

Developed following a one-day conference for women who had earned degrees in science but were currently unemployed or underemployed. Contains employment trends, job descriptions, and employer profiles for a range of scientific and technical fields. Also provides the names of women scientists and engineers interested in encouraging others to pursue science. While information pertains to the San Francisco Bay Area, the directory is readily adaptable.

Davis, Barbara Gross, and Sheila Humphreys. Evaluating Intervention Programs: Applications from Women's Programs in Math and Science. New York: Teacher's College Press, 1985.
Contains practical evaluation information for program directors, elementary and secondary teachers, career counselors, and others conducting programs to increase the participation of students, especially minorities and females, in math and science.

Educating Americans for the 21st Century. 2 vols. Washington, DC: National Science Board Commission on Precollege Education in Mathematics, Science and Technology, National Science Foundation, 1983.
A plan of action for improving mathematics, science, and technology education in all American elementary and secondary schools such that it may be the "best in the world by 1995."

Futures: From High School to High Tech. Portland, OR: Northwest Regional Laboratory, Center for Sex Equity, 1983.
Fifteen-minute videotape, with booklet, designed to increase awareness of equity issues among high school teachers and counselors. Emphasizes the preparation needed by present-day students in order to cope in a high-tech world.

Haas, Violet B. and Carolyn C. Perucci. Women in Scientific and Engineering Professions. Ann Arbor, MI: University of Michigan Press, 1984.
Conference papers examine career opportunities for women and the current status of women professionals in science, social science, and engineering. Offers ideas and strategies to encourage and increase the participation of women in science.

Hall, Paula Quick. **Problems and Solutions in the Education,**
Employment and Personal Choices of Minority Women in Science.
Washington, DC: American Association for the Advancement of
Science, 1981.
      Analyzes the experiences of minority females in
preparing and pursuing science careers. Documents
discrimination and barriers impeding the access of women and
minorities to science and offers recommendations for
overcoming "the problem."

Humphreys, Sheila M., ed. **Women and Minorities in Science:**
Strategies for Increasing Participation. Boulder, CO:
Westview Press, 1982.
      Surveys current levels of participation of women and
minorities in science. Identifies barriers to participation
and describes a range of intervention programs.

Ingison, Linda J., ed. **What Are the Needs in Precollege**
Science Mathematics and Social Science Education: Views from
the Field. Washington, DC: National Science Foundation,
1980.
      Reports from teacher organizations, science
associations, and administrators, examining the conduct and
the quality of precollege science education, plus
recommendations for improvement.

Kahle, Jane Butler. **Double Dilemma: Minorities and Women in**
Science Education. West Lafayette, IN: Purdue University,
1982.
      Describes a cooperative project run in Alabama and
Indiana to encourage and support minorities in science
education. Includes statistics on women in science.

_____, ed. **Women in Science: A Report from the Field.**
Philadelphia: The Falmer Press, 1985.
      Reviews the role, status, and employment patterns of
women in the sciences, particularly the biological sciences.
Differential entrance patterns, retention and reward systems,
and pay scales discussed, including the underemployment and
underutilization of women.

Keller, Evelyn Fox. **A Feeling for the Organism: The Life**
and Work of Barbara McClintock. New York: W.H. Freeman,

1983.
   Biography of the brilliant geneticist who won the Nobel prize for medicine in 1983. Discusses the development of genetics, a new science, and the work and early recognition of McClintock, who later diverged from the biological mainstream.

_____. Reflections on Gender and Science. New Haven, CT: Yale University Press, 1985.
   Nine essays examine the "genderization of science" from historic, psychoanalytic, and scientific perspectives, reflecting on the sexual division of labor, whereby science remains a masculine preserve. Explores the possibility of a science transcending gender stereotypes.

Kelly, Alison, ed. Science for Girls? Philadelphia: Open University Press, 1987.
   Reflects recent thinking about women and science education, especially from the English perspective.

Kreinberg, Nancy. Ideas for Developing and Conducting a "Women in Science" Career Workshop. Washington, DC: National Science Foundation, 1981.
   A practical handbook on how to present workshops for women to encourage them to consider careers in science and engineering and to provide an opportunity to meet role models.

Malcom, Shirley Mahalay. The Double Bind: The Price of Being a Minority Woman in Science, Report of a Conference of Minority Women and Scientists. Washington, DC: American Association for the Advancement of Science, 1976.
   Surveys the status of minority women in science and provides recommendations for improving their education and employment opportunities.

Mallow, Jeffrey V. Science Anxiety: Fear of Science and How to Overcome It. Clearwater, FL: H & H Publishing, 1986.
   Although much attention has been given to math anxiety, Mallow is one of the first to identify another distinct syndrome affecting girls and women in particular--science anxiety. Describes field-tested techniques that have proven successful in overcoming such anxiety.

Rossiter, Margaret W. <u>Women Scientists in America:</u>
<u>Struggles and Strategies to 1940</u>. Baltimore, MD: Johns
Hopkins University Press, 1982.
    An historical examination of the role of women in the
development of American science and their efforts to
establish themselves as contributing members of the
scientific community.

Smith, Walter S. <u>Making Science Useful: COMETS Workshop</u>
<u>Leader's Guide</u>. Lawrence, KS: University of Kansas School of
Education, 1986.
    A manual for use by workshop leaders who will train
teachers to use COMETS. Includes originals for making
transparencies and handouts plus a script to follow or adapt.
A bibliography of science career education resources for
middle school/junior high science teachers is provided.

Vetter, Betty V. <u>Opportunities in Science and Engineering</u>.
Vetter, Betty V., and Eleanor L. Babco. <u>Professional Women</u>
<u>and Minorities: A Manpower Data Resource Service</u>. Sixth
Edition. Washington, DC: Commission on Professionals in
Science and Technology, 1986.
    Two books that provide statistical information on the
education and employment of women and minorities in
scientific fields.

<u>Within Reach</u>. Washington, DC: American Association for the
Advancement of Science, 1981.
    A guide for parents, teachers, counselors, and program
directors for identifying and establishing programs for youth
with disabilities. Sold as a set with <u>Out of School Programs</u>
<u>in Science and Engineering</u>.

<u>Women and Science: Issues and Resources</u>. Madison, WI:
University of Wisconsin, 1984.
    This videotape, with guide, discusses issues of gender
differences, feminist approaches to scientific objectivity,
and the impact of science on women's lives. Features a
Women's Studies librarian discussing resources and research
strategies in these areas.

<u>Women, Math and Science: A Resource Manual</u>. Ann Arbor, MI:
Center for Sex Equity, University of Michigan, 1983.

Contains citations and abstracts of literature on sex differences in math and science, on the professional concerns of women, and on curricular materials in math and science.

Zimmerman, Michael, and others. Accessibility to the Laboratory and Science Classroom for Disabled Students. Washington, DC: American Association for the Advancement of Science, 1983.
Guidelines for accommodating laboratories for use by students with various physical disabilities.

Career Information

Information on careers in science and technology is often published in booklet or pamphlet form by associations, professional societies, nonprofit groups, and even corporations. Frequently a pamphlet is written for and about women or people of color, while most general pamphlets include a section addressed to the concerns of special populations. Because these ephemera do not lend themselves readily to conventional bibliographic treatment, they are grouped together here under the publisher. In each case, some sample pamphlets are listed; the publisher will send a complete list on request. Single copies are free, and bulk orders for career days and conferences are usually inexpensive.

AMERICAN ASSOCIATION FOR THE ADVANCEMENT OF SCIENCE (AAAS). 1515 Massachusetts Ave., NW, Washington, DC 20036.

A Day's Work, A Life Work. Reports based on visits with women chemists, mathematicians, and engineers.

Associations and Committees of/for Women in Science, Engineering, Mathematics and Medicine.

Associations of/for Racial and Ethnic Minority Science, Engineering, and Health Professionals. Periodically updated listing of relevant associations.

Career Opportunities in the Sciences. Lists scientific organizations with available career materials.

The Resource Directory of Scientists and Engineers with Disabilities. A data bank of names, addresses, fields of expertise, and other information on scientists and engineers with disabilities.

AMERICAN ASSOCIATION OF PETROLEUM GEOLOGISTS. P.O. Box 979, Tulsa, OK 74101. AMERICAN GEOLOGICAL INSTITUTE. 4220 King St., Alexandria, VA 22302.

Careers in Geology.

AMERICAN CHEMICAL SOCIETY. 1155 16th Street, NW, Washington, DC 20036.

Careers in Chemistry: Questions and Answers

Careers Nontraditional.

AMERICAN INDIAN SCIENCE AND ENGINEERING SOCIETY. 1310 College Ave., Suite 1220, Boulder, CO 80302.

American Indian Scientists and Engineers.

AMERICAN INSTITUTE OF CHEMICAL ENGINEERS. 345 East 47th St., New York, NY 10017.

The Chemical Engineer.

AMERICAN INSTITUTE OF PHYSICS. AMERICAN PHYSICAL SOCIETY COMMITTEE ON THE STATUS OF WOMEN IN PHYSICS. 335 East 45th St., New York, NY 10017.

Physics: A Career for You.

Women in Physics.

THE AMERICAN SOCIETY OF MECHANICAL ENGINEERS. UNITED ENGINEERING CENTER. 345 East 47th St., New York, NY 10017.

A Career for the Future.

AMERICAN STATISTICAL SOCIETY, COMMITTEE ON WOMEN IN STATISTICS. 806 15th St. NW, Washington, DC 20005.

Statistics as a Career: Women at Work.

E.I. DU PONT DE MEMOURS 7 CO., INC. Wilmington, DE 19898.

What Mechanical Engineers Do at Du Pont.

What Electrical Engineers Do at Du Pont.

ELECTRONIC INDUSTRIES ASSOCIATION CONSUMER ELECTRONICS GROUP. 2001 Eye St, NW, Washington, DC 20006.

Electronics: Your Bridge to Tomorrow, Your Career as an Electronics Technician.

EXXON. P.O. Box 2180, Houston, TX 77001.

Engineers.

GENERAL ELECTRIC COMPANY. Fairfield, CT. 06431

What's It Like to Be an Engineer.

So You Want to Go to Work.

What's It Like to Be a Technician.

What's It Like Working with Computers.

INTERNATIONAL PAPER COMPANY. International Paper Plaza, 77 West 45th St., New York, NY 10036.

Careers.

JETS, INC. UNITED ENGINEERING CENTER. 354 East 47th St., New York, NY 10017.

Exploring the World of Tomorrow...Today: Engineering, Science, Technology Activities for High School Students.

EASTMAN KODAK COMPANY. Rochester, NY 14650.

Women in Engineering at Kodak

NATIONAL ACTION COUNCIL FOR MINORITIES IN ENGINEERING, INC. 3 West 35th St., New York, NY 10001.

Minorities in Engineering.

Engineering: Your Key to the 21st Century.

NATIONAL AERONAUTICS AND SPACE ADMINISTRATION (NASA). Lyndon B. Johnson Space Center, Houston, TX 77058.

NASA will send biographical information and photos of

their women and minority astronauts.

NATIONAL ASSOCIATION OF TRADES AND TECHNICAL SCHOOLS (NATTS). Department WW, P.O. Box 10429, Rockville, MD 20850.

Working Women: Opportunities for Women in Trade and Technical Fields.

NATIONAL SCIENCE TEACHERS ASSOCIATION (NSTA).   1742 Connecticut Ave. NW, Washington, DC 20009.

NSTA publishes four science education magazines and nearly 100 special publications.

SANDIA NATIONAL LABORATORIES. Albuquerque, NM

Careers for Women in Science and Technology. Intertwines comments and pictures of women in science careers.

SOCIETY OF EXPLORATION GEOPHYSICISTS, COMMITTEE FOR WOMEN IN GEOPHYSICS. P.O. Box 702740, Tulsa, OK 74170-2740.

Women Exploring the Earth.

SOCIETY OF WOMEN ENGINEERS.   345 East 47th St., New York, NY 10017.

Engineering: A Goal for Women.

Womanengineer.

What Are You Doing for the Rest of Your Life: Is Engineering for You?

SPORTS

Linda Villarosa

Title IX — Wins and Losses

Back in 1971 in the state of Connecticut, there lived a girl who loved to run. Unfortunately, however, her high school had no cross country team for girls so she ran alone, without competition. Frustrated, she decided to try out for her school's boys' team, but her state's athletic conference forbade girls from competing on boys' teams. So she took the Connecticut Interscholastic Conference to court, to get a permanent injunction that would bar discrimination against girls in indoor track and cross country.

Unfair as it seems, she lost her case. But not only did superior court Judge Clark Fitzgerald deny her bid, he added the following comments:

> The present generation of our younger male population has not become so decadent that boys will experience the thrill of defeating girls in running contests, whether the girls be members of their own team or of an adversary team. It could well be that many boys would feel compelled to forgo entering track events if they were required to compete with girls on their own teams or on adversary teams. With boys vying with girls...the challenge to win, and the glory of achievement, at least for many boys would become nullified. Athletic competition builds character in boys, we do not need that kind of character in girls..."[1]

Needless to say, the climate was not favorable for the female athlete. And statistics parallel the many horror stories. In a survey conducted in 1966-67, less than 16,000 women were participating in intercollegiate sports. By 1971-72, the numbers had begun to escalate, however, no colleges offered athletic scholarships to women.[2] At the high school level, girls represented only seven percent of all athletes -- less than 300,000 participants compared to 3.6 million boys.[3]

But all that changed in 1972 when Title IX came along, outlawing discrimination in educational programs receiving Federal funds. After the bill passed, women's sports exploded. Physical education saw the end of sex-segregated classes. Girls were no longer shuttled into square dance in health classes but allowed to join into formerly male-dominated activities.

In athletics, the sexes remained segregated, but sports teams on the college level began to progress toward equality. Between 1971 and 1976, women participating in college athletics increased 100 percent; presently, female athletes represent 30 percent of all college competitors.[4] In 1974, 60 schools offered women athletes scholarships, and in 1985 that number had increased to 500 schools offering some 15,000 athletic scholarships. At the high school level, girls participating in sports increased by 523,000 between the 1970-71 and 1972-73 surveys. In 1982, 1.8 million girls comprised 35 percent of all interscholastic athletes.[5]

Title IX's effects have made their mark on elite level athletic competition as well. American women athletes collected 64 medals in the 1984 Olympic Games, more than any other country. Eighty-five percent of these champions competed on the college level thanks to antidiscriminatory legislation. The Los Angeles games also marked the first ever women's Olympic marathon, an event long considered too strenuous for women. An American, Joan Benoit Samuelson won the 26.2-mile event in Olympic record time. Samuelson, a graduate of Bowdoin College in Maine, competed on the intercollegiate level, just after Title IX opened up women's athletic opportunities.

But the same year that America's female Olympic athletes strutted their Title IX-boosted success, the law received a damaging blow. In February of 1984, the Supreme Court narrowed the interpretation of Title IX, ruling that the law applied only to education programs and activities that receive direct Federal assistance. The precedent set by the now infamous Grove City v. Bell decision would allow, for example, a university to cut the number of athletic scholarships offered to women athletes without fear of repercussions based on Title IX. Since most athletic departments receive funds from ticket sales, student fees, alumni donations, and TV revenues rather than from Federal assistance, the new program-specific guidelines would no longer apply.

And that's just what happened. Shortly after the Supreme Court's decision, Mercer University in Macon, Georgia, cut the number of women's basketball scholarships from seven to four, while leaving basketball scholarships awarded to male players untouched. Even as athletic administrators warned against panic, the ax fell at other institutions as well. The Universities of Idaho and Montana cut women's swimming from their rosters of intercollegiate sports teams, while the University of Arizona trimmed synchronized swimming.

Citing a "lack of jurisprudence" in this area, immediately after Grove City, the Department of Education's Office of Civil Rights killed sex discrimination cases pending against the University of Maryland, University of Washington, and West Texas State athletic departments. A complaint concerning Penn State's refusal to grant varsity status to the women's soccer team also was shelved. Sources note that the Department of Education has put some 64 discrimination cases on permanent hold at both the college and high school levels since 1984.[6]

But the women's athletic community refuses to sit idly by in the aftermath of the Grove City decision. As a Congressional bill to restore Title IX's bite pushes its way through the maze of legislative protocol, women athletes and sports administrators have surfaced as some of its most vocal supporters. Representatives from the Women's Sports Foundation, the National Association for Girls and Women in Sports, and the American Alliance of Physical Education, Recreation and Dance have offered some of the strongest testimony in support of the legislation.

Additionally, in late 1984, 20 well-known athletes, including Martina Navratilova, Chris Evert Lloyd, and Wilma Rudolph, sent a telegram to President Reagan expressing concern over the fate of women's athletics due to the Grove City case. Cheryl Miller, Mary Decker Slaney, Mary Lou Retton, and the late Flo Hyman, Olympic athletes who were trained during the post-Title IX years, have lobbied fervently for antidiscrimination legislation.

In an interview explaining how Title IX affected her career, basketball star Miller noted, "I wouldn't be where I am without the scholarship [afforded by antidiscrimination legislation]. In her testimony before the hearings of the U.S. Commission on Civil Rights, former director of the Women's Sports Foundation Eva Auchincloss, added: "I am here to speak to you about the expectations of the constituency I represent....They want corrective legislation for Title IX to provide institution-wide coverage that will assure them that women will have equal opportunities to participate in all educational programs including athletics. To be very clear, they support legislation that will provide protection, and they will not accept legislation that does not provide protection. They want no compromise on this issue."

Without a doubt, neither athletes, nor coaches, nor sports administrators will sit quietly sidelined while the gains reaped from Title IX are snatched away or denied the next generation of female competitors.

Equity and Physical Education

The need for an equity approach to physical education begins in the early grades, where ingrained attitudes reflect inaccurate assumptions about the differences in girls' and boys' physical abilities and interest in sports. Even before kindergarten, boys' play experiences traditionally include more large-motor activities, outdoor play, and ball-throwing than girls'. Young children know all too well that "throwing like a girl" is one of the worst criticisms that can be hurled at a young player.

For the most part, young girls do not have the opportunity to develop their bodies and their physical abilities as much as young boys. This leads to lack of confidence and self-esteem crucial to growth and development. Given this situation, it takes a conscious effort to achieve an equity approach. The physical educator needs to:

o   recognize and address sex-stereotyping in
    physical education classes, from the
    elementary grades through high school

o   plan carefully for coed physical education

o   emphasize cooperation games and health
    activities as well as team sports

o   advocate for more female coaches and
    athletic directors

o   plan programs to create specific
    opportunities for girls in sports

The following bibliography offers resources to help achieve equity in physical education and sports. The Instructional/Curriculum Materials section includes strategies for coed physical education and a listing of multiracial readings, films, and resources for students. The readings are most appropriate for junior high and high school -- for the elementary level, there are many good biographies of individual female sports figures. (See Libraries and Media Centers chapter.) Also included are sections on Teacher/Training Resources, Title IX, and Background Readings. The readings include research articles, information about sex roles as they relate to physical education, women in sports, women and sports, and coaching and administration.

Notes

1. Hollander vs Connecticut Interscholastic, Inc. (Superior Court, 1971). From Bonnie Parkhouse and Jackie Lapin, Women Who Win: Exercising Your Rights in Sport, New York: Prentice-Hall, Inc., 1980.

2. In the 1966-1967 survey, 15,727 college women participated in sports. In the 1971-1972 survey, 31,852 college women participated. Statistics are from the National Collegiate Athletic Association.

3. National Federation of State High School Associates Sports Participation Survey, 1971.

4. Statistics from the National Collegiate Athletic Association.

5. National Federation of State High School Associates Sports Participation Survey.

6. Marcia D. Greenberger and Julie Randolph, "The Impact of Grove City on the Enforcement of Title IX," February 26, 1986. Paper prepared for the National Women's Law Center, Washington, DC.

7. In 1988, over the President's veto, Congress passed the Civil Rights Restoration Act that restores the broad scope of coverage to Title IX of the Education Amendments of 1971.

BIBLIOGRAPHY

Instructional/Curriculum Materials

Strategies for Coed Physical Education

Arrighi, Marguerite A., and Dorothy B. McKnight. Instructional Strategies for Coed Physical Education. Chevy Chase, MD: Athletic & Sports Consultants, 1980.
    Offers strategies for combating sex stereotyping in physical education classes including specific grouping patterns, games and student evaluations, as well as charts to measure teacher behavior.

Barta, S., and T. Anderson. Multicultural Nonsexist Education. Physical Education in Iowa Schools. Des Moines, IA: Iowa Department of Public Instruction, (ERIC No. ED 219 358), 1982.
    Although designed for use in the Iowa school system, this pamphlet is applicable to any physical education program. It provides a self-evaluation checklist and bibliography of resource materials and organizations.

Blaufarb, Marjorie, and J. Canoe. Title IX: Sex-integrated Programs That Work. Washington, DC: AAHPER Publications, 1976.
    Monograph containing descriptions of four junior high and 15 senior high school programs that have been successful in implementing Title IX into their curriculum. Guidelines and issues surrounding these changes are discussed.

Clement, Anne, and Betty Hartman. A Guide to Equity in Planning Secondary School Required Physical Education. Newton, MA: EDC, WEEA Publishing Center, 1980.
    Step-by-step guide to planning coed physical education programs. Includes Title IX guidelines, student evaluations, and a source bibliography.

Frankel, S., E. Radzovicz, and E. Sammons. A Curriculum Resource for Junior High Coeducational Physical Education.

Cortland, NY: Cortland-Madison BOCES, 1982.
Developed by Cortland-area educators, this curriculum guide presents suggestions for planning coed activities. Team, individual, and dual sports as well as cooperative games and health activities are featured. The authors offer specific rule modifications for coed activities, e.g. a team must include a certain number of girls or a female must touch the ball before a goal is scored.

Making It Work! A Booklet of Activities to Encourage the Development of Co-Ed Physical Education Programs. Lansing, MI: Michigan State Department of Education, 1980.
Developed from workshops presented by the state Office for Sex Equity, this booklet contains very specific guidelines for fair coed activities.

Tannehill, Deborah. A Practical Handbook for Co-ed Physical Education. Olympia, WA: Washington Office of the State Superintendent of Public Instruction, 1981.
Contains the Washington State Legislation on Sex Equity and the codes for implementation. A step-by-step approach to the planning, organization, and implementation of a successful coed physical education program. Includes tips on philosophy, goal, and objective development and encourages the development of district-wide packages by physical education personnel. Addresses the consensus process and areas of concern surrounding the instructional process. An extensive bibliography, resource consultants, and examples of quality programs are listed.

Readings/Films/Resources for Students

Appenzeller, Herb, Terry Engler, Nancy Mathews, Linda Riekes, and Thomas C. Ross. Sports and Law. St. Paul, MN: West Publishing Co., 1984.
A readable summary of legal issues in athletics. Crisp, nonsexist language and lively illustrations make this guide practical for high school students and younger. Each chapter offers case studies and questions for discussion. The chapter on women's equity is brief but helpful.

Alexander, Alpha, Nikki Franke, Tina Sloan Green, and Carole A. Oglesby. Black Women in Sport. Reston, VA: American Alliance for Health, Physical Education, Recreation and

Dance, 1981.

An interesting collection of essays on black sportswomen. Discusses myths and realities of black women in athletics and physical education. Also includes biographies, resume-style, of 17 noted black female athletes, coaches, and administrators.

Bentley, Ken. Going for the Gold: The Story of Black Women in Sports. Los Angeles: Carnation Company, 1983.

Interviews with 17 top athletes provide an inspirational overview of black women's contributions to sport. A film by the same title can be ordered from Avandi II Productions in Los Angeles, California.

Hey What About Us?: Sex Role Stereotyping in Physical Activities in Schools. Distributed by Extension Media Center, 2223 Fulton Ave., Berkeley, CA 94720.

A fifteen-minute film that presents situations in which sex-role stereotyping is relatively absent, then compares these incidences with stereotyping that occurs in physical education classes.

Kaplan, Janice. Women and Sports: Inspirational Information for the New Female Athlete. New York: Viking Press, 1979.

Although somewhat dated, this book contains interviews with many well-known women athletes and includes several in-depth studies on society's view and the media image of the woman athlete.

Making It Happen. Distributed by WEEA Publishing Center, EDC, 55 Chapel St., Newton, MA 02160.

Explores the lives of three athletes and examines past and present attitudes surrounding women in sports. Available in 16mm film or 3/4 " video. Seventeen minutes.

Myers, Gail Andersen. A World of Sports for Girls. Philadelphia: Westminster Press, 1981.

Provides useful and inspirational information for the junior high level athlete and up. Materials explain Title IX and offer a sample complaint. Jobs in athletics, scholarships, and prominent athletes in sports from lacrosse to horse racing are discussed.

Sports Beyond Winning. Distributed by Modern Talking Picture Service, Scheduling Center, 5000 Park St., North, St. Petersburg, FL 33709.

A nineteen-minute color videotape to encourage young women to participate in sports. With high school students as role models, the film discusses the benefits of sports.

Stanek, Carolyn. The Complete Guide to Women's College Athletics. Chicago: Contemporary Books, 1981.

For college-bound high school athletes. Includes scholarship information and regulations governing recruitment and participation. The chapter covering Title IX and its implications gives a tidy summary in question-and-answer format.

Surer, Swifter, Stronger. Distributed by The Women's Sports Foundation, 342 Madison Ave., New York, NY 10017.

An inspirational six-minute video featuring upbeat music and quick shots of past and present female athletes in action, illustrating the strength of the sportswoman.

TABS: Organization for Equal Education of the Sexes. Women in Sports Poster. New York: OEES, 438 Fourth St., Brooklyn, NY 11215.

Photos of women engaged in a variety of sports; includes lesson plan on the benefits of sports. Posters of individual sportswomen also available.

Twin, Stephanie L., ed. Out of the Bleachers: Writings on Women and Sport. Old Westbury, NY: The Feminist Press, 1979.

Although somewhat dated, this is still a very thoughtful collection of essays covering female athletes. Highlights Title IX and its application to sport, offering a clear, readable explanation of the law's history, limitations, and possibilities.

The Woman in Sports. Distributed by Walter J. Klein Co., 6311 Carmel Rd., Charlotte, NC 28211.

A film series in three parts, it includes a dramatization of a woman as she chooses to participate in sports, a capsule view of women's sports history, and interviews with well-known sportswomen. Ninety minutes.

Teacher/Training Resources

<u>A.C.T.I.V.E.: All Children Totally Involved Via Equity</u>.
Washington, DC: United States Department of Education, 1980.
    Three-part program designed to help elementary school
physical education instructors identify and change
stereotyped behavior. Comprised of a teacher's manual,
workshop manual, and an assessment guide to evaluate teacher
performance, this comprehensive packet also provides lesson
plans, suggested activities, and a guide for a one-day
teacher workshop.,

Griffin, Pat, and Judy Placek. <u>Fair Play in the Gym</u>.
Distributed by The NETWORK, Inc., 290 South Main St.,
Andover, MA 01810.
    A leader's manual with more than 50 practical activities
to help teachers identify what they can do to eliminate
equity problems in their physical education programs.

McKnight, Dorothy B. <u>Project Missing Link: A Focus on
Instruction</u>. Chevy Chase, MD: Educational Sport Institute,
1980-82.
    This project produced a participant's workbook, leader's
handbook, and 28-minute, color videotape on strategies for
equitable coeducational physical education classes.

_____. <u>Effective Spheres of Influence</u>. Chevy Chase, MD:
Educational Sport Institute, 1983-85.
    A training packet and audio tape to use for observing
the effects of sex-fair teaching approaches on students in
coed physical education classes.

<u>Physical Educators for Equity</u>. Newton, MA: EDC, WEEA
Publishing Center, 1980.
    Seven modules discuss sex-role stereotyping, biological
sex differences, and Title IX among other topics. The
accompanying handbook is designed to help physical educators
reduce sex bias in secondary school classes.

Title IX

Acosta, Vivian and Linda Carpenter. <u>The Status of Women.
Intercollegiate Athletics: A Five Year National Study</u>.

Brooklyn: City University of New York, 1984.

This meticulously prepared report contains the facts and figures behind women's sports at the college level. The authors diagram the effect of Title IX on intercollegiate athletics and discuss a disturbing decrease of women coaching girls and women.

Fair, M.H., N.K. Cook, J.A. Goins, and L.S. Doyle. Participant Workbook. Physical Education. Implementing Sex Equity Using Title IX. Denver: Colorado State Department of Education, 1979.

Workbook developed to help instructors comply with Title IX. Provides information and activities relating to: Title IX guidelines, and examples of compliance/noncompliance; physical activity objectives for females and males; film "An Equal Chance Through Title IX"; assessment inventories and action strategies for elementary levels; issues specific to secondary physical education; and sample questions and answers to questions related to Title IX implementation.

Geadelmann, Patricia L. "Assessment Needed: Coeducational Physical Education: For Better or for Worse?" NASSP Bulletin, 1981, 65 (443): 91-95.

Intended for secondary school principals, this article describes the original rationale for Title IX and then the actual practices of coeducation. The author suggests questions principals should ask about their physical education programs and discusses the need for full implementation of Title IX.

Kneer, Marian E., "Sex Integrated Physical Education." NASSP Bulletin, 1978, 62 (417): 79-84.

Describes factors for principals (and others) to consider when implementing Title IX. The benefits and problems of coed physical education classes are discussed. Suggestions for implementation cover the actual program, scheduling and instruction. The author makes suggestions for assigning administrative roles to achieve compliance.

Mathews, Bonnie, ed. More Hurdles to Clear: Women and Girls in Competitive Athletics. Washington, DC: United States Commission on Civil Rights, 1980.

A comprehensive analysis of Title IX and its effect on physical education and sport. Although dated, it is thorough and offers a wide selection of statistics, charts, and graphs.

Physical Education and Athletics: Strategies for Meeting
Title IX Requirements. Conference proceedings. ERIC/CUE
Urban Diversity Series No. 66, Columbia University, 1979. ED
179 628.
    A compilation of papers to assist educators in
identifying the problems in implementing Title IX. Marjorie
Blaufarb discusses the inequities, both psychological and
physical, that have been contributed to by separate-sex
programs. Dorothy Harris contends that there are more
physiological differences within the sexes than between them,
A. Mae Timer describes what a successful sex-integrated
physical education program would look like and suggests
procedures to follow in order to achieve such a program.

Trunzo, Tina and Leslie Wolfe. Like She Owns the Earth--
Women and Sports. Washington, DC: Project on Equal Education
Rights, 1985.
    A brief summary that explains how Title IX applies to
sport and also discusses the effect of the Grove City case on
athletics. Provides a short historical overview of women's
athletics and dispels women's sports myths.

Women's Sports Foundation. The New Agenda: A Blueprint for
the Future of Women's Sports. Conference proceedings. New
York: Women's Sports Foundation, 1983.
    Summarizes panels and speeches from a 1983 conference
held in Washington, DC. The carefully compiled latter
portion of this summary covers, case by case, rules and
regulations that may adversely affect development and
participation of female athletes.

_____. Title IX Guide. New York: Women's Sports Foundation.
    Upon request, the Foundation will send a package that
includes a simple summary of Title IX, an updated fact sheet,
an explanation of The Civil Rights Restoration Act of 1985,
and a packet of past and recent newspaper and magazine
articles on the law and women's sports. This is by far the
most up-to-date and detailed offering available on Title IX
and its application in athletics and physical education.

Background Readings

Dunkle, Margaret. The Sports Gender Gap: The Complete Do-
It-Yourself Guide to Sex Equity in Intercollegiate Athletics.
Washington, DC: The Equality Center, 1987.
    A practical tool to measure equity in a college athletic
program. Information in this resource guide also can be
applied to high school and community-level programs. A
resource list contains information for minority women in
athletics.

From Here to There: The Physical Education Module.
Bethseda, MD: The Equity Institute, 1983.
    Prepared for physical education teachers, this guide
stresses the importance of physical fitness in getting and
holding high-paying jobs. It also explains how to guard
against sex stereotyping in physical fitness training.

Geadelmann, Patricia L. "Physical Education: Stronghold of
Sex Role Stereotyping." Quest, 1980, 32 (2): 192-200.
    Gives a good overview of the history of sex-role
stereotyping. It traces the development of Title IX, its
intents, and its actual impact on physical education. The
author stresses the need for professional preparation
programs to address this issue in order to produce teachers
qualified to deal with coeducational situations.

Hall, Ann M. and Dorothy Richardson. Fair Ball: Towards Sex
Equality in Canadian Sport. Ottawa, Ontario: Canadian
Advisory on the Status of Women, 1982.
    This study by two feminists covers issues concerning
Canada's sports and physical education programs. It includes
extensive discussion of legal issues in women's athletics
both in Canada and the United States.

Hoferek, Mary J. "Sex Role Prescriptions and Attitudes of
Physical Educators." Sex Roles: A Journal of Research,
1982. 8: 83-98.
    Doctoral study investigating the relationship between
the sex-role perceptions of physical educators and their
attitudes and expectations. The author concluded that: 1)
coed classes can be more inequitable depending on the
specific teacher; 2) curriculum should be constructed in a
way that allows for diversity of attitudes and values; and 3)

physical activity personnel need to teach traditionally cross-sex activities to role model for their students.

_____. "Sex Roles and Physical Activities: Evolving Trends." Quest, 1982, 34: 71-81.
    Discusses the trends in the physical activity profession as they relate to changing sex roles. Points out that segregated classes reinforce low instrumentality and high emotionality in girls and vice versa for boys. Author argues for a move toward a more androgynous conceptualization of sex roles in the physical activity professions.

Howell, Reet, ed. Her Story in Sport: A Historical Anthology of Women in Sports. West Point, NY: Leisure Press, 1982.
    A well-researched compilation looks at women in sport from a historical viewpoint. Howell's work is dizzyingly detailed, but informative.

Illinois State Board of Education. 1981. Presentation made at the Physical Education Grouping and Performance Evaluation Symposium. ED 224 783 and ED 222 490.
    A number of interesting papers provide tips and techniques for grouping in coeducational physical education.

Janis, Laura. "Annotated Bibliography of Minority Women in Athletics." Sociology of Sport Journal, Vol. 2, No. 3, 1985, pp 266-274.
    Contains 25 listings for often difficult-to-find references to and resources for minority sportswomen.

Lapchick, Richard Broken Promises: Racism in American Sports. New York: St. Martin's/Marek, 1984.
    A moving and detailed account of racial prejudice from the early days of sport to the present. Filled with chilling accounts of racism against black athletes, the book offers conclusions and solutions in its final pages.

Oglesby, Carole A., ed. Women in Sport: From Myth to Reality. Philadelphia: Lea and Febiger, Inc., 1978.
    Thirteen authors assess the interaction among women, sport, and society. Their viewpoints represent social,

psychological, physiological, and political aspects of the issue. A pioneer effort in physical education and women's sport and an important book for every equity library.

Parkhouse, Bonnie L. and Jackie Lapin. Women Who Win: Exercising Your Rights in Sports. Englewood Cliffs, NJ: Prentice-Hall, Inc., 1980.

Easy-to-read, provocative offering on the theories -- philosophical and legal -- behind equality in sports. Useful chapters offer case-by-case studies as well as step-by-step advice for fighting sexism in athletics and sports administration.

_____. The Woman in Athletic Administration. Santa Monica, CA: Goodyear Publishing Co., 1980.

A definitive handbook for the female coach, athletic director, trainer and physical education instructor at any level from elementary school to college. Chapter 10, "Athletic Affiliations," guides the female administrator through the maze of laws and regulations of various male-dominated governing bodies at all levels of the athletic/physical system.

Schafer, Susan. Sports Need You: A Working Model for the Equity Professional. Denver: Colorado Department of Education, 1984.

A practical guide that explains how to increase the number of women and minorities in athletic coaching, officiating, administration, and governance. Although some of the examples and policy directives refer specifically to Colorado's educational system, the guide also includes national statistics, goals and step-by-step solutions that can be applied universally.

Scott, Gladys M. and Mary J. Hoferek, eds. Women as Leaders in Physical Education and Sports. Iowa City, IA: University of Iowa, 1979.

Seven female essayists offer their views on sexual politics and power plays present in the physical education system.

<u>Women's Sports and Fitness</u>.   P.O. Box 612, Holmes, PA 19043.
    Popular magazine that covers all aspects of women's
sports and fitness and includes features on individual
sportswomen, a calendar of events, and information on new
equipment and resources.

**Thanks to Chris Shelton of the National Association for Girls
and Women in Sport for her inclusion of bibliographic entries
related to equity and physical education.**

TEENAGE CHILDBEARING

Michele Cahill

The School Experience

Approximately 500,000 babies are born to teenagers in the United States annually, giving the United States the highest rate of teen childbearing in the Western industrialized world.[1] Young women who become mothers as teenagers face serious negative consequences including long-term lower education attainment and economic achievement than their peers who do not become parents as teenagers. Thus, preventing teenage pregnancy is an issue of national concern. While public discussion generally has characterized the issue as a health or moral concern, there is growing evidence that the school experience plays a key role in the dilemma of too-early childbearing. Attention is being focused on the necessity of school involvement in teenage pregnancy prevention and the importance of school in the amelioration of the negative effects of teen childbearing.

School is a central institution in the lives of young people, with responsibility for preparing them for productive futures. More than half of female school dropouts cite pregnancy as their reason for leaving, and there is increasing evidence that young women who have dropped out of school or who have fallen behind grade levels are at very high risk of teenage motherhood. This has led to a recognition that school continuation and achievement are critical elements in pregnancy prevention strategies. Further, if educational equity is the goal, it is essential that a school make a commitment to assisting young mothers to graduate.

Addressing the problem of teenage parenthood, however, is a complicated issue. Teen parenthood is interrelated with problems of poverty and inequality in American society, particularly the economic status of women. Teenage mothers are three times more likely to be single than older mothers, and three-quarters of single mothers under age 25 are living in poverty.[2]

These mothers have multiple barriers to economic self-sufficiency: they have childcare responsibilities, lack of experience as labor force participants, and have not received adequate educational preparation. They are thus vulnerable to long-term poverty in an economy where women working full-time average only two-thirds the income of men. The school experience of females at risk of teenage motherhood and of adolescent mothers themselves is a key variable that can either improve chances of economic self-sufficiency or add to the likelihood of long-term poverty.

Prevention Strategies: Sex Education and Health Services

Adolescents in the United States have become increasingly sexually active at younger ages. Statistics indicate that the average age of first intercourse is 16.2 years and that one-third of 15- to 17-year-old females and nearly one-half of all 15- to 17-year-old males are sexually active. By age 19, 80 percent of males and 70 percent of females have been sexually active. In 1984, there were 125,000 pregnancies to junior high school students.[3]

This increase in sexual activity among adolescents often is pointed to as an explanation for the high rates of teenage pregnancy. Yet cross-national studies by the Alan Guttmacher Institute, which documented the higher U.S. rates of teen pregnancy, also indicated that American teenagers are not more sexually active than those in Great Britain, France, Canada, or Sweden--countries with dramatically lower rates of teenage pregnancy. The reasons for the high rates of teenage pregnancy and parenthood in the United States are multifaceted. The Guttmacher study pointed to the fact that European educational policy more commonly favors sex education, and health facilities and clinics offering contraceptive information are more accessible to teenagers. Thus, one strategy for reducing high rates of teenage pregnancy requires increasing sex education, assisting young people with decision-making, and providing appropriate health services. Yet, all teenage young women are not equally likely to become mothers. Young women from poor families who have low basic skills achievement and those who have dropped out of school are far more likely to become teenage mothers. Addressing their needs requires adding to this more general strategy.

Prevention Strategies: Expanding Life Options

In 1984, Joy Dryfoos, a prominent researcher in the field of pregnancy, postulated a life options theory of teenage pregnancy prevention. She stated that to avoid teenage motherhood young women need both the capacity to control their fertility (sex education, family planning services) and the motivation to postpone childbearing.[4] Motivation requires young women to have expanded life options so that motherhood is not viewed as the primary, or only adult role in which a female has a likelihood of success. It is essential for young women to believe early pregnancy will block personal and career goals and decrease their income and status. This motivation is obviously weakened by sex-role stereotyping, but it is also seriously undermined by academic failure in school.

Karen Pittman of the Children's Defense Fund supports this view. In an article entitled "Enhancing Basic Skills and Life Options to Prevent Pregnancy," Pittman states that "the link between teenagers' basic academic (reading and math) skills and their future life options is readily apparent."[5] She continues:

> Students with serious basic skills deficiencies often have encountered failure so frequently that their self-esteem development in non-academic areas (personal and social development, work knowledge and work attitudes, etc.) generally lags behind that of their more fortunate peers. It is this combination of limited opportunities and a less developed sense of their own potential that places poor and minority youths at particularly high risks of early parenthood.

In the same article, Pittman reports on a study based on data from the National Longitudinal Survey of Young Americans (NLS) that "documents the strong relationship between poor basic skills, limited life options, and teenage pregnancy and childbearing." The study reveals how "teens with similar family incomes and basic skills—whether White, Black or Hispanic—have nearly identical rates of childbearing."[6]

Prevention Strategies: Preventing School Dropout

Clearly, school dropout and early childbearing are interrelated. Studies of the <u>High School and Beyond</u> data indicate that more than 50 percent of females who dropped out of school gave pregnancy and/or marriage as their reason for leaving school. Other research has documented that pregnancy and early motherhood are even more common among adolescents who have already dropped out of school and are unemployed. The negative consequences of teenage childbearing can continue over a lifetime. Denise Polit, in a summary of the research on these negative consequences, concluded:

> The single, best-documented consequence of an early pregnancy is truncated education....Girls who become mothers during their teenage years can expect diminished lifelong educational attainment in comparison with classmates who postpone childbearing even when socio-economic and motivational factors are controlled.[8]

It appears that improving the educational achievement of young women from poor families and preventing school dropout among them would have significant impact on their vulnerability to early childbearing. This is not a simple task. As with other types of dropout prevention, teenage pregnancy prevention is complex. It involves both broadening the roles of schools and changing how most schools regard and treat female students--attitudes of teachers and staff, vocational options, curricula, and support services. This involves schools in controversial areas where community values are often in conflict. The struggles over on-site child care and school-based clinics reflect the depth of negative feelings about condoning or "rewarding" behavior that has traditionally defined "bad girls." Yet concern for equity demands that schools assist young women and young men to be responsible about their sexuality and not support punitive responses to adolescent female sexuality. Teenage childbearing must be recognized as a concern of dropout prevention programs, and early intervention must be initiated.

Equity and Young Mothers

In addition to playing a key role in prevention, schools are crucial to the achievement of educational equity for teenage mothers. As has been discussed earlier, the diminished educational attainment characteristic of teenage childbearing leads to diminished economic status. Most teenage mothers are unable to make up for lost education.

Sixty percent of women heading households receiving AFDC
began receipt as an adolescent mother. Harvard researchers
Mary Jo Bane and David Ellwood's study of national
longitudinal data demonstrated that while most exits from
AFDC occurred within the first two years, a significant
minority of single mothers and their children remained for
long periods (8 to 10 years). These were women facing the
most serious obstacles in the labor market--women who are
high school dropouts with three or more children.[9]

While the importance of schools addressing the need of
teenage mothers to complete their educations is evident, the
policies and practices required to meet these needs are
controversial. They require schools to recognize that
traditional practices and policies (attendance, counseling
arrangements, course sequencing, etc.) result in high
dropout among this group, and that flexibility, additional
services, and new arrangements are necessary. These must be
built upon an expanded view of sex equity evidenced in
curricula that examine the lives of girls and women and
encourage achievement and staff attitudes and school policies
that actively support strengthening the capacity of girls for
future economic self-sufficiency.

Most schools began this process of change during the
last decade by eliminating overt discrimination in their
practices regarding teenage mothers. In a recent report for
the Council of Chief State School Officers, Margaret Dunkle
of The Equality Center points out that prior to Title IX
(1972):

> Less than a third of the country's school districts
> offered pregnant students any education at all.
> Most students who were not expelled were either
> kept at home or segregated in special programs. Of
> those students who left school, 85% never
> returned.[10]

The problem today is not this active discrimination of
the past, but the school's implicit acceptance of motherhood
as an end to the need for employment preparation. As one
junior high school principal observed, "A diploma will make
no difference to these girls."[11] Attitudes such as these
form the basis of current discrimination practices. Teen
mothers' need for assistance with scheduling, child care, and
related problems are often seen as extraneous to the school's
responsibility. The results are very low rates of school
completion for young mothers.

Some school districts, however, have taken on the task of ensuring sex equity for young mothers. These districts are leaders in demonstrating new educational arrangements and programs that assist young mothers in completing their education and that strengthen the capacities and motivations of girls to avoid too-early parenthood. Many of these programs are collaborations between schools and health, social service, and youth-serving agencies. They include comprehensive school-based clinics, day-care centers, and case management programs that offer counseling, child care, service referral, and academic assistance to teen mothers.

Schools that are involved in prevention programs also have developed curricula with other agencies emphasizing life planning, decision-making skills, and comprehensive approaches to family life education. The collaborative nature of these programs indicates the complexity and difficulty of the tasks, but affirms the willingness of schools and many community agencies to face the controversies and work together to meet the challenge.

Most female students will go on to hold paid employment for most of their adult lives while also fulfilling parenting roles. Many will be the sole economic support for themselves and their children. This is difficult under the best of economic circumstances, but impossible for girls who are not educated for economic self-sufficiency. Girls need schools to encourage self-sufficient futures and to provide the academic and social support they need to achieve the competencies required for these successful futures. Schools must evaluate traditional practices, revise course offerings, and devise new programs and arrangements for preparing girls for economic self-sufficiency or they will be failing to provide them with an equitable education.

The bibliography has been assembled in order to help schools address the issue of teenage childbearing and educational equity. It is divided as follows: Background Reading, Readings from an Equity Perspective, Readings Describing School-Based Programs, Curricula and Resource Materials, Resource Groups, and Publishers.

The books, periodicals, curricular materials, films, and resource groups are listed to provide readers with a broad introduction to the multiple dimensions of the problem of teenage childbearing. Material covers the antecedents and consequences of teenage childbearing; provides information on resource groups working in the area of teenage pregnancy and school dropout; and points readers to both specific curricula and teaching materials (where they exist) and to the publishing houses and libraries where follow-up information can be found. While the list includes more than fifty entries (overviews, statistics, studies of the life experiences of young mothers, sex education and life planning curricula, research and advocacy material, etc.), they do not all represent an explicit equity orientation. Much has been written about teenage pregnancy and even more about sex education for adolescents. Yet the field has relatively few publications that have a strong sex equity perspective. Consequently, in compiling this bibliography, some materials were included that provide useful information but do not have an equity focus.

Notes

1. Charles F. Westoff, Gerard Cabot, and Andrew D. Foster, "Teenage Fertility in Developed Nations: 1971-1980," <u>Family Planning Perspectives</u>, Vol. 15, No. 3, May/June 1983, pp. 185-110.

2. <u>Preventing Teenage Pregnancy: A Literature Review</u> (Washington, DC: The Center for the Study of Social Policy, August 1986), p. 12.

3. Karen Pittman, <u>Preventing Children Having Children</u>, Adolescent Pregnancy Prevention Clearinghouse Paper No. 1 (Washington, DC: Children's Defense Fund, 1985).

4. Joy G. Dryfoos, "A New Strategy for Preventing Unintended Teenage Childbearing," <u>Family Planning Perspectives</u>, Vol. 16, No. 4, July/August 1984, pp. 193-195.

5. Karen Pittman. <u>Preventing Adolescent Pregnancy: What Schools Can Do</u>. Adolescent Pregnancy Prevention Clearinghouse Paper No. 6, (Washington, DC: Children's Defense Fund, September 1986), p. 4.

6. <u>Ibid</u>.

7. Ruth B.I. Ekstrom, Margaret E. Goertz, Judith M. Pollack and Donald A. Rock, "Who Drops Out of High School and Why? Findings from a National Study" <u>Teachers College Record</u>.

Vol. 87, No. 3, Spring 1986, p. 376.

8. Denise F. Polit and J.R. Kahn, "Teenage Pregnancy and the Role of the Schools," unpublished paper available from Humanalysis, Inc., Saratoga Springs, NY.

9.   Mary Jo Bane and David Ellwood, "The Dynamics of Dependency: The Routes to Self-Sufficiency," report prepared for the Assistant Secretary for Planning and Evaluation, Office of Evaluation and Technical Assistance, Office of Income Security Policy, U.S. Department of Health and Human Services, June 1983, p. 111.

10.   Margaret C. Dunkle, Adolescent Pregnancy and Parenting: Evaluating School Policies and Programs from a Sex Equity Perspective. (Washington, DC: Council of Chief State School Officers Resource Center on Educational Equity, 1985), p. 3.

11.   Dunkle, Op. Cit., p. 1.

BIBLIOGRAPHY

Background Reading

Ascher, Carol. Pregnant and Parenting Teens: Statistics, Characteristics and School-Based Support Services. No. 1 in Trends and Issues series. New York: ERIC/Clearinghouse on Urban Education, April 1985.
    Briefly summarizes important research and issues.

Children's Defense Fund, Adolescent Pregnancy Clearinghouse publications (see listing of Resource Groups for address).

   Preventing Children Having Children (1985)

   Adolescent Pregnancy: Whose Problem Is It? (Jan. 1986)

   Adolescent Pregnancy: What the States Are Saying (March 1986)

   Building Health Programs for Teenagers (March 1986)

   Model Programs: Preventing Adolescent Pregnancy and Building Youth Sufficiency (July 1986)

   Preventing Adolescent Pregnancy: What Schools Can Do (Sept. 1986)

   Welfare and Teen Pregnancy: What Do We Know? What Do We Do? (Nov. 1986)

   Adolescent Pregnancy: Anatomy of a Social Problem in Search of Comprehensive Solutions (Jan. 1987)

   Child Care: An Essential Service for Teen Parents (March 1987)

   Teenage Pregnancy: An Advocate's Guide to the Numbers (January/March 1988)

   Provide highly readable synopses of research, program interventions, and policy issues, with many references to programs and resources. Especially pertinent are Preventing Children Having Children and Preventing Adolescent Pregnancy.

Furstenburg, Frank, J. Brooks-Gunn, and S. Philip Morgan. <u>Adolescent Mothers in Later Life</u>. New York: Cambridge University Press, 1987.

A good longitudinal study on the life experience of young mothers highlighting long-term consequences of teen childbearing.

Hayes, Cheryl, ed. <u>Risking the Future: Adolescent Sexuality, Pregnancy and Childbearing</u>. Washington, DC: National Academy Press, 1987.

Provides excellent, in-depth discussions of the problem. Good chapters on programs designed to prevent or delay teen pregnancies and to assist pregnant and parenting teens. Report of the National Academy of Sciences.

Miller, Shelby H. <u>Children as Parents: Final Report on a Study of Childbearing and Childbearing Among 12-15 Year Olds</u>. Edison, NJ: Child Welfare League of America, 1983.

A pertinent study for those concerned with very young mothers.

Moore, Kristin, and Martha Burt. <u>Private Crisis, Public Cost: Policy Perspectives on Teenage Childbearing</u>. Baltimore, MD: Urban Institute Press, 1982. (Note: Offices of the Urban Institute are in Washington, DC, but publications should be ordered through the Urban Institute Press, 301-338-6951.)

Addresses the issue from a public policy perspective, with emphasis on intervention options. Useful summary in last chapter.

Nickel, Phyllis Smith, and Holly Delany. <u>Working with Teen Parents: A Survey of Promising Approaches</u>. Chicago: Family Resource Coalition, 1985.

A handbook for the development and establishment of programs. Includes resource and program listings.

<u>Teenage Pregnancy: The Problem That Hasn't Gone Away</u>. New York: Alan Guttmacher Institute, 1981.

Provides an excellent, concise discussion of the problem, with many charts and illustrations.

Readings from an Equity Perspective

Ascher, Carol. <u>Improving Schooling to Reduce Teenage</u> <u>Pregnancy</u>. No. 28 of <u>ERIC Digests</u>. New York: ERIC/Clearinghouse of Urban Education, Dec. 1985.
    In concise form describes intervention options and school-based programs to reduce teen pregnancy.

Dunkle, Margaret C. <u>Adolescent Pregnancy and Parenting:</u> <u>Evaluating School Policies and Programs from a Sex Equity</u> <u>Perspective</u>. Washington, DC: Council of Chief State School Officers, Resource Center on Educational Equity, 1985.
    Provides a step-by-step guide for evaluating sex-equitable treatment of pregnant and parenting students.

_____, and Jill E. Reid. <u>Education and the Teenage Pregnancy</u> <u>Puzzle: Report Card #5</u>. Washington, DC: The Mid-Atlantic Center for Sex Equity, 1985.
    Fosters discussion about teen pregnancy among educators through questions and answers.

Equality Center. <u>Building a Brighter Future: Ideas for</u> <u>Educators on Child Care for Teen Parents</u>. Washington, DC: The Equality Center, 1988.
    A booklet describing strategies that schools can use to help teen parents find child care.

McGee, Elizabeth. <u>Too Little, Too Late: Services for Teenage</u> <u>Parents</u>. A report to the Ford Foundation, October, 1982.
    Outlines the basic issues and trends in programs for adolescent parents.

_____. <u>Training for Transition: A Guide for Helping Young</u> <u>Mothers Develop Employability Skills</u>. New York: Manpower Demonstration Research Corporation, 1985.
    Geared to helping educators who work with young student mothers preparing for eventual employment.

Moore, Kristin A., and L.J. Waite. "Early Childbearing and Educational Attainment," <u>Family Planning Perspectives</u>, 1977, 9(5): 220-234.
    Good analysis of relationship between early childbirth

and subsequent schooling.

Mott, Frank L., and Marsiglio. "Early Childbearing and
Completion of High School, Family Planning Perspectives.
September/October 1985, 17(5): 234-237.
    Brief, good analysis of relationship between early
childbearing and high school graduation.

Readings Describing School-Based Programs

Creating Family Life Education Programs in the Public
Schools: A Guide for State Education Policy Makers, by Susan
N. Wilson. 1985. National Association of State Boards of
Education, 701 North Fairfax Street, Suite 340, Alexandria,
VA 22314.
    An excellent handbook designed to help educators
implement family life education programs, using the New
Jersey experience as a successful example. Suggests methods
of dealing with controversy.

In School Together: School-Based Childcare Serving Student
Mothers--A Handbook. Academy for Educational Development,
1987. (See list of Resource Groups for address.)
    An excellent guide on the establishing of school-based
childcare for student mothers, with guidelines on assessing
need, staffing, curricula, etc.

Opportunities for Prevention: Building After-School and
Summer Programs for Young Adolescents. Adolescent Pregnancy
Prevention Clearinghouse, Children's Defense Fund, 1987.
(See list of Resource Groups for address.)
    Summarizes steps for creating a variety of after-school
and summer programs for young adults.

Programs at a Glance. Center for Population Options, 1986.
(See list of Resource Groups for address.)
    Describes selective diverse programs--for teen parents,
for young men, programs in religious institutions, etc. Most
useful to get a sense of what is possible and, especially, of
what is being done in local areas.

School-Based Health Clinics: A Guide to Implementing Programs. Center for Population Options, 1986. (See list of Resource Groups for address.)

    An excellent handbook covering all aspects of setting up a school-based clinic: assessing need, building community support, working with the media. Includes sample surveys, adolescent health fact sheets, etc.

Sexuality Education Strategy and Resource Guides. Set of six guides: Programs for Adolescents, Programs for Parents, Programs for Young Men, Programs in Religious Settings, Small Group Workshops, Peer Education Programs. Center for Population Options, 1983. (See list of Resource Groups for address.)

    An excellent series of pamphlets dealing with various aspects of the issues. The pamphlet, Small Group Workshops, is especially useful for professionals.

Curricula and Resource Materials

Curricula

Bingham, Mindy, Judy Edmondson, and Sandy Stryker. Choices: A Teen Woman's Journal for Self-Awareness and Personal Planning and Challenges: A Teen Male's Journal for Self-Awareness and Personal Planning. Santa Barbara, CA: Advocacy Press, 1984.

    Encourages young people to question sex-role stereotypes, to identify their individual values, and to plan for the future with regard to decisions about sex, careers, marriage, and parenthood.

Center for Population Options. Life Planning Education: A Youth Development Program. Washington, DC: Center for Population Options, 1985.

    Combines sex education with career and values exploration in a comprehensive curriculum.

Human Sexuality: Values and Choices. A Guide for Parents of Young Adolescents. 1985. A collaborative project of St. Paul Maternal and Infant Care Project and Search Institute, 122 West Franklin Ave., Minneapolis, MN 55404.

    Provides a very comprehensive family life curricula

stressing value formation, decision-making and goal setting, and communication skills. Includes activities and "games" for involving students.

Resource Materials

Barr, Linda, and Catherine Monserrat. Teenage Pregnancy: A New Beginning. Reprinted by New Futures, Inc., Alburquerque, NM, 1987.
    A prenatal health book written especially for teenagers. Reading level 5th grade. Also available in Spanish.

Bell, Ruth, et al. Changing Lives: A Book for Teens on Sex and Relationships. New York: Random House, 1981.
    Developed by the authors of Our Bodies, Ourselves, this book offers a frank exploration of such sexual issues as puberty, premarital sex, sexual response, birth control, and homosexuality. The diagrams, pictures, and personal stories from teenagers make this a popular resource book. Also available in Spanish.

Center for Population Options. The Missing Ingredient: Involving Men in Family Planning. Washington, DC: Center for Population Options, 1986.
    Brief reports on training staff, on school-based clinics serving males, on funding resources, and marketing programs.

Eagan, Andrea Boroff. Why Am I So Miserable If These Are the Best Years of My Life? New York: Avon Books, 1979.
    Covers various topics related to sexuality; encourages girls to make decisions for themselves that capitalize on changing role options for women.

It Happened to Us: Teens Speak Out about Pregnancy and Parenting. 1988. The NETWORK, Inc., 290 S. Main St., Andover, MA 01810.
    Booklet of vignettes based on interviews with more than 30 female and male adolescents. Questions to stimulate discussion follow each first-person account.

Gordon, Sol, and Judith Gordon. Girls Are Girls and Boys Are Boys. Fayetteville, NY: Ed-U Press, 1979.

Discusses human reproduction and the physical differences between boys and girls, and explicitly discourages stereotypical thinking about sex roles. For children 6-10.

Lindsay, Jeanne Warren. <u>Do I Have a Daddy?</u> Buena Park, CA: Morning Glory Press, 1982.

Depicts a young child questioning his mother about his father. With a special section on single parents. Comes with brief teacher and student guides. For young children.

_____. <u>Teens Parenting: The Challenges of Babies and Toddlers.</u> Buena Park, CA: Morning Glory Press, 1982.

An excellent handbook for young mothers. Reading level 6.6. Comes with student and teacher guides.

<u>Moving Forward Tomorrow.</u> 1988. The NETWORK, Inc. 290 S. Main St., Andover, MA 01810.

A set of six posters, four in English and two in Spanish. Each poster is 18" x 24" with a bright colored border around a black-and-white photo of a teen. The captions are quotations taken from interviews with pregnant and parenting teens.

Myers, Walter Dean. <u>Sweet Illusions</u>. New York: Teachers and Writers Collaborative, 1986.

Geared to young adults; deals with issues of sexuality and pregnancy. The book is interactive--that is, each chapter concludes with an exercise involving a question posed by one of the characters.

Waxman, Stephanie. <u>Growing-Up--Feeling Good: A Child's Guide to Sexuality.</u> Los Angeles: Panjandrum Books, 1979.

Provides an excellent introduction to human sexuality for young children.

Videos

<u>Breaking Stereotypes: Teens Talk about Raising Children.</u> 1988. Educational Equity Concepts, Inc., 114 E. 32nd St., New York, NY 10016.

Fifteen-minute video that features teen parents talking

about sex-role stereotypes in relation to young children. Discussion guide included.

Choices: The Mating Game. The Ounce of Prevention Fund, Suite 1820, 180 N. LaSalle St., Chicago, IL 60601.
 Fifty-eight minute videotape for teens about sexual decision-making.

How to Say No. Emory/Grady Teen Services Program, Box 26158, Grady Memorial Hospital, 80 Butler Street S.E., Atlanta, GA 30335.
 Program and curriculum, consisting of manual, cassette, and slides.

In Due Time. ODN Productions, 74 Varick Street N.W., New York, NY 11113.
 Provides first-person account of a young woman who chose to delay parenthood and why.

Looking for Love. Educational Cable Consortium, 24 Beechwood Rd., Summitt, NJ 07901.
 Depicts young black and Hispanic women talking about how pregnancy and motherhood affected their lives.

Mixed Messages: Teens Talk about Sex, Romance, Education, and Work. 1988. Educational Equity Concepts, Inc., 114 E. 32nd St., New York, NY 10016.
 Fifteen-minute video in which teens express their feelings about the double standard and explore myths and realities about sex, romance, education, and work. Discussion guide included.

No Time Soon. ODN Productions, 74 Varick St., New York, NY 10013.
 Provides a young man's perspective on teenage pregnancy prevention.

Your What?! Boston Women's Health Book Collective, 47 Nichols Ave., Watertown, MA 02172.
 Portrays one pregnant teen's efforts to figure out which choice (parenthood, adoption, or abortion) is best for her.

Resource Groups

Academy for Educational Development, School & Community Services Division, 100 Fifth Ave., New York, NY 10011.

Provides technical assistance, conducts research and evaluations, and publishes reports on school improvement policies and programs, including dropout prevention and adolescent pregnancy prevention programs. Operates the Support Center for Educational Equity for Young Mothers, which provides training and technical assistance to educators and policy makers on improving educational opportunities and economic changes for women who bore their first child as a teenager; initiates research and reports on effective strategies.

Bank Street College of Education, 610 W. 112th St., New York, NY 10025.

Educational resources on child development and child care. Bank Street's Teen Fathers Collaboration has resources for designing programs serving teen fathers and provides referral to agencies involved in vocational training, family planning, and employment opportunity services.

Center for Population Options, 1012 14th Street, N.W., Suite 1200, Washington, DC 20005. Support Center for School-Based Clinics, 5650 Kirby Dr., Suite 203, Houston, TX 77005.

National organization with primary objective of reducing the incidence of unintended teenage pregnancy. Provides training in the development and implementation of family life education programs. Publications on life planning and sexuality education. Also operates Support Center for School-Based Health Clinics, which acts as a national resource for clinics; sponsors programs to increase communication among practitioners; assists program developers and staff; and provides policy analysis and information on evaluation.

Children's Defense Fund, 122 C St. N.W., Washington, DC 20001.

National child advocacy and research organization; operates Adolescent Pregnancy Prevention Clearinghouse; monitors government activities; has information on subsidized care and federal and state policies; provides wide array of publications. Resource list available.

The Equality Center, 220 I St. N.E., Suite 250, Washington, DC 20002.

Policy and research center on educational equity; specialists on Title IX compliance and working with state education departments on policy regarding pregnant and parenting teenagers.

Sex Information and Education Council of U.S. (SIECUS), New York University, 32 Washington Pl., New York, NY 10003.

Operates library on human sexuality and sex education; publishes numerous annotated bibliographies on a wide range of sex education topics, including one of family life curricula and one of sex education literature arranged by age. Publishes monthly newsletter.

Publishers

These publishers offer a range of materials (print and video) on family life and sex education, reproductive health, life options, decision-making, etc. Write for a catalog of available materials.

ED-U (PRESS), 7174 Mott Rd., Fayetteville, NY 13066.

Focus (INTERNATIONAL, INC.), 14 Ocean Dr., Huntington Station, New York, NY 11748.

Morning Glory Press, 6595-F San Haroldo Way, Buena Park, CA 90620.

Network Publications, ETR Associates, P.O. Box 1830, Santa Cruz, CA 95061-1830.

The bibliography for the Teenage Childbearing chapter was prepared jointly by Michele Cahill and Elayne Archer of the Academy for Educational Development

VOCATIONAL EDUCATION

Barbara A. Bitters

Women and Work

While 65 percent of all women 18-64 years of age were in the workforce in 1985, occupational segregation on the basis of sex still exists. Women continue to make up large proportions of traditional "female" occupations such as administrative support workers (80 percent female) and retail and personal service sales workers (69 percent female). The wage gap between men and women also still exists. Women are paid 64 cents for every dollar paid to men. In addition, one out of six families (17 percent) was maintained by a woman in 1985, and women represent 61 percent of all persons (16 and over) who had incomes below the poverty level in 1984.[1]

For women of color and women with disabilities, the statistics are even more startling. In 1985, half of all black and Hispanic women workers were concentrated in low-paying clerical or service jobs and earned 10 to 16 percent less than their white counterparts. Over half of the families headed by black and Hispanic women had incomes below the poverty line.[2]

Three out of every four disabled women (76.5 percent) are not in the labor force. Of the 25 percent who are in the labor force, 15.5 percent are unemployed (double the rate of nondisabled women). Of those who are employed, 28.8 percent are clustered in the lowest level service jobs. In 1980, two out of three disabled women had incomes below the poverty line (nearly triple the rate for nondisabled women and 10.6 percent higher than the rate for disabled men).[3]

These disturbing statistics on the economic status of women have their antecedents, in part, in the educational system and particularly in the vocational education segment of that system. In the broadest sense, vocational education prepares students for the dual roles of earning wages and maintaining a household and/or family. It provides students the opportunity to formulate an understanding of work, work systems, and work rituals; to explore work choices; to develop employability skills and attitudes, and to develop specific competencies for a chosen occupation.

What is Vocational Sex Equity?

The term "sex equity" describes an environment in which individuals can consider options and make choices based on their abilities and talents, not on the basis of gender stereotypes and biased expectations. The achievement of vocational sex equity enables women and men, regardless of race, ethnicity, and disability, to develop skills needed in the home and in the paid work force, skills that are best suited to an individual's informed interests and abilities. It opens economic, social, and political opportunities for all people. Sex equity in vocational education involves creating an educational environment that allows all students to <u>choose</u> vocational programs and careers without regard to biased expectation and to <u>enter</u>, to <u>participate</u> fully in, and <u>benefit</u> from those programs.

What Are the Issues?

Historically, vocational education enrollments have been highly sex segregated. Schools heavily reinforced traditional sex-role stereotypes in course offerings, curriculum materials, and counseling and guidance programs, which served to reflect and perpetuate outdated, limited occupational and family roles for both females and males. In fact, prior to the mid-1970s, females still were encouraged to prepare solely for the role of full-time homemaker or were led to believe they would work only a few years in a low paying, dead-end "female" occupation. Verheyden-Hilliard wrote in 1975 that girls in vocational education were being prepared for "Cinderellahood" rather than jobs.[4] For female students with disabilities the situation is greatly exacerbated. Typically, vocational education has offered male students with disabilities far more in the way of options and services. In a landmark 1974 article, Patricia Gillespie and Albert Fink described how sex bias in vocational training programs for students with disabilities limits the development of female students, leading to the economic dependence and lines of poverty that are confirmed by the statistics stated earlier.[5]

Access

Access to nontraditional courses and to some vocational
schools was legally and practically denied to females and
males prior to Title IX of the Educational Amendments (1972)
and the Vocational Education Act (1976).[6] Many schools had
policies requiring completion of different vocational courses
by males and females prior to graduation. Courses like
"Bachelor Living" and "Powder Puff Mechanics" maintained the
separation of the sexes in vocational education. Females'
access to quality vocational, work study, job placement,
cooperative, and apprenticeship programs was limited and/or
stereotyped. Membership in certain vocational student
organizations was restricted to members of one sex. (The
Future Farmers of America voted to allow female members in
1969.) In 1974, almost 50 percent of all female students in
vocational education were in consumer home economics,
training for unpaid work in the home. Another 29 percent of[7]
females were training for entry-level clerical occupations.
Male students were concentrated in agriculture and industrial
education.

Administrative and vocational staff patterns still
reflect traditional sex distributions in instructional areas.
Across the country males hold substantial majorities of
positions in the program areas of Agricultural, Marketing,
Technical, Trade and Industrial, and Industrial Arts.
Females hold similarly sizable majorities of positions in
Health Occupations, Home Economics (Wage-Earning and
Consumer), and Business. Administrative positions are held
predominantly by males. The lack of nontraditional educator
role models acts as a barrier for students who are unable to
see someone like themselves succeeding in a nontraditional
vocational area.

Sex-Biased Attitudes

Attitudes of educators, students, parents, and employers
reflect outdated and inaccurate information about labor force
participation and a clear belief that there are "men's" jobs
and "women's" jobs. These attitudes limit students' career
aspirations and occupational choices. Frequently traditional
attitudes about the "proper" role and abilities of females
contribute to a hostile learning environment for females who
have made nontraditional vocational choices. More recently,
sexual harassment of young women in vocational classrooms and
labs nontraditional for their sex is being recognized as an

important issue to be addressed.[8]

Boys are discouraged from pursuing programs in cosmetology, nursing, health, administrative support services, and other fields nontraditional for their sex. Assumptions are made about the financial aspirations of boys, and questions about their masculinity are often raised.

Vocational Guidance and Counseling

Prior to Title IX and the Vocational Educational Act of 1976, practices, materials, and assessment tools reflected traditional sex-role stereotypes, with different scales used to measure interests and aptitudes of females and males. Research in the 1970s revealed that adolescent males were aware of a greater number of occupations, had higher occupational aspirations, and expected to achieve them. Adolescent females were aware of a limited number of occupations, had lower aspirations and expectations of career achievements. Many counselors have not kept pace with the changing labor market or the changing roles of males and females, and few actively have incorporated this information into their counseling practices.

Support Services for Females

Lack of support services in the educational setting act as greater barriers to female participation than male participation in vocational education. This is particularly true for low-income women, older women returning to school after many years, women of color, single parents, women with disabilities, and women seeking nontraditional occupations. Support services needed include: child care, transportation assistance, accessible transportation and classrooms, financial aid, flexible class scheduling, special counseling and guidance, remedial classes, role models, peer support groups, community mentors, pre-vocational assessment, and job development and placement services.

Unequal Opportunities

Manifestations of sex bias in the teaching/learning environment create unequal educational opportunities for females. Even in coeducational classrooms, examples of sex bias persist in: vocational texts and instructional materials that not only reflect, but exaggerate traditional, stereotyped roles and a "traditional" division of labor; curriculum that is geared to the interests and needs of only one sex; instructional practices that divide students into single sex groups; student evaluations that use different criteria for grading males and females; teacher expectations that differentiate between male and female students; unequal funding for equipment, labs, and student projects in female intensive vocational programs; and a higher ratio of students to teachers in female intensive vocational programs.

Follow-up studies of vocational education students indicate that differences in "pay off" or benefits exist between male and female graduates. A wage-gap exists one year after graduation and increases over time. Males seem to move up career ladders more quickly. Male nontraditional workers may not experience the same level of hazing, harassment, or constant demands to prove their competence.

Economic and Social Changes

The conditions and practices in vocational education outlined above pose a stark contrast to the changes relating to women's participation in the paid labor force taking place from the 1960s up to the present day. Testimony presented before education committees of the U.S. Congress from 1970 to 1984 emphasized the gap between preparation in vocational education and the reality girls and women faced after graduation. Inequality between male and female workers is reflected in and partially created by the sex segregation, bias, role stereotyping, and discrimination present in vocational stereotyping.

Deep-rooted and enduring social and economic changes have occurred during the last twenty years. Despite this, few educators and counselors are informing students how these workforce and social changes might affect their lifestyles and work plans. Vocational educators have to broaden their perceptions of the educational needs of male and female students of all races and various mental and physical abilities. Students must leave school better prepared to function successfully in a society characterized by changing conditions and expectations.

Activities and Strategies

Vocational and sex equity activities are focused on career, vocational education, and employment and training activities and programs. To be effective, equity change agents need to be informed about:

o Career and vocational needs of males and females regardless of sex, race/ethnicity, or disability from kindergarten to returning adult students. This includes special target groups such as teen parents, single parents, displaced homemakers, and at-risk students.

o Various vocational education program areas, vocational guidance, career education, and employment/training programs.

o Variety of institutions and organizations that deliver vocational education: comprehensive high schools; regional vocational schools and centers; postsecondary vocational, technical, and community colleges; community-based organizations; and employers.

o Functions and relationships between the state and local educational agencies and teacher preparation programs and how equity goals can be infused in each organization's current agenda.

o How to coordinate effectively other state and local government agencies and programs (e.g. JTPA and Welfare) and statewide advocacy/interest groups.

Local level strategies encompass areas ranging from policy-making to awareness training. Vocational equity specialists conduct staff development workshops; community, employers, and parent equity awareness programs; and student awareness activities. They develop affirmative guidance programs, which include student recruitment and the provision of support services.

In the curriculum area, equity specialists develop materials to supplement the existing models and revise and

reconstruct the traditional vocational education curriculum.
In working with administrators, equity specialists assist
school systems in evaluating their equity needs and in
planning actions to achieve greater equity. At the policy
level, they revise or develop policies, procedures, and
practices that support equity.

At the state level, equity strategies include: statewide
data collection and analysis, planning, and policy
development; equity resource development; provision of
assistance to local school districts, i.e., advice on
compliance with nondiscrimination requirements; funding,
monitoring, and evaluating local equity projects; and intra-
agency/inter-agency networking and coordinating to maximize
the achievement of common equity goals. Equity specialists
also provide staff development, curriculum development,
special project and program development, and information on
promising equity strategies and methods.

The initial search for vocational sex equity materials
took place in the ERIC database, using the following
descriptors in various combinations: female(s), male(s), sex
equity, equity, equal educational opportunities, vocational
education, career education, agriculture, business education,
home economics, health occupations, marketing education,
industrial arts, and technology education. In addition,
catalogs and materials in current use by vocational sex
equity professionals were explored.

The bibliography is divided into two categories:
Curriculum and Teacher/Training Resources. While the
majority of the listings are for grades seven through twelve,
a few curricular resources for K-6 have been listed as well
as some postsecondary materials that address the needs of
reentry women. Criteria for inclusion were: publication in
1980 or after unless the resource is considered a "classic";
representation of diverse topics/target populations;
successful use by the reviewer and/or equity professionals in
vocational education.

Annotations were not included for products from the
following sources because the catalogs are readily available:
Educational Development Center/The Women's Educational Equity
Act Publishing Center, the Ohio Center for Research in
Vocational Education, and the Women's Bureau, Department of
Labor. Readers seeking resource material are urged to

contact their states' vocational sex equity administrator
(formerly coordinators) through the state education agency
and/or the state board for vocational education.

Notes

1. Women's Bureau, U.S. Department of Labor, Twenty Facts on
Women Workers (Washington, D.C.: 1986).

2. National Commission on Working Women, An Overview of
Women in the Workforce (Washington, D.C.: 1986).

3. Frank Bowes, Disabled Women in America: A Statistical
Report Drawn from Census Bureau Data (Washington, D.C.: The
President's Committee on Employment of the Handicapped, n.d.
1980-1982 statistics).

4. Mary Ellen Verheyden-Hilliard, "Cinderella Doesn't Live
Here Anymore," Womanpower (November 1975).

5. Patricia H. Gillespie and Albert H. Fink, "The Influence
of Sexism on the Education of Handicapped Children,"
Exceptional Children, Vol. 41, No. 3, (1974), pp. 158-159.

6. The Vocational Education Act prohibiting sex
discrimination in vocational education was passed· in 1976
with guidelines issued by the Office of Civil Rights in 1980.
In 1984, The Act, now known as the Carl D. Perkins Vocational
Educational Act, was reauthorized to continue through 1989.

7. Mary Ellen Verheyden-Hilliard, "Cinderella Doesn't Live
Here Anymore."

8. See Sexual Harassment in the Schools. This publication,
prepared by the Northwest Women's Law Center for the State of
Washington (under a grant from the Women's Educational Equity
Act) includes definitions, legal remedies, and a bibliography
of research strategies. Pages 36-37 contain a sample Sexual
Harrassment Policy for High Schools and Vocational Schools.
"Sexual Harrassment in the Schools," a 15 minute slide/tape
show on sexual harrassment in the secondary and vocational
schools, is listed in the bibliography, and the
Teacher/Training Resources section lists several exemplary
programs at the high school level.

9. Charlotte J. Farris, Expanding Adolescent Role
Expectations (Ithaca, NY: Cornell University, 1978).

BIBLIOGRAPHY

Curriculum

American Institutes for Research. <u>Classroom Activities to Combat Stereotyping in Career Choice</u>. Palo Alto, CA: American Institutes for Research, 1980. ED187886.
    Provides student activities designed to reduce sex-role, race, and disability stereotyping in career choice and career education. Related staff awareness and training document is included. A classic.

Bingham, Mindy, Judy Edmondson, and Sandy Stryker. <u>Challenges: A Young Man's Journal for Self-Awareness and Personal Planning</u>. Santa Barbara, CA: Advocacy Press, 1984.
    Provides written activities in journal style to help young men become aware of career and changing sex-role issues. Considered a pre-career education curriculum. Designed to be used with <u>Choices</u> (see below).

     . <u>Choices: A Teen Woman's Journal for Self-Awareness and Personal Planning</u>. Santa Barbara, CA: Advocacy Press, 1983.
    Provides written activities in journal style to help young women become aware of career and changing sex-role issues. Considered a pre-career education curriculum. A classic.

Bingham, Mindy, and Sandy Stryker. <u>More Choices: A Strategic Planning Guide for Mixing Career and Family</u>. Santa Barbara, CA: Advocacy Press, 1987.
    Continuation of <u>Choices</u>. Provides continued direction and planning ideas with special emphasis on managing both career and family with the resources available.

Bitters, Barbara. "Gender Equity and Teen Parents--An Important Connection." <u>Career Survival Kit for Teen Education and Employment</u>. Ann Arbor, MI: University of Michigan, 1985.
    A student introduction to sexual harassment issues, legal rights, and suggested ways of dealing with harassment.

Dougherty, Barbara, Jan Novak, and LaVonne Reschke. <u>Ready, Set, Go!</u> Madison, WI: Madison Vocational Studies Center, 1986.

A project aimed at assisting/guiding women and girls who are disabled with personal growth, career decision-making, education and employment success. Also discusses how to secure the support services needed. Materials are based on the experiences of twelve girls and women with disabilities. Project products include a two-volume staff handbook, student/client workbook, and three videotapes.

Educational Equity Center for the Pacific. <u>Oceans of Options: Sex Equity Lessons for the Classroom.</u> San Francisco: Far West Laboratory for Educational Research and Development, 1983.

Sex-equity activities for elementary school children. Includes bias-free career education materials.

Equal Goals in Occupations Project. <u>Rainbow, Shave Ice, Crackseed, and Other Ono Stuff: Sex Equity Goodies for the Classroom.</u> Honolulu, HI: Office of the State Director of Vocational Education, 1984.

Sex equity activities for use in the vocational classroom grades 7-12. Activities were created from vocational equity classics.

Farris, Charlotte, et al. <u>Move On Together: Classroom Activities For Vocational Equity</u> Utica, NY: Project MOVE, SUNY College of Technology, 1981.

A collection of 50 tested classroom teaching activities by occupational course. A good example of how to infuse equity into existing vocational courses.

Gassman, Roberta, and Nancy Deutsch. <u>Increasing Options through Life/Work Planning.</u> Madison, WI: Wisconsin Department of Public Instruction and Women's Education Resources, 1986.

A life-work planning workbook based on Bolles model for students 13-18 years. Recently revised, it stresses the need for both girls and boys to prepare for the dual roles of family work and paid work outside the home. Used extensively by counselors, home economics teachers, and JTPA youth programs.

Gassman, Roberta, Nancy Deutsch, and Lonnie Weiss. Maximizing Options for Students in Business. Madison, WI: Wisconsin Department of Public Instruction and Waunakee Community Schools, 1983.
    Instructional materials and teachers guide for grades 9-12. Presents important emerging issues in business education, the impact of microcomputer technology, sex equity, occupational segregation, wage inequity, and career survival and upward mobility skills.

Los Angeles Unified School District. CAREERWAYS: A Multimedia Real-Life Career Education Program for Grades 7-12. Los Angeles: Los Angeles Unified School District, n.d.
    A multimedia program (great up-beat videotapes) designed to raise student awareness about work, career, and stereotyping. Validated and disseminated by the National Diffusion Network (NDN)

Mahrt, James, and Joyce Fouts. Expanding Career Options: A Model Sex Equity Program Wayne, MI: Wayne County Intermediate School District, 1980. ED206850 and ED206951.
    A compilation of activities on sex bias and stereotyping for teachers 7-12. Activities were compiled and adapted from exemplary projects.

Matthews, Martha, and Shirley McCune. Try It, You'll Like It! A Student's Introduction to Nonsexist Vocational Education. Washington, DC: Resource Center on Sex Roles in Education, 1978. ED170520.
    Probably the first secondary-level student guide to considering nontraditional jobs. The employment statistics are now out of date. A classic.

Michigan Career Education and Vocational Education Resource Center. Achieving Sex Equity Through Students (ASETS). East Lansing, MI: Michigan State University, 1984-85.
    After raising student and teacher awareness of sex equity in career and vocational education, this model provides a guide for male and female teams of students to work with other students in their home school.

_____. Expanding Career Options (ECO). East Lansing, MI: Michigan State University, 1982-85.

A four-week lesson guide designed to create awareness of vocational sex equity issues and assist students in exploring alternatives to traditional work and family roles. The trainer's guide and counselor's guide outline a two-day and one-day workshop for educators.

Sadker, David. Being a Man: A Unit of Instructional Activities on Male Role Stereotyping. Washington, DC: The American University, 1980.

Provides classroom strategies and eight lesson plans that explore attitudes and feelings about male sex-roles and stereotypes. To be used with junior high school students. A classic.

Project ESTEEM. Sexual Harassment: It's Uncool. 1988. Honolulu: Hawaii Department of Education, P.O. Box 2360, Honolulu, HI 96804

A poster, with accompanying brochure, describing the many forms sexual harassment can take.

TABS: Organization for Equal Education of the Sexes, Inc. Career Posters. New York: OEES, 438 Fourth St., Brooklyn, NY 11215.

Posters of contemporary women working in a wide variety of jobs and occupations. Multicultural; each includes a brief biography. In addition, there are a wide variety of posters on women, including a series on women with disabilities, that provide excellent role models.

University of New Mexico. Choosing What's Best for You. Albuquerque: University of New Mexico, 1982.

Student workbook with exercises on self-image, relationships, education, and career futures. Infuses equity concepts and provides students with the opportunity to discuss stereotyping, male/female roles, and discrimination in schools or on the job.

Teacher/Training Resources

American Vocational Association. Women in Vocational Education Administration. Alexandria, VA: American Vocational Association, 1985.

A computerized directory of women in vocational

administrative positions and several articles by women
leaders in vocational education.

Bitters, Barbara. "Equity and the Vocational Curriculum."
Madison, WI: Wisconsin Department of Public Instruction,
Vocational Equity Office, 1987.
   Describes four stages for infusing equity into the
vocational curriculum.   Also discusses student equity
competencies.

Bowe, Frank. <u>Disabled Women in America</u>. Washington, DC: The
President's Committee on Employment of the Handicapped, 1984.
   Reports findings about disabled women in America from
1981 and 1982 Current Population Survey. Areas covered are
age, education, residence, geographical area, marital status,
employment, income, and occupational category.

<u>Career Opportunity News</u>. Garrett Park Press, Garrett Park,
MD 20896.
   Newsletter publishes information on emerging careers,
job opening predictions, and women in the workforce; includes
resources.

Center for Women's Services. <u>Road Map to Change: A Workbook</u>
<u>for the Development of Nonbiased Instructional Materials</u>.
Kalamazoo, MI: Western Michigan University, 1979.
   A workbook to prepare educators to review and identify
sex bias in vocational education instructional materials.

Chasek, Arlene. <u>Futures Unlimited: Expanding Choices in</u>
<u>Nontraditional Careers</u>. New Brunswick, NJ: Rutgers, The
State University of New Jersey, 1985.
   A conference planning handbook adapted from the
"Expanding Your Horizons in Science and Mathematics" model
developed by the Mills College Math/Science Network. Write
for information about other <u>Futures Unlimited</u> resource
materials such as posters and videotapes.

Christian, M. <u>Breaking through Barriers: Workers Who Are</u>
<u>Disabled</u>. Lincroft, NJ: Brookdale Community College and New
Jersey Department of Education, 1984.
   Descriptions of female role models with disabilities:

dancer, printer, student, office worker, auditor, boutique manager, computer engineer, social worker, research neurochemist, actor, lecturer, mechanic, and teacher.

Dunphy, Gail. Careers Don't Come in Pink or Blue. A Career/Life Planning Workshop Guide for Teachers. Providence, RI: Rhode Island Department of Community Affairs, 1985.
　　Guide to teach students how to explore the many career options available and create awareness of how sex bias and stereotyping negatively affects career and life choices. Written to try and prevent young women from becoming future Displaced Homemakers.

Equity Works! Educational Equity Concepts, Inc., 114 E. 32nd St., New York, NY 10016.
　　Two 20-minute videotapes are excellent for training. 5 to 50 Plus covers a range of topics. Vocational Education features four nontraditional students and their principal talking positively about equity in vocational education.

Farris, Charlotte. Expanding Adolescent Role Expectations: Information, Activities, Resources for Vocational Educators. Utica, NY: Project MOVE, SUNY College of Technology, 1978.
　　This "aging" document is still one of the most helpful because of the two-page fact sheets that summarize research findings. A classic.

Gedney, Curt, and Lynn O'Hern. Puzzles, Patterns, Pathways. Tucson, AZ: University of Arizona, 1986.
　　An excellent counseling manual focusing on the needs of single parents and homemakers in transition. Contains strategies for helping women in transition look inward (self-concept/esteem, emotions and values) and outward at career and education choices.

Gibbs, Gloria. Sex Equity in the Construction Trades. Salem, OR: Oregon State Department of Education, 1981.
　　Sex equity instructional models for construction occupations.

Good, James, and Mary Ann DeVore. Expanding Options: A Model

to Attract Secondary Students into Nontraditional Vocational
Programs. Columbia, MO: University of Missouri, 1981.
      Good compilation of influence factors and strategies to
increase enrollments at the secondary school level.
Materials are targeted at attracting females to building
trades, electronics, and welding; males to health services.

Gutek, Barbara, and Laurie Larwood. Women's Career
Development. Newbury Park, CA: SAGE Publications, 1987.
      Ten essays in career development issues for women. The
last chapter looks at five concerns: career preparations, the
opportunities available in society, the influence of
marriage, the influence of pregnancy and children, and timing
and age. The authors use these topics to discuss career path
options and to stimulate additional research.

Harrison, Laurie, and Peter Dahl. Executive Summary:
Vocational Education Equity Study. Palo Alto, CA: American
Institutes for Research, 1979.
      A summary of the congressionally mandated study to
determine the extent to which sex discrimination and
stereotyping exist in vocational education programs.
Discusses the progress as of 1978 that has been made to
reduce or eliminate sex-role stereotyping, bias, and
discrimination in vocational education. The full study is
four volumes.

Institute for Information Studies. The Dream's Not Enough:
Portraits of Successful Women with Disabilities. Falls
Church, VA: Institute for Information Studies, 1981.
      Provides information sources for women with disabilities
interested in nontraditional professional careers, including
professional groups, women's groups, disability groups, lists
of publications covering life stories of women who succeeded
in nontraditional careers, and career counseling resources.

The Institute for Women's Concerns. Increasing Sex Equity--
The Impact of the 1976 Vocational Education Amendments on Sex
Equity in Vocational Education. Washington, DC: National
Advisory Council on Vocational Education and National
Advisory Council on Women's Education Programs, 1980 and
1982.
      A joint report of two national advisory council's study
of the 1976 VEA sex equity provisions. Includes analysis of

15 different states' enrollment trends, state plans, and reports. Outlines issues that are still relevant in the vocational equity field.

Jones, S. "If You Are Disabled and Female, You're Probably Out of Work." In Mainstream Magazine of the Able-Disabled, 9 (10), 11, 1985.
  Statistics from a study done for the President's Committee on Employment of the Handicapped showing the high unemployment rate of disabled women.

Klein, Freada, Nancy Wilber, et al. Who's Hurt and Who's Liable: Sexual Harassment in Massachusetts Schools. Quincy, MA: Massachusetts Department of Education, 1986. ED 215254.
  This guide defines sexual harassment, explains the legal issues, describes administrative strategies, presents student activities, and contains classroom lessons. Intended for administrators, counselors, teachers, and students.

Knight, James. Developing Model for Recruitment, Retention, and Placement of Female Students in Secondary Vocational Education Programs Which Have Traditionally Been for Males. Columbus, OH: Agricultural Curriculum Materials Service, Ohio State University, 1980. ED195823.
  One of the early studies of ten "successful" vocational programs in recruiting, retaining, and placing female students in nontraditional areas. Conclusions will be helpful in designing sex equity programs.

Larson, Beverly. Promoting Sex Equity in the Classroom: A Bibliography. Des Moines: Iowa Department of Public Instruction, 1982.
  Includes all the classics. Intended for vocational instructors, counselors, advisory council members, teacher educators, and curriculum specialists. Includes print, audio-visual, and nonprint materials.

Lizotte, Paul, and Roger Lizotte. Women Working. Salem, NH: Tri-Equity, n.d.
  Describes nontraditional technical careers for women. Designed to be used by counselors working with high school or adult women. There is a companion booklet, Working Women: Physical Fitness.

Marks, E., and A. Lewis. <u>Job Hunting for the Disabled</u>.
Woodbury, NY: Barron's Educational Series, 1983.
      Shows the job hunter how to define goals, conduct a job
search, and build a rewarding career.   Includes a self-
assessment questionnaire, sample resumes, and cover letters.

Marzone, Jean. <u>Promising Programs for Sex-Fair Vocational</u>
<u>Education</u>.   San Francisco: Far West Laboratory for
Educational Research and Development, 1981.   ED208195.
      Documents forty-seven programs/approaches to sex fair
vocational education developed at the state level.

Massachusetts Department of Education. <u>A Guide to Making Low</u>
<u>Cost Videotapes of Nontraditional Role Models</u>.   Quincy, MA:
Massachusetts Department of Education, 1983.
      This practical guide gives advice on creating videotapes
for use in recruitment and career education.

McCune, Shirley, and Martha Matthews. <u>Building Sex Equity in</u>
<u>Vocational Education: An Inservice Training Program</u>.
Washington, DC: Resource Center on Sex Roles in Education,
1980.
      A model training program.   Includes four workshops
addressing the need for sex equity in vocational education,
legal mandates (does not include the most recent federal
requirements under the Carl Perkins Act), building individual
skills, and programs for change in vocational education.

McGrath, Mimi, and Rhonda Pekelo-Bielen.   <u>You Can Do It!</u>
<u>Volume 1, Planning Your Approach</u> and <u>You Can Do It!   Volume</u>
<u>2, Choosing Strategies That Are Right for You</u>.   Quincy, MA:
Massachusetts Department of Education, 1983.
      Massachusetts takes a comprehensive equity approach
(race, sex, disability, economic status, etc.) in most of
their publications.   These describe successful strategies for
recruiting students, especially "priority population
students."

_____. <u>Future Shares: Expanding the Career and Educational</u>
<u>Opportunities of Vocational School Students</u>.   Quincy, MA:
Massachusetts Department of Education, 1984.
      A four-part workbook of strategies and techniques that
vocational educators can use to promote sex equity in their

programs. Focus of activities is on nontraditional training, but the goal is to help both staff and students understand sex equity issues.

Michigan Career Education and Vocational Education Resource Center. NETWORK Implementation Guides. East Lansing, MI: Michigan State University, 1983.
    Eleven practical, short, "how-to" guides for implementing sex equity strategies in vocational education.

National Alliance of Business. Women in Poverty: Roads to Independence. Washington, DC: National Alliance of Business, 1986.
    Two-page summaries of nineteen programs that help poor women become economically self-sufficient. Programs funded under welfare reform efforts, JTPA, and vocational education. The summaries (see titles below) are available from the Ohio Center for Research in Vocational Education at Ohio State University. (Call 800-848-4815 for annual catalog or write to The Ohio State University, 1960 Kenny Road, Columbus, Ohio, 43210.)

    Factors Influencing Nontraditional Vocational Education Enrollments: A Literature Review. 1979. A classic.

    Entrepreneurship for Women: An Unfulfilled Agenda. 1981.

    Equity from a Vocational Education Perspective. 1982.

    ERIC Update on Career and Vocational Education Programs for Female, Handicapped, and Disadvantaged Students. 1984.

    Guess Who's Coming to Work. 1986.

    A Guide for Vocational Education Sex Equity Personnel. 1985.

    Guidelines for Sex-Fair Vocational Education Materials. 1978. A classic.

    Sex Equity Strategies, 2d. ed. 1980. A classic.

    Sex Fairness in Vocational Education. 1977. A classic.

Otto, Luther B. How to Help Your Child Choose a Career. New York: M. Evans and Company, 1984.

An excellent parent education program on careers, labor market information, and educational options. Includes a discussion of changing sex roles and the need for educational equity. This book is to be used with an eight-hour workshop for parents.

Polit, Denise. Building Self-Sufficiency: A Guide to Vocational and Employment Services for Teenage Parents. Jefferson City, MO: Humanalysis, 1986.

A handbook that summarizes the state-of-the-art with regard to the provision of vocational and employment-related services to teen parents. Based on responses from 200 teen parent specialists nationwide.

Project on the Status of Women. The Classroom Climate: A Chilly One for Women? and Out of the Classroom: A Chilly Campus Climate for Women? Washington, DC: Association of American Colleges, 1982 and 1984.

Examines the postsecondary experience of women: how men and women are treated differently and the effect on female students' confidence and achievement. Both are classics.

Ruffner, R.H. "Just Where's the Barrier? A New Look at Employer Attitudes." In Disabled USA, 4 (10), 3-6, 1981.

Findings based on a survey of employers show the barriers to employment of persons who are disabled: lack of marketable skills, inadequate job preparation, difficulty locating qualified employees, system disincentives which discourage entering the job market, and insufficient information and corporate training programs dealing with disability.

Sanders, Jo Schucat. The Nuts and Bolts of NTO. New York: Women's Action Alliance, 1981.

The most comprehensive guide available for educators and job training program operators on the special techniques needed to help women and girls take advantage of occupational preparation that leads to higher wage/higher benefit, nontraditional, technical, and skilled jobs. A classic.

_____, Antonia Stone, and Women's Action Alliance. <u>The
Neuter Computer: Computers for Girls and Boys</u>. New York:
Neal Schuman Publishers, 1986.

Designed to help parents, educators, and policy-makers
provide computer equity for females and males. Includes a
self-test, activities for computer excellence, strategies for
computer equity, and guidelines for planning and evaluating a
computer equity program in a school. Important to vocational
education because 50 to 70 percent of jobs in the future will
involve computers.

Schulzinger, Rhoda, and Lisa Syron. <u>Inch by Inch--Report on
Equal Opportunity for Young Women in New York City's
Vocational High Schools</u>. New York: Full Access and Rights to
Education Coalition, Center for Public Advocacy Research,
1984.

A report on the problems and progress in New York City
Schools with regard to sex segregation and bias in vocational
education.

Scotch, R.K. <u>From the Good Will to Civil Rights:
Transforming Federal Disability Policy</u>. Philadelphia: Temple
University Press, 1983.

Reviews the letter and spirit of the Vocational
Rehabilitation Act from the 1970s to the 1980s and discusses
how legislation applies to rights such as advocacy,
employment, and accessibility.

Scott, Joyce, Rhonda Pekelo-Bielen, and David Coughlin.
<u>Making It Work: An Inservice Program for Vocational
Educators</u>. Quincy, MA: Massachusetts Department of
Education, 1983.

An inservice package designed to train vocational
educators in retention, placement, curriculum, and learning
environment adaptation for priority populations.

Shelton-Walters, Christine, and Carole Oglesby. <u>Women
Working: Physical Fitness</u>. Salem, NH: Tri-Equity, n.d.

Excellent resource for women interested in
nontraditional careers. Outlines steps for both emotional
and physical fitness in preparation for physically demanding
work.

Smith, Amanda, and Charlotte Farris. Pioneering Programs in Sex Equity: A Teacher's Guide. Arlington, VA: The American Vocational Association, 1980.
  Comprehensive guide for teachers on the issues, facts, and how-to of promoting sex equity in vocational education.

Smith, Amanda. New Pioneers: A Program to Expand Sex Role Expectations in Elementary and Secondary Education. Raleigh, NC: North Carolina Department of Public Transportation, 1978. ED145192.
  A week-long inservice workshop guide for educators. A classic.

Stearner, S.P. Able Scientists—Disabled Persons: Careers in the Sciences. Oakbrook, IL: John Racila Associates, 1984.
  Contains over 25 biographical sketches illustrating people with disabilities who have careers in the sciences (approximately one-third are women).

University of the State of New York. Expanding Student Opportunities in Occupational Education: Methods to Reduce Sex-role Stereotyping in Program Choice. Albany: New York State Education Department, 1982.
  Report of a study to develop activities and materials to assist secondary-level students to move beyond stereotyped career choices. Discussion and student activities included.

Wells, Janet, ed. A Good Start: Improving Opportunities for Women Under the Vocational Education Act. Washington, DC: Federal Education Project, Lawyer's Committee for Civil Rights Under Law, 1982.
  A summary of the congressional hearings considering the impact of the VEA 1976 sex equity provisions and recommendations for the Carl Perkins Vocational Education Act of 1984. Good summary of status of males and females in vocational education and what state and federal agencies are doing and not doing to eliminate inequity.

Weston, Kathleen. The Apprenticeship and Blue Collar System: Putting Women on the Right Track. Sacramento: California Department of Education, 1981.
  A systems approach to getting women into apprenticeship, blue collar, and skilled jobs.

Wider Opportunities for Women. <u>Bridging the Skills Gap:</u>
<u>Women and Jobs in a High Tech World</u>. Washington, DC: Wider
Opportunities for Women, 1983.

Three products are available from a one-year project:
"Changing Technologies: Changing Jobs for Women?," which is a
general overview of the issues of a changing labor market;
"High Technology: A Primer," which clarifies and defines
"high technology"; and "Women and High Technology: An
Annotated Bibliography."

Wisconsin Board of Vocational, Technical and Adult Education.
<u>Excellence Through Equity</u>. Madison, WI: Wisconsin Board of
Vocational, Technical and Adult Education, 1983.

Resources for achieving sex equity at the postsecondary
vocational-technical school level. Background readings and
activities.

_____. <u>Exploring Nontraditional Training Options: Focus on</u>
<u>Women</u>. Madison, WI: Wisconsin Board of Vocational, Technical
and Adult Education, 1983.

Outlines nontraditional pre-enrollment courses for women
at a number of post-secondary VTAE districts in Wisconsin.

_____. <u>Changing Roles of Men & Women: Implications for</u>
<u>Vocational Education</u>. Madison, WI: Wisconsin Board of
Vocational, Technical and Adult Education, 1984.

A graduate level course for instructors in the
postsecondary VTAE system in Wisconsin. Goals of the course
are to increase participant's understanding of sex-equity
related issues and to foster local activities.

Women's Bureau. Washington, DC: U.S. Department of Labor,
1978-86.

Good materials (see titles below) addressing women and
employment.

<u>The Coal Employment Project: How Women Can Make</u>
<u>Breakthroughs into Nontraditional Industries</u>. 1985.

<u>Employment-Focused Programs for Adolescent Mothers</u>.
1986.

<u>Employment Programs for Rural Women</u>. 1985.

From Homemaking to Entrepreneurship: A Readiness Training Program. 1985.

National Women's Employment and Education Project. 1985.

Time of Change: 1983 Handbook on Women Workers. 1983.

20 Facts on Women Workers. Fact Sheet No. 86-1. 1986.

The United Nations Decade for Women, 1976-1985: Employment in the United States. 1985.

A Woman's Guide to Apprenticeship. 1980.

Women in Nontraditional Careers (WINC), Curriculum Guide. 1984.

Women Who Maintain Families. Fact Sheet No. 86-2. 1986.

A Working Woman's Guide to Her Job Rights. 1984.

Young Women and Employment: What We Know and Need to Know About the School-to-Work Transition. 1978. ED163113. A classic.

Women's Educational Equity Act Publishing Center. Newton, MA: EDC/Women's Educational Equity Act Publishing Center, 1977-86.
Materials (see titles below) developed under the Women's Educational Equity Program Act.

ASPIRE: Awareness of Sexual Prejudice is the Responsibility of Educators.

Born Free: Training Packet to Reduce Sex-Role Stereotyping in Career Development.

Career Educational Resource Kit. An Annotated Bibliography of Nonsexist Resources.

Career Planning for Minority Women.

Choices/Changes: An Investigation of Alternative Occupational Role Models.

Choosing Occupations and Life Roles.

Connections: Women and Work and Skills for Good Jobs.

Critical Events Shaping Women's Identity. A Handbook
for the Helping Professions.

Every Women's Right. The Right to Quality Education and
Economic Independence.

Expanding Options.

Freeing Ourselves. Removing Internal Barriers to
Equality.

It's Her Future.

Learning from Experience.

Life Skills for Women in Transition.

Minority Woman's Survival Kit. Personal and
Professional Development for Minority Women.

Placing Rural Minority Women in Training Situations for
Nontraditional Jobs.

Project Choice: Creating Her Options in Career
Exploration.

Revising the Curriculum. Teacher Skill Guide for
Combatting Sexism.

Whole Person Book I and II: Toward Self-Discovery and
Life Options.

Wong, Shirley. Resources and References for Sex-Fair
Vocational Education. San Francisco: Far West Laboratory for
Educational Research and Development, 1981. ED208230.
     Bibliography of vocational equity resources. Includes
references for materials developed in each of the fifty
states which are not often listed in ERIC or other sources.

LIBRARIES AND MEDIA CENTERS

Marylin A. Hulme

I like reading books in the bulk. Lately my diet
has become a trifle monotonous; history is too much
about wars; biography too much about great men;
poetry has[1] shown a tendency, I think, to
sterility...

Librarians are in a unique position within a school
system to effect change through an open and representative
collection of materials: trade books, magazines, journals,
audiovisual materials, and all types of supplementary
materials. This bibliography is included in this volume to
provide the school librarian and media specialist with
information and resources to search out materials for the
school library which provide nonstereotyped information and
positive role models for all female and male students.
Included is a basic list of reference materials specifically
on issues pertaining to women, people of color, different
ethnic groups, people with disabilities, and the issues of
sex roles and stereotyping.

School librarians and media specialists already will
have an excellent background in general conventional library
matters and the expertise to deal with students in the
library classroom, teaching them library skills and providing
them with a wide selection of materials. What some may not
be aware of, however, is the need to examine the collection,
the collection development strategies, and selections
policies from the perspective of educational equity, which
extends to include bulletin boards and displays, and even the
subject catalog.

In addition, librarians, like most teachers (and indeed
all of us) no doubt unwittingly show bias toward students in
terms of equal treatment and access to services. This
introduction, then, serves to alert readers to educational
equity as it relates the role of the school librarian and to
issues of equity in school library collections.

The Role of the School Librarian Vis a Vis Equity

When librarians discuss equity in the school library and focus on their role in addressing issues of sex roles, stereotyping and bias, the following questions need to be addressed:

o   Girls will read books about males to a greater degree than boys will read books about females. Are there "girls' books" and "boys' books"?

o   What can be done to encourage all students to read good books regardless of the gender of the major character?

o   Classics are laden with sex, race, and disability stereotypes, as are most fairy tales and folk stories. How can the librarian raise awareness and help young children cope with them?

o   How does the librarian make decisions on weeding when materials are considered condescending, stereotyped, patronizing, or biased? When does weeding become censorship?

o   How does the librarian guide recreational reading? To what uses are displays and book selections put?

o   How can the librarian help the classroom teacher deal with stereotyped materials?

The librarian's equity role within the school community can and should include participating in the textbook evaluation and selection committee, working with teachers to encourage literacy, and keeping an eye out for censorship. Librarians should provide all groups of the school's population with materials that are appropriate for them and that encourage them to read and explore, celebrate special days and holidays with resources from a wide variety of sources, and organize displays and exhibits showing the achievements of women, people of color, different ethnic groups, and people with disabilities. Librarians also should take care to employ female and male students equally as library aides in all jobs.

Equity in School Library Collections

In the 1970s, an enormous effort was undertaken to make publishers and the public aware of the discrimination and bias that existed in educational materials used by students every day. Studies were formulated; the classic "Dick and Jane as Victims," which is still referred to today, demonstrated how strongly stereotyping and bias affected students' view of the world and of themselves with little relevance to their own reality.[2] Under pressure from civil rights groups, publishers hastened to produce guidelines on how to eliminate stereotyping and bias from textbooks; these also spread their influence into trade books, especially in the areas of nonfiction and biography. Early feminist small presses filled the void by producing inexpensive paperbacks, which were the bane of the school librarian as they were fragile and did not last long. Some went out of business once the traditional publishers turned their attention to being sensitive to the changes in society and the demand for nonstereotypic stories, career education books, history, and biography. One area quick to expand and become more representative was sports and athletics, where publishers found they easily could include women gymnasts and tennis stars along with the football and baseball heroes.

Since that time, the literature on women, people of color, ethnic groups, people with disabilities, and sex roles in educational equity have grown and entered the mainstream of publishing and bibliographic control. It becomes necessary, therefore, for the school librarian to be able to locate and identify useful sources quickly. This bibliography, which focuses on the needs of students in grades K through 12, has been designed to address that need. Most of the work in the area of women's and multicultural studies addresses the needs and concerns of the postsecondary institution. Far fewer materials addressing these issues have been published for the public school.

Only books are considered for this listing; readers are referred to the ERIC system for the full range of periodical literature. Similarly, standard library works of reference, familiar to most librarians, are omitted. This listing is designed to be used as a collection development and selection tool, and as a reference to other areas, such as biography, textbook concerns, and bibliography.

This bibliography is divided into eight sections: General, Early Childhood/Elementary, Secondary, Biography, Periodicals, Audiovisual Materials, Textbooks, and Desegregation Assistance Centers. Items were selected for inclusion if they were nonsexist and included a multicultural perspective whenever possible. Issues of race, ethnicity, and disability were considered, and, although every item may not answer to all the criteria, overall the bibliography does. With the exceptions of some early classics, the cut-off date has been set at 1979. Books that are out of print have been so noted and are usually available in libraries and resource centers, such as those at the U.S. Department of Education's Desegregation Assistance Centers, located around the country. (See bibliography listing.)

The General section contains general reference books, resource guides, and directories that are not grade-level specific and that cover a wide range of topics. Wherever possible, entries are listed under the most specific heading. Included are some older items of interest to librarians, such as Joan Marshall's On Equal Terms and Sanford Berman's The Joy of Cataloguing.

The Early Childhood/Elementary and Secondary sections attempt to pull together a wide range of nontraditional resources and books, discussing stereotyping in children's literature and writings of and on various groups. For example, resources on women artists, black writers, and Nobel prize winners are included here as a basis for further exploration.

All the entries in the Biography section are concerned with women and include only general guides and directories. No individual biographies are included, nor are collective biographies of any length. The items are considered signposts, encouraging the student to explore further. There is very little available on nonwhite sources, and it was not possible to find any entries on women with disabilities.

The recommended titles listed in the Periodicals section address classroom equity issues and provide reliable reviews of equitable supplementary materials for both student and teacher use. Periodicals of specific subject interest are located under the appropriate subject section in other chapters of this book.

The next two sections address areas of special interest and concern: Audiovisual Materials and Textbooks. The

<u>Audiovisual Materials</u> section includes filmographies dealing with women's history, changes in the workforce, and issues of staff development in gender and minority issues. Samples of listings generated by special collections in State Departments of Education and Desegregation Assistance Centers are included so that librarians may add these useful sources to their usual ones when borrowing films and videos. The <u>Textbooks</u> section covers textbook selection and the censorship issue, which of course spills over into the domain of the library. The last section lists <u>Desegregation Assistance Centers</u>.

Notes

1. Virginia Woolf, <u>A Room of One's Own</u> (New York: Harcourt Brace Jovanovich, 1929), p. 69.

2. Women on Words and Images, <u>Dick and Jane as Victims: Sex Stereotyping on Children's Readers</u> (Princeton, NJ: WWI., 1975).

3. Joan Marshall, ed., <u>On Equal Terms: A Thesaurus for Nonsexist Indexing and Cataloguing</u> (New York: Neal-Schuman, 1977) and Sanford Berman, <u>The Joy of Cataloguing: Essays, Letters, Reviews, and Other Explosions</u> (Phoenix, AZ: Oryx Press, 1981).

4. For a discussion of censorship issues, see Marylin Hulme, "Mirror Mirror on the Wall: Biased Reflections in Textbooks and Instructional Materials," in <u>Sex Equity in Education: Readings and Strategies</u>, edited by Anne O'Brien Carelli (Springfield, IL: Charles Thomas Publishers, 1988).

BIBLIOGRAPHY

General

Allen, Martha Leslie, ed.   <u>Index/Directory of Women's Media</u>.
Washington, DC: Women's Institute for Freedom of the Press;
Forestville, MD: Anaconda Press, 1986.   (Index of <u>Media
Report to Women</u>, 1982-85).
      Contains listings of women's periodicals, presses,
publishers, news services, radio and TV groups and programs;
women's video, cable, film, music, art, graphics, theater and
writer's networks; public relations, editorial, and
advertising services for women; women's speaker bureaus;
courses on media and women; women's resource distributors;
organizations for media change; women's resource
distributors, bookstores, libraries and selected catalogs.
Also includes a directory of more than 300 "media women and
media concerned women."

Berman, Sanford.   <u>The Joy of Cataloguing: Essays, Letters,
Reviews, and Other Explosions</u>.   Phoenix, AZ: Oryx Press,
1981. (O.P.)
      The writer is well-known in the library world for his
constant attempts to improve subject access to equity
materials (see also his "Out of the Kitchen -- But Not into
the Catalog," <u>Technical Services Quarterly</u>, 2:1/2,
Fall/Winter 1984, pp. 167-72).   In this book, he documents
the unreliability of standard "authorities" and demonstrates
that equity in library subject headings can be accomplished.

<u>Bibliography of Bilingual Materials for Career/Vocational
Education: A List of BESC Library Holdings</u>.   Springfield, IL:
State Board of Education, 1980.
      Contains materials for career exploration, job search,
and vocational training for use with secondary students,
although equally useful in proposal writing, program
planning, and staff development.   Resources in Spanish,
Chinese, and Vietnamese.

Carelli, Anne O'Brien, ed.   <u>Sex Equity in Education: Readings
and Strategies</u>.   Springfield, IL: Charles Thomas Publishers,
1988.

A comprehensive and practical reference that discusses the problems and provides solutions to encourage educators to eliminate sex-role stereotyping. Topics covered in the twenty-three chapters include early childhood and sex-role socialization, educators response to contemporary families, teaching practices, administration, computer equity, equity in math, science, and technology, and bias in textbooks.

Cotera, Martha P. and Nella Cunningham, eds. Multicultural Women's Sourcebook: Materials Guide for Use in Women's Studies and Bilingual/Multicultural Programs. Newton, MA: EDC/Women's Educational Equity Act Publishing Center, 1982.

The over 2,000 entries included in this annotated bibliography belie statements that materials on ethnic women are not available. This is a good source of information and materials on U.S. women of various cultures including Asians, Afro-Americans, Cubans, Mexicans, Puerto Ricans, Middle Easterners, Native Americans, Jewish women, and women of European heritage. A comprehensive listing of sources and a publishers' directory are provided.

Danky, James, P. and Elliot, Shore, eds. Alternative Materials in Libraries. Metuchen, NJ: Scarecrow Press, 1982.

This comprehensive handbook on alternative materials incorporates aspects of acquisitions and cataloguing and provides references for materials on issues such as the women's movement, solar power, and ethnic groups. Also includes a directory of library collections of contemporary alternative materials.

Doss, Martha Merill, ed. Women's Organizations: A National Directory. Garrett Park, MD: Garrett Park Press, 1986.

This comprehensive publication lists, in alphabetical order, organizations that address women's needs, especially their educational and career goals. Indexes by city and state provide access to local services.

Haber, Barbara. Women in America: A Guide to Books, 1963-1975. Boston: G.K. Hall, 1978.

A comprehensive bibliography of books by and about American women that emerged with the new wave of feminism in the 1960s. The materials in this guide cover a broad range of issues from black and Native American women to women and work, including law and politics. Some annotations are lengthy and detailed, others brief.

Hulme, Marylin A. Current Bibliographies: Selected Listings
of Equity Materials. New Brunswick, NJ: Consortium for
Educational Equity, Rutgers, The State University. v.p.
(annual)
    Each annotated bibliography in this packet covers one
topic, either a subject area such as science or a type of
material such as posters. Materials listed either deal with
equity issues or provide access to alternative materials that
contain information on hitherto neglected populations. All
items listed are available for borrowing from the
Consortium's Resource Center.

Hutchison, Barbara. BIAS (Building Instruction Around Sex
Equity). Portland, OR: Northwest Regional Educational
Laboratory, Center for Sex Equity, 1982. 5 vols.
    This inservice training package contains workshops
designed to assist teachers, librarians and parents to
recognize and address sex-role stereotyping and bias in
books. Activities and handouts familiarize participants with
educational equity issues and help them implement change in
their schools. Volume two is an annotated bibliography of
nonsexist supplementary books; volume three and four address
parents specifically. Bibliography available from Oryx
Press, Phoenix, AZ.

Klein, Gillian and Edith W. King. Resources for Teaching
about Anti-Racism and Multi-Ethnic Education: Recent
Outstanding Materials from Britain Selected Especially for
American Teachers. ERIC, 1984. Ed #260160.
    A great opportunity for American educators to learn and
benefit from work being done in Britain regarding
multicultural/multi-ethnic education, world studies,
development studies, and intercultural perspectives.
Introduction cites texts appropriate for discussing race
relations in the classroom, and succeeding chapters describe
nearly 60 books on print and prejudice and on supporting
children's bilingualism.

Klein, Susan S., ed. Handbook for Achieving Sex Equity
through Education. Baltimore: Johns Hopkins University
Press, 1985.
    A comprehensive general reference that focuses on

research and educational strategies to aid in the achievement of sex equity through education as well as the achievement of sex equity in educational activities and settings. Topics covered include the nature and value of sex equity, administrative strategies, educational practices, subject content areas, special populations, and early education environments.

Kumagai, Gloria L., ed. "Minority Women: An Annotated Bibliography" in America's Women of Color: Integrating Cultural Diversity into Non-Sex-Biased Curricula. Newton, MA: EDC/Women's Educational Equity Act Publishing Center, 1982.

Enumerates resources for elementary and secondary students and teachers that can be used to learn about minority women and to develop culturally diverse sex-fair curricula. This is one part of a training program that includes a teacher-training manual, curriculum guides, and filmstrips.

Mariampolski, Sharon Wolf,, ed. MSDAC Resource Library Annotated Bibliography. Second Edition. Manhattan, KS: Midwest Sex Desegregation Assistance Center, 1986.

This bibliography, though not up-to-date, includes books, films, filmstrips, recordings, and booklets that promote sex-fair education. Each entry contains a description of material and is accompanied by a recommended level of use and group of people most likely to find materials useful. Materials can be borrowed from the Center.

Marshall, Joan K., ed. On Equal Terms: A Thesaurus for Nonsexist Indexing and Cataloguing. New York: Neal-Schuman, 1977.

This thesaurus, though old, is an excellent tool for librarians to use in generating new subject headings that provide access to materials, topics, and issues previously considered unimportant or tangential.

"Minority Women" in Sex Equity in Education: Content Specific Bibliographies. Lansing, MI: Michigan Department of Education, 1984.

Elementary and secondary school teachers and librarians will find this annotated bibliography useful for locating materials on girls and women of color. Included are curriculum, student reading, counseling, and workshop materials, in addition to biographies and history texts. Addresses are given for organizations and associations that are lesser-known publishers.

Nelson, Margaret F., and M. Frances Walton. Ohoyo Ikhana: A Bibliography of American Indian-Alaska Native Curriculum Materials. Wichita Falls, TX: Ohoyo Resource Center, 1982.

Sections on classroom materials with grade level recommendations, resource materials on developing a bias-free curriculum, and additional bibliographies containing Indian materials. For brief overviews of American Indian and Alaskan educational issues a list of select articles is provided. Extensive indexing gives access by region, a/v type, and source.

Osterweil, Wendy, ed. Alternative Press Publishers of Children's Books: A Directory. Second Edition. Madison, WI: Cooperative Children's Book Center, 1985.

Every library with a children's collection -- public, school, or college -- could use this directory of 150 publishers. Coverage of feminist and nonsexist publishers is fairly comprehensive, and the distributor information provided is especially valuable, as is the inclusion of Canadian presses. The bilingual index by 17 languages and the geographical index by state and province are equally useful.

Resource Bibliography. Nacogdoches, TX: The Sex Desegregation Assistance Center, Stephen F. Austin State University, 1986.

This published (and somewhat out-of-date) catalog records the extensive collection of the Southwest Sex Desegregation Assistance Center Library. Includes books, kits, posters, records, filmstrips, films, and videotapes about women, sex-role stereotyping, human relations, and career education. All can be borrowed from the Center.

Rix, Sara E., ed. The American Woman, 1987-88: A Report in Depth. New York: W.W. Norton, 1987.

An excellent resource of statistics and information on the American woman, reflecting her status in the country, which provides readers, researchers, and writers with answers to many questions and data for analysis on the social, political and economic changes in women's roles.

Seager, Joni, and Ann Olson. <u>Women in the World: An International Atlas</u>. New York: Simon & Schuster, 1986.
    Maps and charts graphically depict women's condition and experiences throughout the world, showing commonalities and differences. Topics include marriage, work, motherhood, health care, politics, resources, and education and government.

Sivard, Ruth Leger. <u>Women...a World Survey</u>. Washington, DC: World Priorities, 1985.
    This booklet provides comparative statistics pertaining to women by nation, conditions of employment, infant mortality, work, education and health, to underscore their contention that "there is no major field of activity and no country in which women have attained equality with men." Good source of data.

Tyler, Karen Beyard, and Alleen Pace Nilson. <u>Promoting Educational Equity Through School Libraries</u>. Tempe, AZ: Arizona State University, 1978. 5 vols.
    The only known training manual for increasing understanding of equity issues among librarians and teachers, and helping them eliminate bias and exclusion in their school libraries. Included are an instructor's guide, quizzes, and activities.

Valiant, Sharon. <u>Crossing Cultures II: Third World Women</u>. New Brunswick, NJ: Rutgers University Consortium for Educational Equity, 1983.
    A useful resource booklet provides classroom teachers with materials, activities, and ideas on Third World women. Focusing on Asian, Asian-American, black, Hispanic, and Native American women, information is included that is generally not present in school libraries.

<u>Women's Action Almanac: A Complete Resource Guide</u>. New York: Women's Action Alliance; William Morrow, 1980. (O.P.)
    A good example of a guide to women's issues, programs, organizations, commissions, and associations, though now somewhat out-of-date. Especially useful is the listing by state of women's resources and organizations.

The Women's Annual...The Year in Review. Boston: G.K. Hall,
1980- (annual).
    While this annual review seems to be increasingly geared
to the college level rather than to the general reader, it
conveniently brings together the major events and issues
concerning women in the humanities, sciences, law, politics,
and also popular culture.

Women's History Network: Directory. Santa Rosa, CA:
National Women's History Project, 1984- (annual).
    An alphabetical listing by state of women and men eager
to share what they know about promoting women's history. For
easy and direct contact, addresses, phone numbers, and a
description of individual's area of expertise is included.

Women's Library Resources. Trenton, NJ: New Jersey
Department of Community Affairs, Division on Women, 1981.
    A brief and limited guide to public library resources
includes selected lists of classic feminist works, reference
books on women, nonsexist children's books, feminist
publishers, and periodicals. Also contains samples of
resource file headings and guidelines for establishing a
community information and referral service.

Women's Organizations and Leaders Directory. Washington, DC:
Today Publications and News Service, 1973- (annual).
    Wide-ranging directory of women's societies, clubs,
professional associations, political organizations,
institutions and their officers. Updated annually and fully
indexed.

Early Childhood/Elementary

Abrams, Eileen. A Curriculum Guide to Women's Studies for
the Middle School, Grades 5-9. Old Westbury, NY: The
Feminist Press, 1981. (O.P.)
    The twenty activities in this guide may be used with
related curriculum units to add a women's studies dimension.
Grouped into four major sections: "All about Stereotyping,"
"Women in the Past," "Women in Today's World," and "Taking
Charge of Our Lives." Includes a reading and resources list.

Bracken, Jeanne, and Sharon Wigutoff. <u>Books for Today's Children: An Annotated Bibliography of Non-Stereotyped Picture Books</u>. Old Westbury, NY: The Feminist Press, 1979.

Picture books listed have been examined for sex-role presentation and categorized based on authors' recommendations. An accompanying subject index is useful for locating quality books on such topics as working mothers, disabilities, multiracial ethnicities, sensitive males, etc.

_____. <u>Books for Today's Young Readers: An Annotated Bibliography of Recommended Fiction for Ages 10-14</u>. Old Westbury, NY: The Feminist Press, 1981.

Examines a selected list of junior novels, published between 1977 and 1980, which present positive images of a pluralistic society, challenging traditional sex-role expectations. A great help to parents, librarians, and teachers who want to recommend and encourage reading outside the usual middle school (5-8) canon.

Broderick, Dorothy M. <u>Image of the Black in Children's Fiction</u>. New York: R.R. Bowker, 1973. (O.P.)

Although the books examined are older and many have since been published that are less stereotyped, this historical, literary, and critical analysis of the image of black people that emerges from children's books raises relevant issues.

<u>Interracial Books for Children: Bulletin</u>. Council on Interracial Books for Children, 1841 Broadway, New York, NY 10023; v. 8, nos. 6 and 7, 1977.

This double issue of the <u>Bulletin</u> is devoted to a discussion of disability. Topics covered include handicapism, media portrayals of people with disabilities, and how to counter handicapist stereotypes in the classroom. A unique resource for disability issues.

_____. (v. 13, nos. 4 and 5, 1981).

A five-year update on handicapism in children's books. Includes criteria for selection, reviews of books for young readers, middle grades, and older readers, articles and resources.

Davis, Enid. The Liberty Cap: A Catalogue of Non-Sexist Materials for Children. Chicago: Academy Press, 1977.
   One of the first books to list and evaluate picture books, easy readers, fiction and nonfiction for children, in addition to films, photographs, records, cassettes, and toys. The articles, resource lists, and indexes illustrate an exemplary commitment to locating children's books with positive images.

Dick and Jane as Victims: Sex Stereotyping in Children's Readers. Expanded Edition. Princeton, NJ: Women on Words and Images, 1975. (Also slide/tape show.)
   This now classic report is an early analysis of sex-role stereotyping in elementary school readers. Its approach and structure set the tone for many other reports on the continuing pervasiveness of sex-role stereotyping in children's books and readers.

Gallagher, Kathleen, and Alice Peery. Bibliography of Materials on Sexism and Sex-Role Stereotyping in Children's Books. Chapel Hill, NC: Lollipop Power, 1972- (annual).
   A comprehensive listing of materials that specifically address the issue of sexism in children's literature. Also includes selected bibliographies and curricular materials, publishers of nonsexist, nonracist children's books, and mail-order sources of nonsexist toys, educational supplies, and books.

Hirschfelder, Arlene B. American Indian Stereotypes in the World of Children: A Reader and Bibliography. Metuchen, NJ: Scarecrow Press, 1982.
   This anthology of essays scrutinizes the presentation of American Indians in children's story and textbooks, analyzing the stereotypes and describing the misuse of Native American religion and customs. Included is an annotated bibliography of books and articles about Indian imagery in children's literature and suggested ways to correct the inauthentic, offensive, and unreal images of American Indians.

Identifying Racism and Sexism in Children's Books. New York: Council on Interracial Books for Children, 1978. (2 filmstrips/tapes and guide.)
   Sex and race stereotypes are identified in well-known books and counterbalanced with examples of unbiased

materials. The program is useful for elementary school teachers and librarians.

The Lion and the Unicorn. Vol. 11, No. 1, April 1987. Special Issue: "Literature of American Minorities."
This issue of The Lion and the Unicorn, a theme- and genre-centered journal in children's literature, focuses on minority issues. Topics include older people, the Chinese-American experience, gypsy images, Orientalism, black history, and Jewish American books. Also included is one of the few published articles on "Disability Bias in Children's Literature."

Newman, Joan E. Girls Are People Too! A Bibliography of Non-Traditional Female Roles in Children's Books. Metuchen, NJ: Scarecrow Press, 1982.
Listed are books whose female characters demonstrate nontraditional sex-role behavior. Includes fiction and nonfiction with a special emphasis on books about women of color and women with disabilities. Selections are rated good, fair, or excellent and accompanied by suggested reading levels. The appendix constitutes a unique feature: a chronology of notable events and personalities in the history of women.

Resources for Reading Free: Liberated Titles for Elementary Students. Andover, MA: New England Center for Equity Assistance, 1984.
Teachers and librarians will find this packet useful for identifying sex-fair reading materials. Included are two articles on racism and sexism in literature and sample lesson plans for detecting bias in reading. Several bibliographies of recommended reading annotate materials on Asian, black, and Hispanic women and biographies of women in science.

Secondary

Alarcon, Norma, and Sylvia Kossnar. Bibliography of Hispanic Women Writers. Bloomington, IN: Chicano-Riqueno Studies, 1980. (O.P.)
Critical works on Hispanic women writers have been extrapolated from the MLA International Bibliography, 1922-1978, to form this specialized bibliography. Entries are listed alphabetically by the name of the individual writer and indexed chronologically. No annotations are provided.

Baraka, Amiri, and Amina Baraka. <u>Confirmation: An Anthology</u>
<u>of African-American Women</u>. New York: William Morrow, 1983.
    Written to "confirm" that a whole body of American
literature has been consistently ignored and to draw
attention to its existence and excellence, <u>Confirmation</u>
presents excerpts from the works of forty-nine black women
writers, some published here for the first time.

Butler, Matilda, and William Paisley. <u>Women and the Mass</u>
<u>Media: A Sourcebook for Research and Action</u>. New York:
Human Sciences Press, 1980.
    This first systematic study of sexism in the media
presents information and strategies by which concerns for
media "isms" can be translated into legal, economic, and
social action.

Chapman, Anne, ed. <u>Feminist Resources for Schools and</u>
<u>Colleges: A Guide to Curricular Materials</u>. Third Edition.
New York: The Feminist Press, 1987.
    High school and undergraduate teachers and librarians
will find this annotated listing of current nonsexist
curricular materials invaluable for expanding their curricula
and collections. Entries include books, articles, pamphlets,
films, and tapes covering a wide array of subject areas:
Art, English, History, Mathematics, Science, Social Science,
and special interdisciplinary studies on women (including
women and disabilities), the family, mothering, and gender
roles.

Evans, Mari, ed. <u>Black Women Writers (1950-1980): A</u>
<u>Critical Evaluation</u>. Garden City, NY: Anchor Press, 1984.
    Fifteen black women writers each have made a five-to-
seven page statement on "why and how I write." Critical
overviews of their work, as well as a selection of
bibliographic materials and current biographical information,
are included.

Green, Rayna. <u>Native American Women: A Contextual</u>
<u>Bibliography</u>. Bloomington, IN: Indiana University Press,
1983.
    Offers nearly 700 works by or about Native North
American women. Films, recordings, journal articles,
government reports, and books are included. Green's
introduction provides a critical review of the literature and

an informative history of writing by and about Native
American women.

Harris, Ann Sutherland, and Linda Nochlin. <u>Women Artists
1550-1950</u>. New York: Alfred A. Knopf, 1981.
      Presents the work of eighty-four painters from the
Renaissance to the mid-twentieth century, based on the first
international exhibition of art by women. Commentaries
consider the work of each individual artist in the context of
her time, provide a short biography, and discuss the
techniques and the principles of her art. Two critical
essays encompassing all the periods are provided by the
authors.

Partnow, Elaine, ed. <u>The Quotable Woman: 1800-1981</u>. New
York: Facts on File, 1982 and <u>The Quotable Woman: From Eve
to 1799</u>. New York: Facts on File, 1985.
      Nearly 2,300 women spanning from the 9th century B.C. to
present day, representing a variety of professions and
nations, are quoted within these two volumes. They are
presented in chronological order according to the year of
their birth and alphabetically within each year. A
biographical index provides limited background information.

Rosenfelt, Deborah Silverton, ed. <u>Strong Women: An
Annotated Bibliography of Literature for the High School
Classroom</u>. Old Westbury, NY: The Feminist Press, 1976.
(O.P.)
      Provides high school teachers and librarians with
inexpensive readings by and about women, emphasizing the
strengths and accomplishments of women. Materials include
anthologies, autobiographies, biographies, plays, novels,
short stories, and poetry.

Searing, Susan E. <u>Introduction to Library Research in
Women's Studies</u>. Boulder, CO: Westview Press, 1985.
      Part One, "Using the Library," is an introduction to
library research strategies and techniques in women's
studies. Part Two, "Tools of Research," provides a detailed
listing of bibliographies and other sources of women's
studies materials. Exhaustive coverage as far as North
American sources are concerned.

Shaffer, Susan M., and Barbara J.A. Gordon. Resource
Notebook. Washington, DC: Mid-Atlantic Center for Sex
Equity, 1980.
     An easy reference source for educators to locate
materials, organizations, information, and general resources
related to sex equity and the implementation of Title IX.
Also offered are strategies for ensuring equity in
vocational/technical education.

Sherr, Lynn, and Jurate Kazickas. The American Woman's
Gazetteer. New York: Bantam Books, 1976. (O.P.)
     Two years of research, travel, and writing produced this
collection of feminist shrines, this travel guide to all the
places in America where women made history. The geographical
dictionary is arranged alphabetically by state, county, city,
and occasional mountain. A valuable tool for teachers as
well as those interested in touring the country in the
footsteps of the nation's female heroes.

Shiels, Barbara. Winners: Women and the Nobel Prize.
Minneapolis, MN: Dillon Press, 1985.
     The life stories of the eight women Nobel prize winners
of the latter half of the century. An introductory section
provides a fascinating look at Alfred Nobel and the Nobel
Prize. Also included are mini-biographies of the other women
winners and a suggested reading list.

Sims, Janet L., ed. The Progress of Afro-American Women: A
Selected Bibliography and Resource Guide. Westport, CT:
Greenwood Press, 1980.
     The first major listing of nineteenth- and twentieth-
century materials on the Afro-American woman, including
audiovisuals, biographies, magazines, and organizations. No
annotations are provided.

Slatkin, Wendy. Women Artists in History: From Antiquity to
the 20th Century. Englewood Cliffs, NJ: Prentice-Hall,
1985.
     Documents the careers and accomplishments of
approximately forty women artists from eleven successive
eras. Also included is introductory material for each era
and an annotated bibliography for further information on the
history of women artists.

Stanford, Barbara Dodds, and Karima Amin. <u>Black Literature</u>
<u>for High School Students</u>. Urbana, IL: National Council of
Teachers of English, 1978.

    In addition to articles about the history and the
teaching of black literature, this book contains a number of
supplementary bibliographies and course guides designed to
direct teachers to works available from black writers and to
offer strategies for presenting these works to students.

Walker, Barbara G. <u>The Woman's Encyclopedia of Myths and</u>
<u>Secrets</u>. San Francisco: Harper & Row, 1983.

    Relates the fascinating stories behind word origins,
legends, superstitions, customs, archeological, and
anthropological findings.

Wong, Shirley and Matilda Butler. <u>Resources and References</u>
<u>for Sex-Fair Vocational Education</u>. San Francisco: Far West
Laboratory, 1981.

    The second of four reports issued by the Sex Equity in
Vocational Education Project documents more than 600
resources for use by administrators, teachers, counselors,
and students. Specific sections address recruitment of women
for nontraditional vocations, parent/community involvement,
and meeting the needs of displaced homemakers.

Biography

Anderson, Owanah. <u>Ohoyo One Thousand: A Resource Guide of</u>
<u>American Indiana/Alaska Native Women</u>. Wichita Falls, TX:
Ohoyo Resource Center, 1982.

    This compilation of 1,004 notable American Indian women
includes brief biographies and narratives detailing each
woman's occupation, tribe, and advocacy on behalf of women
and Indians. Names are indexed by skill, tribe, and state.

Davis, Marianne W., ed. <u>Contributions of Black Women to</u>
<u>America</u>. Columbia, SC: Kenday Press, 1982. 2 vols. (v. I,
Arts, Media, Business, Law, Sports; v. II, Civil Rights,
Politics and Government, Education, Medicine, Sciences).
(O.P.)

    Finally, a biographical sourcebook on black women in
America! Divided by the topics listed above, these two
volumes relate black women's achievements and accomplishments
in many different areas and at many different levels. Each

section is accompanied by a bibliography and an index.

Herman, Kali. Women in Particular: An Index to American Women. Phoenix, AZ: Oryz Press, 1985.
    This useful reference work lists women who appear in a variety of biographical dictionaries and directories, such as American Biographical Dictionary, Current Biography, Dictionary of Literary Biography, and other sources too numerous to mention. All are cross-referenced and indexed by field and career, religious affiliation, ethnic and racial group, and geographical location.

McCullough, Joan. First of All: Significant "Firsts" by American Women. New York: Holt, Rinehart and Winston, 1980. (O.P.)
    Fascinating tidbits and little-known facts about more than 160 women who were pioneers in aviation, business and finance, politics, law, science, sports, and the armed services. The "firsts" from Soap Box Derby to Mississippi steamboat captain.

Notable American Women: A Biographical Dictionary, 1606-1950 (3 vols.) and Notable American Women: The Modern Period. Cambridge, MA: Belknap Press of Harvard University Press, 1971-1980.
    The biographical dictionary of American women, a must for every school library.

O'Neil, Lois Decker, ed. The Women's Book of World Records and Achievements. Quality Paperback Series. New York: Da Capo, 1983.
    A basic reference work celebrating women's world records and achievements in the late nineteenth and twentieth centuries. Contains more than 5,000 women activists, heroes, humanitarians, and notable firsts.

Robinson, Doris. Women Novelists, 1891-1920: An Index to Biographical and Autobiographical Sources. New York: Garland Publishing, 1984.
    Identifies English-language biographical and autobiographical works as well as obituary notices for women novelists who wrote at the turn of the century or whose novels were first translated at that time. Extensive cross-

referencing according to married names, pen names, and pseudonyms, in addition to supplemental indexes of black women writers and others identified by country.

Siegal, Mary-Ellen. Her Way: A Guide to Biographies of Women for Young People. Second Edition. Chicago: American Library Association, 1984.
     Each of the short profiles is followed by a selected list of individual biographies useful for both youngsters and adults. A bibliography of collective biographies is arranged by author; supplemental indexes list women by nationality, ethnicity, and vocation.

Simpson, Lucy Picco, ed. The Teaching About Series... Brooklyn, NY: Organization for Equal Education of the Sexes. 4 vols. Contents: 1) Women and Girls with Disabilities (1987); 2) Women in American History (1988); 3) Asian American Women (in press); 4) Black Women (in press).
     Each introductory teaching packet contains a poster, background information, teaching strategies, and bibliography on a specific group of women. Useful resource kits.

_____. Women of Achievement: A Packet of Twenty-Four Biographies and Miniposters. Brooklyn, NY: Organization for Equal Education of the Sexes, in press.
     A resource packet for junior and senior high school students containing information on 24 American women, both historical and contemporary, a resource list/bibliography, and teaching activities. Each woman is profiled in a brief biography accompanied by a small poster.

Uglow, Jennifer, S., ed. The International Dictionary of Women's Biography. New York: Continuum, 1982.
     Relates the essential details of the lives and activities of 1,500 women mostly from North America, Europe, and the British Commonwealth. Entries are indexed by subject; many provide further references to an autobiography or biography.

Weiser, Marjorie P.K., and Jean S. Arbiter. Womanlist. New York: Atheneum, 1981.
     Celebrates women's accomplishments, for good or ill, all over the world. Brief listings under: Games, Honors,

Naming, Rulers, Suffrage, Art, Fads and Fashion, Law, Victims, etc.

Periodicals

<u>Association of Black Women in Higher Education</u>. 30 Limerick Dr., Albany, NY 12204.
   Newlsetter covers issues of interest to black teachers and students.

<u>The Disability Rag</u>. Avocado Press, P.O. Box 145, Louisville, KY 40201.
   Monthly periodical with a progressive slant on disability issues. (Available in print and on tape.)

<u>Equal Education Alert</u>. Project on Equal Education Rights (PEER), 1413 K St. NW, Washington, DC 2005.
   News bulletin focuses on fast-breaking developments in sex equity in education, mostly of a legal nature.

<u>Feminist Collections</u>. Office of Women Studies Librarian-at-Large, University of Wisconsin, 112A Memorial Library, 728 State St., Madison, WI 53706.
   Reviews books and journals of interest to women's studies.

<u>Feminist Periodicals</u>. Office of Women's Studies Librarian-at-Large, University of Wisconsin, 112A Memorial Library, 728 State St., Madison, WI 53706.
   Contents pages from current issues of major feminist periodicals are reproduced; includes annotated listing of all journals selected.

<u>Feminist Teacher</u>. Editorial Collective, Ballantine 442, Indiana University, Bloomington, IN 47405. (v. 1, 1984-).
   Publishes articles on nonsexist teaching techniques and strategies, and reviews and evaluates supplementary classroom materials. Issued quarterly.

<u>Hulme, Marylin A. A Plethora of Periodicals for Equity in Education</u>. New Brunswick, NJ: Consortium for Educational

Equity, Rutgers, The State University, 1985.

The Consortium's Resource Center maintains a core collection of periodicals and magazines catalogued in this list. Available materials deal with sex discrimination and bias, equity in education, women's studies for the K-12 curriculum, children's literature, sex-role stereotyping, and the issues of gender in education and employment. The collection provides excellent sources for equitable materials and information on equity in education, and includes some review journals.

Interracial Books for Children: Bulletin. Council on Interracial Books for Children, 1841 Broadway, New York, NY 10023. (v. 1, 1970-).

In this bulletin, CIBC regularly analyzes learning materials for stereotypes and other forms of bias, recommends new books, and provides consciousness-raising articles and alternative resources. IBCB is published irregularly eight times a year.

Journal of Educational Equity and Leadership. Sage Publications, 275 South Beverly Drive, Beverly Hills, CA 90212. Sponsored by the University Council for Educational Administration in cooperation with Arizona State University. (v. 1, 1981-).

Published four times a year; designed to support affirmative action programs and to free education from discriminatory practices. Provides educational leaders with ideas for advancing educational equity and a forum for examining research findings and emergent practices in equity. Includes book reviews.

Kaleidoscope. Kaleidoscope Press, United Cerebral Palsy and Services for the Handicapped, 326 Locust St., Akron, OH 44302.

A semi-annual literary and fine art magazine concerning issues inherent to the experience of disability and the arts. Often covers issues of women and disability.

Voice of Youth Advocates. 3936 West Colonial Parkway, Virginia Beach, VA 23452. (v. 1, 1978-).

Published by librarians, this review journal is of special interest to those working with adolescents and young adults. Featured are articles on such topics as career development, sex education, and growing up female. Extensive book and media reviews. VOYA is issued bi-monthly April through February.

Women in Libraries. ALA/ASSRT Task Force on Women, Attn: L. Kahn, 2 Manchester, 2A, Newark, NJ 07104. (v. 1, 1970-).
    Addresses the concerns of women librarians and library administrators, and provides information about professional activities and resources. The newsletter is published quarterly.

Women's Studies Quarterly. The Feminist Press at The City University of New York, 311 East 94 Street, New York, NY 10128. (v. 1, 1972-).
    Contains suggested syllabi and resource lists for integrating women's studies into the high school classroom. Also features articles on current women's issues and educational concerns.

Audiovisuals

Artel, Linda. Women and Work - New Options: A Guide to Nonprint Media. San Francisco: Women's Educational Equity Communication Network, Far West Laboratory, 1979. (O.P.)
    The films, filmstrips, videotapes, cassettes, slides, and photographs listed in this guide present women exploring new career options. Nearly all of the items were previewed and evaluated in terms of their content and visual quality.

_____, and Susan Wengraf. Positive Images: A Guide to Non-Sexist Films for Young People. San Francisco: Booklegger Press, 1976.
    One of the first filmographies to deal with sex-equity issues for young people. This has become a model for subsequent volumes.

Film Bibliography. Nacogdoches, TX: The Technical Assistance Center of the Southwest, Stephen F. Austin State University, 1986.
    Lists films and videotapes available for loan from the TACSW. Topics include women's issues, race desegregation, human relations, and career education.

Hulme, Marylin A. <u>Media List: An Annotated Listing of</u>
<u>Educational Equity Audiovisual Materials</u>. New Brunswick, NJ:
Consortium for Educational Equity, Rutgers, The State
University. v.p. (annual)
     Materials include films, filmstrips, slide/tape shows,
videotapes and audio tapes, listed here alphabetically by
title and divided into the three sections: Elementary (K-6),
Secondary (7-12), Staff Development.   Most serve as
supplementary materials for classroom use, incorporating the
contributions of women and minorities in a wide variety of
fields. All materials can be borrowed from the Consortium's
Resource Center.

<u>List of Media</u>. Trenton: New Jersey Department of Education,
Office of Equal Educational Opportunity. v.p. (annual)
     This is but one example of a state education
department's holdings of audiovisual materials in sex equity,
which may be borrowed by educators within that state.

Nordquist, Joan. <u>Audiovisuals for Women</u>. Jefferson, NC:
McFarland, 1980.
     Lists and describes 16mm films, videotapes, filmstrips,
slides, and recordings by and about women. Materials cover a
wide range of women's issues and are useful for supporting
and integrating women's studies in the high school.   A
directory of distributors is included.

Oshana, Maryann. <u>Women of Color: A Filmography of Minority</u>
<u>and Third World Women</u>. New York: Garland Publishing, 1985.
     Reviews English-language films whose characters include
women of color, specifically American leading and supporting
actors belonging to a minority group or to the Third World.
Stereotypical casting is also discussed.

<u>Screening Educational Equity: A Filmography</u>. Washington,
DC: Mid-Atlantic Center for Race Equity, 1983. v.p.
     A selection of films and videotapes portraying a wide
variety of accurate and vivid multicultural experiences. All
are highly recommended for classroom use.

Shaffer, Susan M.   <u>Spotlight on Sex Equity: A Filmography</u>.
Washington, DC: Mid-Atlantic Center for Sex Equity, 1980.
67 p. index.

Annotated listing of sex-equity media resources including films, filmstrips, and slide presentations appropriate for educators' use. Resources are cross-referenced under a number of headings: career development, history, multi-ethnic, sexism, special needs, women's achievements, etc.

Sullivan, Kaye. <u>Films for, by and about Women</u>. Series II. Metuchen, NJ: Scarecrow Press, 1985. (Series I, 1980).
A comprehensive list of current films including subjects such as adoption and children's rights not previously covered. Many are produced or directed by women; others are about women or women's concerns. Women filmmakers are identified in separate index with film titles. Full ordering information is provided.

Textbooks

Alspektor, Rose Ann, and Jeana Wirtenberg. <u>Fair Textbooks: A Resource Guide</u>. Washington, DC: United States Commission on Civil Rights, 1979. (Clearinghouse Publication 61)
A compilation of materials and procedural resources with textbook, curriculum, and administrative guidelines and textbook evaluation instruments. Includes a listing of publishers, state education department directories, and other organizational resources.

<u>As Texas Goes, So Goes the Nation: A Report on Textbook Selection in Texas</u>. Washington, DC: People for the American Way, 1983.
Describes in detail the textbook selection process in Texas, focusing on the Gablers who have provided the raw materials necessary for activists to lead censorship crusades. Also analyzed is the nationwide impact the Texas process has made on the availability, quality, and accuracy of certain textbooks, particularly science.

Britton, Gwyneth, and Margaret Lumpkin. <u>A Consumer's Guide to Sex, Race and Career Bias in Public School Textbooks</u>. Corvallis, OR: Britton and Associates, 1977.
Introductory articles document the changes in textbooks relative to sex and race bias and career stereotyping before and after publishers issued guidelines for creating positive sexual and racial images. Authors conclude that changes as

of this publication had been statistically insignificant. An evaluation kit is provided for discerning the existence of bias in reading, literature, and social studies curriculum materials. A list of textbook series, analyzed by the authors, has been included.

Carroll, James and others. We the People: A Review of U.S. Government and Civics Textbooks. Washington, DC: People for the American Way, 1987.

Reviews textbooks on civics and government commonly used in high schools for breadth of courage, engagement, and treatment of Constitutional themes. Although sound in scholarship, the books evaluated were found to be dull, uninspiring, and generally avoided controversial issues. The amount of discussion of gender bias and ethnocentricity was not consistent and very much dependent upon the interest and sensitivity of the individual reviewer.

Censorship or Selection: Choosing Books for Public Schools. New York: Columbia University Graduate School of Journalism, 1982.

Transcript of a TV program featuring authors Kurt Vonnegut and Judy Blume, Moral Majority vice president Ronald Godwin, and several community activists and educators. Addresses issues concerning the selection of books for public school libraries and the removal of certain books through public pressure.

Cotera, Martha P. Checklists for Counteracting Race and Sex Bias in Educational Materials. Newton, MA: EDC/Women's Educational Equity Act Publishing Center, 1982.

Provides guidelines and checklists to be used in selecting and evaluating curricular materials for use in bilingual/multicultural programs. Materials covered include elementary readers, fiction, and math, science, and social studies texts.

Fitzgerald, Frances. America Revised: History Schoolbooks in the 20th Century. Boston: Little, Brown and Company, 1979.

This analysis of U.S. history books discusses the change brought about by the failure of the "melting pot" theory and pressure from political interest groups and pedagogical "fads." Fitzgerald concludes that history texts manipulate children rather than inform them. Sex and race bias also are addressed.

Glazer, Nathan, and Reed Ueda. Ethnic Groups in History Textbooks. Washington, DC: Ethics and Policy Center, 1983.
    Examined herein are six popular high school American history texts, their ability to deal with American diversity, and whether much attention is paid to ethnic groups. The authors' detailed analysis and conclusions will be of value to parents, educators, and those involved in textbook development.

Guidelines for Selecting Bias Free Textbooks and Storybooks. New York: Council on Interracial Books for Children, 1980.
    Informs teachers, librarians, counselors, administrators, and parents about the issue of biased content in textbooks and storybooks. Provides a variety of evaluation instruments for careful, bias free selections. Guidelines are included for children's books, literature anthologies, dictionaries, biographies, career education textbooks, etc.

Help Wanted: Sexism in Career Education Material. Princeton, NJ: Women on Words and Images, 1976. (Slide/tape and guide.)
    This classic study identifies sex-role stereotyping in a wide variety of career education materials.

Jenkinson, Edward B. The Schoolbook Protest Movement: 40 Questions and Answers. Bloomington, IN: Phi Delta Kappa Education Foundation, 1986.
    In a question and answer format, this book provides basic information on issues of censorship, choice, bias and parents' rights. A debate with the Gablers, conservative textbooks reviewers who have influenced state textbook adoption lists, is included.

Moyer, Wayne A., and William V. Mayer. A Consumer's Guide to Biology Textbooks. Washington, DC: People for the American Way, 1985.
    Useful for teachers, supervisors, and administrators interested in improving science education. Gives critical reviews of 18 biology textbooks, representing those currently available for high schools. Also discusses creationism

versus evolution with regard to including this information in textbooks.

Sadker, Myra, and David Sadker. Beyond Pictures and Pronouns: Sexism in Teacher Education Textbooks. Newton, MA: EDC/WEEA Publishing Center, 1980.
   This analysis of teacher training materials reveals that the issue of sexism is rarely discussed in teacher education texts and that the texts themselves are often sexist.

_____. Sex Equity Handbook for Schools. New York: Longman, 1982.
   Bias in instructional materials is one of the issues discussed in this useful reference book. The authors identify the main ways in which sexism is perpetuated in books and texts, including contextual invisibility, stereotyping, and historical distortions and omissions.

Desegregation Assistance Centers

Region A: CT, ME, MA, NH, RI, VT
New England Center for Equity Assistance
The Network
290 South Main Street
Andover, MA 01810

Region B: NJ, NY, PR, VI
Consortium for Equity
New York University, Metro Center
School of Education, Health, Nursing & Arts Professions
32 Washington Place, Suite 72
New York, NY 10003

Region C: DC, DE, MD, PA, VA, WV
Mid-Atlantic Center for Equity
The American University School of Education
4400 Wisconsin Ave., NW
Washington, DC 20016
Sheryl Denbo, Director

Region D: AL, FL, GA, KY, MS, NC, SC, TN
University of Miami
School of Education & Allied Professions
P.O. Box 248065
Coral Gables, FL 33124

Region E: IL, IN, MI, MN, OH, WI
Center for Equity
University of Michigan
School of Education
1033 School of Education Building
Ann Arbor, MI 48109-1259

Region F: AR, LA, NM, OK, TX
Intercultural Development Research Association
5835 Callaghan Road, Suite 350
San Antonio, TX 78228

Region G: IA, KS, MO, NB
McRel Equity Center
Mid-Continent Regional Educational Laboratory
4709 Belleview
Kansas City, MO 64112
Shirley McCune, Director

Region H: CO, MT, ND, SD, UT, WY
Mountain West Educational Equity Center
Weber State College
3750 Harrison Blvd.
Ogden, UT 84408-1210
Dianne Siegfried, Director

Region I: AZ, CA, NV
Arc Associates
Southwest Regional Laboratory for Education
Research & Development
4665 Lampson Ave.
Los Alamitos, CA 90720
Harriet Doss Willis, Director

Region J: AK, ID, HI, OR, WA, American Samoa, Guam, Northern
     Mariana Islands, Pacific Trust Territory
Northwest Regional Educational Laboratory
Center for Equity
101 SW Main Street, Suite 500
Portland, OR 97204
Ethel Simon-McWilliams, Director

I would like to acknowledge the assistance of Patricia K. Bailey, Douglass College intern, in the compilation and word processing of this bibliography.

ABOUT THE AUTHORS

Beryle Banfield

Currently Beryle Banfield is Director of Creative Approaches to Instructional Resources, a consulting firm. She also serves as Curriculum Specialist and Director of Women's Equity Projects at Metro Center, New York University. In her long history as a leader in the field of educational equity, Beryle Banfield has been an elementary school Assistant Principal, a middle school Principal, citywide Curriculum Coordinator for the New York City Board of Education, and, for fifteen years, she was President of the Council on Interracial Books for Children.

Barbara A. Bitters

Barbara Bitters is the Vocational Equity/Single Parent Administrator for the Wisconsin Department of Public Instruction. From 1979 to 1989, she served as the Special Advisor on Women's Issues for the Office of Vocational and Adult Education, U.S. Department of Education. She was Associate Director of the Freedom for Individual Development Project funded by the Women's Educational Equity Act in 1976-1977 and has been a lecturer in the University of Wisconsin-Madison Women's Studies Program.

Michele Cahill

Michele Cahill is Senior Program Officer for the Division of School and Community Services at the Academy for Educational Development (AED). As part of her work at AED, she directs the Urban Middle School Adolescent Pregnancy Program. She is a co-author of In School Together: School-Based Child Care Serving Student Mothers. Formerly Michele Cahill was Co-Founder and Director of the Women and Communities Project at the Women's Education Institute in New York City and taught Urban Studies and Public Policy at St. Peter's College in New Jersey.

Patricia B. Campbell

For the past seven years Patricia Campbell has directed Campbell-Kibler Associates, an educational consulting firm specializing in computers in education, sex and race equality, educational research and evaluation, and materials development. She has written more than sixty-five articles, books, and book chapters and has made more than 150 presentations to national and regional professional associations, colleges and universities, equity organizations, and the media.

Linda Colón

Linda Colón was the Administrator of Educational Equity Concepts from 1983-1987. During that time she was part of the program development and training team for Project Inclusive and co-authored Including All of Us: An Early Childhood Curriculum About Disability. After taking a three-month parental leave, Linda Colon has returned to the organization as a member of the development team and bilingual trainer for Beginning Science Equitably, a program to foster physical science skills in young children. In addition, she is active in Puerto Rican issues and is a Board Member of the New York Chapter of the National Conference of Puerto Rican Women.

Merle Froschl

Merle Froschl is a Founder and Co-Director of Educational Equity Concepts. She has been a leader in promoting educational equity since the early 1970s, when she was Project Co-Director of the "Women's Lives/Women's Work Series" at The Feminist Press. From 1980-1982 she was Director of the Non-Sexist Child Development Project at the Women's Action Alliance. A special focus of her work at Educational Equity Concepts has been to develop programs and materials for mainstreaming and to address the special needs of women with disabilities. Merle Froschl has co-authored several books including What Will Happen If...Young Children and the Scientific Method and Including All of Us: An Early Childhood Curriculum about Disability and is a nationally sought after speaker on issues of educational equity.

Marylin A. Hulme

Marylin Hulme is Assistant Director of the Consortium for Educational Equity at Rutgers University. The Consortium is part of the Region II Equity Assistance Center along with Teachers College, Columbia University and Metro Center, New York University. She is the author of "Bias in Instructional Materials," a chapter in Sex Equity in Education: Readings and Strategies, edited by Anne O'Brien Carelli. Formerly Marylin Hulme was the Assistant Science Librarian at McMaster University, Ontario, Canada. She is a member of her local school board in New Jersey.

Melissa Keyes

Melissa Keyes is the Sex Equity Consultant at the Wisconsin Department of Public Instruction. She has served two terms as Chair of the National Coalition for Sex Equity in Education (NCSEE) and is a founder of the Wisconsin Consortium for Sex Equity in Education. Melissa Keyes also has been a high school teacher.

Frances Arick Kolb

Frances Arick Kolb is Associate Director of the New England Center for Equity Assistance, a division of The NETWORK, Inc. Currently she is Project Director for the Women's Educational Equity Act Technical Assistance Project. Frances Kolb is a nationally known speaker on women's rights and constitutional rights and is the author of a book on oral history, Portraits of Our Mothers.

Ellen Rubin

Ellen Rubin is the Special Education Staff Specialist at Educational Equity Concepts where she participates in program development, conducts inservice training, and is in charge of the resource collection for the organization's programs in the area of disability. Before joining Educational Equity Concepts in 1983, Ellen Rubin had been a special educator and counselor in a variety of programs serving children with special needs. She is a co-author of Including All of Us: An Early Childhood Curriculum about Disability and a member of the Commissioner's Advisory Panel for the Education of Children with Handicapping Conditions.

Walter S. Smith

Walter Smith is a Professor of Science Education and Chair of the Department of Curriculum and Instruction at the University of Kansas, Lawrence. He has been a long time advocate of educational equity, particularly in the area of science. He was the Project Director for COMETS (Career Oriented Modules to Explore Topics in Science), published by the National Science Teachers Association (NSTA). Walter Smith has been an active member of NSTA for many years, serving on the Board of Directors and on various committees.

Barbara Sprung

Barbara Sprung is a Founder and Co-Director of Educational Equity Concepts. She has been active in the field of educational equity since the early 1970s. As Director of the Non-Sexist Child Development at the Women's Action Alliance from 1972-1978, she pioneered in the development of nonsexist, multicultural, and inclusive early childhood programs and materials. Barbara Sprung has authored and edited several books including Non-Sexist Education for Young Children: A Practical Guide and What Will Happen If...Young Children and the Scientific Method. She is a nationally known speaker on issues of early childhood and equity.

Linda Villarosa

Linda Villarosa is the Managing Editor of Runner's World magazine in Emmaeus, Pennsylvania. A runner herself, she has long been an advocate for equity for female athletes. Formerly Linda Villarosa was Project Director of the Center for Athletes' Rights in Education at Sports for the People.

Joy Wallace

Currently Joy Wallace is Editor of the Expanding Horizons Newsletter, a publication to encourage black female adolescent students to take math. She also is a consultant to the Math/Science Network in Oakland, California and to the EQUALS and Family Math programs at the Lawrence Hall of Science, University of California, Berkeley. Joy Wallace has given math and computer equity workshops across the country and recently conducted an equity training session for the marketing staff of the Apple Computer Company.

Pamela J. Wilson

Pamela Wilson is the Supervisor of Guidance and Counseling for the Wisconsin Department of Public Instruction. Formerly she was a drama teacher and school counselor at the high school level. She also has worked with gifted students at the University of Wisconsin Guidance Institute for Talented Students and has been Mayor of her small Wisconsin community.

Leslie R. Wolfe

Leslie Wolfe is the Executive Director of the Center for Women Policy Studies and the former Director of the Project on Equal Education Rights (PEER) of the NOW Legal Defense and Education Fund. She was Director of the Women's Educational Equity Act Program in the U.S. Department of Education from 1979 to 1983. Once a college level English teacher, Leslie Wolfe has devoted the bulk of her career to promoting educational equity.

ABOUT EDUCATIONAL EQUITY CONCEPTS, INC.

Educational Equity Concepts, Inc. is a national, nonprofit organization founded in 1982 to foster equal educational opportunity. The organization designs innovative programs and materials to help eliminate sex, race, and disability bias; offers a broad range of training and consulting services; and engages in a variety of public education activities.

Because Educational Equity Concepts believes that equal opportunity should "begin at the beginning," the organization has developed a number of unique and nationally-respected early childhood programs. However, Educational Equity Concepts is equally committed to increasing opportunities for young people and adults who have not had the chance to "begin early." And so the organization's program areas span the educational continuum: early childhood, elementary, young adult, and community education.

In all of its programs, materials, and services, Educational Equity Concepts' approach is "inclusive," making the connections between factors of sex, race, disability, and socioeconomic status that can limit individual growth and potential at any age. The organization's programs and materials are concentrated in areas where serious voids exist and where women and children have been adversely affected by sex, race, and disability bias. The content areas include early science, mainstreaming at all levels, teen pregnancy and parenting, and women with disabilities.